D1082848

England's Ruins

For my parents
and
the ID 450 Feminist Collective

England's Ruins

*Poetic Purpose and the
National Landscape*

Anne Janowitz

Basil Blackwell

Copyright © Anne Janowitz 1990

First published 1990

Basil Blackwell, Inc.
3 Cambridge Center
Cambridge, Massachusetts 02142, USA

Basil Blackwell Ltd
108 Cowley Road, Oxford, OX4 1JF, UK

Library of Congress Cataloging in Publication Data

Janowitz, Anne F.
  England's ruins: poetic purpose and the national landscape / Anne Janowitz.
      p.   cm.
  Includes bibliographical references.
  ISBN 0–631–16756–0
  1. English poetry–History and criticism.   2. Ruins in literature.
  3. Politics in literature.   4. Landscape in literature.
  5. Nationalism in literature.   6. Sublime, The, in literature.
  7. Romanticism–England.   I. Title.
  PR508.R84J36   1990
  821.7'09145–dc20   89–27440
                                                              CIP

British Library Cataloguing in Publication Data

A CIP catalogue record for this book is available from the British Library.

Typeset in 11 on 13 pt Erhardt
by Vera-Reyes, Inc.
Printed in Great Britain by
T. J. Press Ltd, Padstow, Cornwall

Contents

Acknowledgments

England's Ruins belongs to the critical field of Romanticism; its analytical premise is that poetic purpose is explicable by attending to historically situated manifestations and versions of *topoi* and structures.

Scholarly work of various kinds on the romantic fragment has been undertaken in the twentieth century by Philippe Lacoue-Labarthe and Jean-Luc Nancy, Marjorie Levinson, Thomas McFarland, Balachandra Rajan, and D. F. Rauber. The terrain of imaginative ruin sentiment was mapped by Rose Macauley and a substantial work on the literary thematics of ruin was accomplished by Laurence Goldstein. I am indebted to all of their work on the subject.

My most profound intellectual debts, however, are to critics not principally known for their investigation of romantic texts. Though I have not explicitly stated so in this study, the writings of Michael McKeon and of Raymond Williams have been the models whose examples have most inspired me by their work in and commitment to exploring the complex relations among poetic structures, social experiences, and political intentions.

Many scholars, colleagues, and friends in the United States and Britain offered me comradely support, helpful advice, and generous readings of portions of this study in manuscript. Thanks to Yasmin Anwar, Craig Baldwin, Joe Boatman, Daria Donnelly, Terry Eagleton, Maud Ellmann, John Fitzpatrick, Alex Fraser, Albert Gelpi, Michael T. Gilmore, Eugene Goodheart, Allen Grossman, Alan Hudson, Wyn Kelly, Jon Klancher, Catherine LaFarge, Tia Lombardi, Jerome McGann, Robin Miller, Pamela Mosher, Andrew Murphy, Sara Nugent, Christina Root, Barbara Rosenbaum, Nancy Ruttenburg, Jon Spayde, Susan Staves, Paul Tickell, Deborah Valenze, Nancy Waring, Georgia Warnke, Carolyn Williams, and Patsy

Acknowledgments

Yaeger. My parents, Adeline Tintner and Henry Janowitz, have been very helpful.

Eugene Goodheart, Allen Grossman, Paul Hamilton, and Michael McKeon each read the manuscript in its entirety and offered valuable comments. An exemplary colleague, Michael T. Gilmore has read my work and listened to my notions for the last five years with seriousness and patience. His advice has been invariably valuable.

Stephan Chambers has been a helpful and enthusiastic editor and the staff at Basil Blackwell made the final stages of production easy and pleasant.

I wish to thank the Department of English and American Literature at Brandeis University for allowing me leave time to complete work on this study. The project was supported by a grant from the American Council of Learned Societies and a year as an Andrew R. Mellon Faculty Fellow in the Humanities at Harvard University, 1988–89.

Anne Janowitz
Brandeis University

Historical Pontefract, from *The Sieges of Pontefract Castle*, ed. Richard
Holmes (Pontefract, 1887; courtesy Harvard College Library)

Picturesque Pontefract, from J. S. Fletcher, *Pontefract* (London, 1920): from a drawing by T. Hearn, November 1798 (courtesy Harvard College Library)

1

Introduction: The Ruin Poem in English

I

At the center of this study is a shifting image of ruins in the landscape: the ruins of Ludlow Castle seen by moonlight by a pensive, melancholic moralist; the ruined tower of Dornadilla, presenting evidence of how the often bloody differences between Scotland and England were absorbed into a scar-bearing union; a ruined cottage in the Dorset countryside serving as the local habitation for Wordsworth's meditation on waste and loss. Castle or abbey, peasant or aristocratic dwelling, the ruin is an image that often appears when "Britishness" is evoked. When Rose Macauley wrote her elegant survey, *Pleasure of Ruins*, she concluded that the then recent devastation of Europe from the bombs of World War II had come to replace the picturesque benignity of ruin with an immediate and frightening reality: of *Ruinenlust*, "we have had our fill."[1] The twentieth-century intention to ruinate has irrefragably changed that peculiar pleasure of ruin which comes from the contemplation of the absolute pastness of the past within the aesthetically controlled shape of temporal transience.

Though there are plentiful historical precedents for a culture's obsession with the prospect or retrospect of decline, it is noteworthy that the rigid optimism of Mrs Thatcher's government has done little to ameliorate the burgeoning rhetoric of "the decline of Britain." Alongside discussions such as Martin Wiener's *English Culture and the Decline of the Industrial Spirit* and Alan Sked's *Britain's Decline*, the figure of decay has become contemporary and widespread, and ruin is a familiar trope in films, music, and novels.[2] Contemporary ruinists work with a lexicon of images drawn from both city and country, a set of domestic ruins emblematizing the effects of the end of the British Empire.

V. S. Naipaul's *The Enigma of Arrival*, for example, superimposes contemporary economic decline upon the more ancient ruin of

Stonehenge, and in the temporal mix Naipaul evokes Wordsworth's "A Night on Salisbury Plain," in which the perversity of Pitt's government is similarly shaded into the poet's experience wandering across the Wiltshire Downs. Most frequently, however, contemporary images of ruin, such as Stephen Frear's direction of Hanif Kureishi's *Sammy and Rosie Get Laid* and Derek Jarman's *The Last of England*, focus on urban decay: physical ruin associated with both poverty and the racism inextricable from and remaining as a legacy of British imperialism. These images of waste suggest their lineage of descent from Blake's poem of urban ruin, *Jerusalem*, an anomalous text in the early nineteenth century for locating the site of ruin in the city rather than the countryside. The intention of the contemporary image of urban ruin is critical and oppositional; that of landscape ruin tends to be presented as iconic of British "heritage."[3] Naipaul is like Wordsworth in that his unhappiness over decline is answered by a retrogressive nostalgia; Jarman is like Blake in his presentation of a version of the urban "Voice of Honest Indignation."

How perplexing it is, then, when scanning images of London squats and squalid Underground stations, and sensing in Johnny Rotten's lyric line, "It was the sound of the city collapsing," resonances with texts written two centuries earlier,[4] to recall that the moment in British history when the ruin was as important a cultural image as it is today was just as England, in its represented form as "Britain," was emerging as a dominant nation-state, and launching a global empire. The eighteenth-century "ruin sentiment" in painting and architecture, variously documented, was what we might think of as a "cultural affect" attending Britain as the nation moved into its imperial phase, while also indexing an imperial anxiety.[5] While the ruin image of the late 1980s appears simply, perhaps even banally, to mirror a condition of economic decay, its meanings were more complex in the eighteenth century and well into the nineteenth. The paradox of eighteenth-century ruin was that the figure of decay was at the same time the image used to authorize England's autonomy as a world power.

The logic of this authority can be briefly outlined. In its shift from an agricultural into an industrial nation, and from a mercantile into a global capitalist economy, England became also "Britain," the self-representation of a homogeneous nation made up out of various and disparate cultural groupings within England and Wales and also beyond, in Scotland and – by the opening of the nineteenth century – in Ireland. The nation I am here calling "Britain" is one of those "imagined communities" so compellingly analyzed by Benedict Anderson in his study of the origins and forms of nationalism. "Communities are to be distinguished," he writes, "not by their falsity / genuineness but by the style in which they are imagined."[6] The growth of "Britain" demanded the fashioning of a common history which would unite its regionally and economically diverse inhabitants into a single group, whose members would identify their interests with those of Britain as an entity. The making of the English working class was as much the making of the British working class, and the competing claims of nation and class were at the center of the many material and ideological struggles of nineteenth-century "Britons." As Anderson makes the point, nationality is imagined as *community* because, "regardless of the actual inequality and exploitation that may prevail in each, the nation is always conceived as a deep, horizontal comradeship."[7] The authority of antiquity was one thread in the fabric of a common nationality, and was visibly available in architectural ruin, the physical trace of historical event in the countryside.

If nations are imagined communities, they are built out of the hopes and intentions of actual, imagining agents. Though the spectacle of ruins in the landscape offers evidence of a nation possessed of a long history, the materials that ruinists draw on to make figures may produce different meanings within some other group's imagination. The detritus of a Scottish castle may remind the Scottish viewer most powerfully of a defeat suffered, while Martello towers assert to the Irish the continuous and material presence of English domination. So, too, the evidence of ruined castles may remind those in opposition to central government that there has been a time when government was neither central nor uncontested. That particular danger was thought to have been avoided, for example, by the seventeenth-century parliamentary orders to demolish what was left of castles in order to prevent further occupations in as yet unimagined civil wars. When the revolutionary process was halted by the Restoration, many of what M. W. Thompson calls these "stricken" castles were abandoned.[8] Nature took on the project of the reclamation of the stones. The physical situation of cultural ruins within the countryside linked the rhetoric of ruin to that of land. This turned out to be fortunate in the creation of British nationalism: as assimilated into the later eighteenth-century aesthetic of the picturesque, ruins were admired as blending into the countryside, while the sense of "country" as rural terrain and "country" as nation also began to melt one into the other. In such a seemingly self-evident and therefore "unimagined" coincidence between country and country – the "naturalizing" of the nation – was born the myth of rural England, as well as the myth of the homogeneous coherence of the nation. Such a rhetoric naturalizes as well the violence of nation-making, which evacuates from cultural artifacts the labor that made them, the human events that took place in them, and the cost to both ancient and local defeated communities, whose worlds provided the ruins upon which arises the structure of British nationalism.[9]

Interestingly, Martin Wiener's argument that rural nostalgia, a cultural bias against industrialization, contributed to the actual industrial decline of Britain, links our contemporary concern with British ruin to its earlier version. In order to coerce its culturally complex populations into the industrial and globally imperialist age, the hegemonic English group which imagines the community of "Britain" calls upon the figure of ruin to secure its past, but by the ancillary naturalizing of the image precipitates a retrogressive ideology of ruralness which industrialization itself can neither exhaust nor even catch up with.

The ruin provides an historical provenance for the conception of the British nation as immemorially ancient, and through its naturalization subsumes cultural and class difference into a conflated representation of Britain as nature's inevitable product. But at the same time, ruin imagery cannot help asserting the visible evidence of historical and imperial impermanence, for the ruin has been traditionally associated with human and cultural transience. The building of a national identity is closely linked to the sense of some earlier or some other nation's ruin, and the artifacts of empire are subject to decomposition, to a return into those "lone and level sands" which Ozymandias' shards refer to and threaten to be overtaken by. The counterpoising of culture to nature is a persistent theme of ruin sentiment in both art and poetry, as moldering time shows its power above the designs and vanities of human communities.

A traditional riposte to the ruinous claims of time has been the assertion of the permanence of art. Poetry in particular is a sturdy monument because it has the property of preserving itself through immaterial as well as material means: "Not marble, nor the gilded monuments / Of princes shall outlive this pow'rful rhyme." Buildings fall down, but poems stand, structurally sound. When Shakespeare presents his version of what Blake will scorn as the Natural Man, physical decay is assimilated to a barren ruin, the speaker's hair falling like leaves from autumnal boughs, "bare ruin'd choirs, where late the sweet birds sang."[10] We are reminded here also that the ruin of the monasteries, an act predating the picturesque aesthetic by at least two hundred years, was a constitutive moment of English absolutism. The unification of England was symbolized in the destruction and appropriation of the Roman Church's buildings and lands, a sixteenth-century version of the violent coexistence of ruin and national unity. For the most part, however, Shakespeare's ruin imagery asserts the immortality of poetry against the impermanence of buildings. Culture insists on its difference from nature, and therein lies the triumph of poetic art.

The passage from culture *to* nature, then, which the eighteenth-century image of ruin performs is quite remarkable for its ability to shift the opposition of art and nature into a convergence of not only materials, but also intentions. So William Gilpin, theorist of the picturesque, surprisingly describes Fountains Abbey in 1772 as "a sacred thing. Rooted for ages in the soil, assimilated to it, and become, as it were a part of it; we consider it as a work of nature, rather than of art."[11] What is true for the artifact is true for the nation: in the eighteenth-century ruin sentiment the cultural entity (Britain) was also forged as inextricable from the natural entity (the countryside), not merely superimposed but blended, and the nation came to be understood *as* nature. Such inevitability came, in turn, to fuel the engine of British chauvinism, which mustered colonial and domestic communities (who might have imagined themselves in other ways) into the forces and agents of the British Empire. Though we are used to thinking of the imperialist ideology as appearing only in the later nineteenth century, the foundations of imperialism – economic and ideological – were built earlier.

In the period that this study principally covers, from the middle of the eighteenth century through the masterful reimagining of "Brittannia" by William Blake in *Jerusalem* between 1804 and 1820, poetic texts were frequently the site of ruin sentiment conspiring with national aspiration. Benedict Anderson convincingly foregrounds the importance of a vernacular print market to the growth of nationalism,[12] and though the poems with which this inquiry begins were written for and read by only small audiences, the representation of the British nation to its ruling class began to include within its myths an ever widening set of intended readers. We will find in Wordsworth's poetry an orientation towards that broadest, most homogeneous conception of the "people," crucial to the instantiation of British nationalism, and which was purveyed, conveyed and internalized through the education of ever larger groups of persons in the nineteenth century.

The compatibility of poetry and nation-making is clear in epic forms: poems which preserve the founding of the nation in a permanent image. But the close links can be understood also as an aspect of the importance of vernacular language in establishing nationhood. This domestic relation finds fullest flower in Wordsworth's critique of poetic diction and in his abstraction of locale into a self-evident "natural" discourse of a "man speaking to men," before withering into the jingoism of later nationalist poetry. In *The Prelude* Wordsworth constructs a psychology out of his abstraction and so makes a nationalist epic from materials apparently personal and individual. With respect to the ruin poem, the connection between poetry and the nation is established within the tradition of the ruin theme, which was often and closely linked to the ancient poetic *topos* of the immortality of poetry. From the Anglo-Saxon poem written about the ruins of the Roman baths at what would become Bath, through the Anglo-American Eliot asserting that he will shore his poetic fragments against ruin, the ruin subject has been integral to the thetic life of English poetry, and in the immortality-of-poetry *topos* was a ready vehicle for asserting the immortality of the nation.

II

Though the histories of poetic forms and themes are fairly autonomous, we can nonetheless map out the fortunes of thematic and structural features within literary history which, while not absolutely mandated by ideological necessity, are allied to it. A genealogy of ruin poetry, then, though it must begin centuries before the political possibility of a British nation, interestingly adapts to a more general tendency, in the later eighteenth century, of de-historicization and de-contextualization. In the period which this study most closely investigates, the project of naturalizing the nation meets up with a shift within ruin poetry away from narrative forms and toward lyric forms conceived in spatial terms. The de-temporalization that poetry enacts upon itself links the intentions of ruin poetry to those of the formulation of a supra-historical Nation.

Those poetic intentions can be, in their most general terms, spoken of as a shift from temporal to spatial claims. The thematic core of such a myth-making enterprise can be observed in the ubiquitous ruined castle poem, which floods the periodical press in the later eighteenth century, and whose narrative structure is altered into a progressive diminishment of time, until the histories which the ruins tell are only of the individual who contemplates them, rather than of the violent events of the past which have taken place in them. The structural counterpart of such a privatizing impulse is to be found in the birth of the romantic fragment poem – a ruin for whose central category of temporal decline has been substituted an equally important assertion of spatial incompletion. The succession of the immortality-of-poetry *topos* by the inexpressibility *topos* also agrees with spatialization usurping temporality in ruin poetry. The fragment, while positively open-ended, also bears the burden of incompletion and so is often linked to the inexpressibility problem.

The naturalizing of the nation and the spatialization of poetic temporality are congenial partners in the making of a national consciousness and alongside it a national literature. Matthew Arnold notes this crucial connection. In an 1879 essay on Wordsworth, Arnold names the poet's importance to the image of the nation: Wordsworth "is one of the very chief glories of English Poetry; and by nothing is England so glorious as her poetry."[13] But to specify the moment when Wordsworth had gone some way toward redeeming ruin in a national landscape, we need first to sort out the strains which make up a genealogy of ruin poetry. Briefly scanning the ruin family from its beginning in Old English poetry to High Modernism, we can then focus on the network of relations among ruins, fragments, and nation-making.

"The Ruin," an Old English meditation on Roman remains, is thought to be the first topographical poem in English, and is also

England's first ruin poem. It provides a useful place to begin sketching in the largest shape of the ruin as a species persistent in English poetry both because it offers a point of departure, and also because the text is not only about but is a material ruin. It thus adumbrates an important category in romantic poetry: the fragment as a distinctive poetic genre. The page of the *Exeter Book* on which "The Ruin" appears has been damaged by fire, and the poem offers evidence of having suffered cultural degeneration, as the scoring marks on the first page suggest that the object had at some point been used as a cutting board.[14] The accidents of the text's physical life are tied to its thematic concerns, for what is with hindsight striking about the poem is that in it the immortality-of-poetry *topos* is entirely absent: human and architectural ruin are figured as fully homologous. The speaker does not offer, nor can the reader locate, any mediating structure by which the poetic act can forestall or substitute for the collapse of text, speaker, or community. The permeability of the flesh is entirely identified with that of stone. Just as the roofs fall, so "corpses fell widely" ("Crungen walo wide" [l. 25a]).[15] There is no intimation here of a transcendence of physical decay through poetic monumentalization. Stone and earth merge, and along with them collapse temporal differentiations. In a cruelly and accidentally iconic line, the text reads: "Still decays the . . ." ("Wonath giet se" [l. 12a]). The possibility of a limitless future of ruin is also hinted at: "The grip of the earth holds the powerful workers, decayed, departed" [ll. 6b–8a] "until a hundred generations will have passed away" ("oth hund cnea / wertheoda gewiten" [ll. 8b–9a]). Because of the physical state of the *Exeter Book* page, we cannot know if "The Ruin," like the other Old English elegies, "The Wanderer" and "The Seafarer," was composed with a closural transcendent recompense for the transience of humans, their communities and their artifacts. "The Ruin" serves as a kind of degree 0 for the ruin poem and the immortality-of-poetry *topos*. The poem documents the decay of both stone and flesh, but it does not assert its permanence against ruin. This is neither a missionary nor a reconstructive poem.

We meet a somewhat more optimistic version of the coincidence of ruin and fragmentation again, after many generations, in *The Waste Land*. Here the poet attempts to arrange cultural fragments into a new coherence which may serve as a pattern for transcendence and immortality. It was in the Renaissance, however, that the immortality-of-poetry *topos* was most unproblematically a fixture of poetic practice, and served as well to build the sense of nationhood by offering the poem as the permanent image of the nation. We should note, however, that in the cosmopolitan aristocratic Europeanism of Renaissance poetry, nation was conceived in more genealogical than geographical terms. The site of national origin was taken to be external to physical terrain, and derived from the classical tradition, in which the nearest genealogical link to be found was in a mythological parent-child relation between Rome and England. In looking at English versions of the theme of the ruins of Rome in chapter 2, I map this early integration of national and poetic issues. In the aftermath of the war of imperialism in the early twentieth century, the modernist poem made up out of an assemblage of fragments situates itself once again in the aristocratic pan-Europeanism we associate with the claims of the Renaissance. Eliot and Pound attempt to find in cultural materials a simulacrum of a nation without locating that nation as a geographical entity.

Michael McKeon's work on the growth of the ideology of aesthetic autonomy in the later eighteenth century enables us to gauge how the shift of poetic practice away from more overtly public stances strips the immortality-of-poetry *topos* of its preservative function.[16] In the intersection of the ruin motif and the emergence of romanticism occurs a significant weakening of the *topos*. The trajectory of the immortality-of-poetry *topos* from the sixteenth to the late eighteenth century as it appears in ruin poetry approaches and then merges with its ruined objects of observation, drawing in its wake a collapse of the distinction between poem and building, self and object of contemplation. The secure distance between architectural ruin and poetic structure which is a feature of the immortality claim in ruin poetry is eroded in romantic poetry, and we find the speaking poetic persona collapsing into the ruins he images. So, to complete a circle back to Rome, in a romantic instance of the theme of the ruins of Rome, Byron stands in the Colosseum "a ruin amidst ruins"; while back in England, Blake's Daughters of Albion, observing the devastations of Luvah wrought by governmental oppression, "looked on one-another & became what they beheld" (*Jerusalem* 34: 50).

The weakening of the *topos* coincides with both thematic and structural alterations in ruin poems. In one strain of eighteenth-century poetry the security of poetic monumentality had been augmented by the transparency of ruin, which offered to the poet-observer the chance to investigate and make sense of cultural detritus. The observer alters ruins – transitively moralizes them – as he reflects upon them, and so redeems ruin through implicit poetic monumentality. After surveying the "huge heaps of hoary, moulder'd walls" (l. 83) from Grongar Hill, John Dyer can poetically shape them into the lesson of transience:

> But transient is the smile of fate!
> A little rule, a little sway,
> A sun-beam in a winter's day
> Is all the proud and mighty have
> Between the cradle and the grave.
>   (ll. 88–92)[17]

But insofar as the ruin gives evidence of ineluctable genesis and decay, it challenges the structure of the present, and threatens to eradicate temporal difference, swallowing up the present into an unforeseeable yet inevitable repetition of the past. Here poetic and national intentions converge in the later eighteenth century as the naturalizing of ruin promotes a feeling for, rather than an assertion of, the permanence of the nation. In such cases, the immortality-of-poetry *topos* becomes redundant, a distractingly artificial account of what is meant to be read as natural effusion or meditation. Arnold writes of Wordsworth that "Nature herself seems, I say, to take the pen out of his hand, and to write for him with her own bare, sheer, penetrating power."[18]

The structural result of the crisis of the immortality of poetry *topos* can be construed as a kind of internalization of ruin; that is, the coming into being of the fragment as an identifiable kind of poem. The temporality of ruin – a whole now worn away – gives up poetic space to the shape of a fragment – the poetic incompletion, or part of a whole. The poem that has broken down may become the poem which is not yet finished. The relationship between ruin and fragment can be thought of as a dialectic in which the temporal figure of degeneration, spatialized, generates hope. Memory is superseded by longing. In this way the fragment and the ruin meet and modify one another in the romantic period.

III

In 1813, Francis Jeffrey, reviewing Byron's *The Giaour, A Fragment of a Turkish Tale*, archly observed: "The Taste for Fragments, we suspect, has become very general, and the greater part of polite readers would no more think of sitting down to a whole epic than to a whole Ox."[19] This taste was certainly not born in the first decade of the nineteenth century, but it did assume a characteristically romantic form. Recent critical work on romantic poetry has looked with interest at both ruin and fragment, and though my chief concern in this study is with the convergence of nationalism and the ruin motif, the place of the fragment among the varieties of ruin poetry needs to be specified. In 1969, D. F. Rauber wrote an essay on the appropriateness of the unfinished poem to the Romantic mode. Rauber argued that the stance of romanticism, "centered upon an aspiration for the infinite," renders an unfinished form particularly apt.[20] Thomas McFarland, in *Romanticism and the Forms of Ruin*, performs a phenomenology of fragmentation and ruin in romanticism which he presents as an emblem of the necessary mortal limitations of all human productions.[21] Marjorie Levinson's *The Romantic Fragment Poem: A Critique of a Form* investigates romantic fragments such as Keats's two "Hyperion" poems and Wordsworth's "Nutting" with an eye to detailing the historical determinations of the form through a complex set of theoretical and psychoanalytical strategies and insights.[22] While Levinson's focus is on the fragment as a poetic structure, she offers an intriguing suggestion that the groundwork for the availability of the fragment as a readable romantic form can be located in the hoax poems of the later eighteenth century – in particular, Chatterton and Macpherson's bogus antiquarian works. She argues that a shift took place from an historical reading of their works to an aesthetic one: "The hoaxes, judged to have affected various kinds of irresolution in order to suggest the condition of genuinely antique texts, brought out the rhetorical and thematic uses [of textual irresolution] and thus the potential literariness of the feature."[23] If we enlarge the range of fragment characteristics to include thematic as well as formal ones, we can situate the genre within the larger family of the ruin poem. For the most immediate forerunner of the autonomous romantic fragment can be found in the eighteenth-century ruin landscape, occupying a plot adjacent to that occupied by the forerunner of what M. H. Abrams has defined as the "greater Romantic lyric."[24] While Abrams finds the source of this closurally secure romantic lyric genre in topographical local poetry, we can also isolate in the topography of ruins the elements which press towards the romantic fragment. In its most general form, the ruin "kind" of topographical poem presents a visible ruin in a landscape which provides a physical demonstration of the vanity of human constructions. The speaker then reads a humbling moral lesson in the detritus. Typically, the ruin motif is introduced in order to point out the vanity of pomp and glory. In his pioneering study of the ruin theme in literature, *Ruins and Empire*, Laurence Goldstein gracefully calls this poetic stance "the prophet's scorn for worldly splendor."[25] "The mouldering monuments of Fame / Your vain deluded hopes betray," writes John Hughes; and Dyer asks, "O luxury . . . What dreary change, what ruins are not thine?"[26] Goldstein, who might be set among other optimistic romanticists, interprets the romantic poets' response to the theme of the transience of empire as a turning to the domestic landscape and its consolations, which afford the poet "self-mastery, and through self-mastery, joy."[27] I am compelled to see the transformations in ruin poems in a more ideological light. First, the eighteenth-century ruin motif itself undergoes significant alterations, and the naturalizing of the ruin results in part from the notional requirements of industry and empire: the landscape functions as much as a political as a rural site (see chapter 3). Second, the prophetic "scorn for worldly splendor" is, in part, a function of confidence in the immortality of poetry, a confidence which takes a less public and more attenuated, naturalized form in the romantic period, but which is thereby no less closely linked to public issues.

Since we have also come to see, through critics like Anne Mellor and McFarland, that romanticism was built as much from anxiety, frustration, and irresolution as from the poetic shapes of self-mastery and joy, we might juxtapose the "greater romantic lyric" of domestic comfort to an alternative response to the ruined landscape, which occupies one line of filiation in the ruin tradition.[28] As the overt sources of reflection shift from the external world to the poet's subjective response to that world, the ruin theme is transposed into a structural element, and the ruin engenders the fragment.

Observing the "Taste for Fragments" edge out that for ruin, we can begin to distinguish between a ruin and a fragment. The salient difference is that between a temporal and spatial construct. If something is ruined, then presumably it once had a full form that has been eroded through time. A fragment, on the other hand, is simply a part of a whole. It may be part of a linguistic, temporal whole, or it may be part of a spatial, visual whole. Presented as a part of a temporal whole, the fragment alludes to a poetic unity somehow prematurely stopped. As a part of a spatial or visual whole, the fragment suggests that it is to be the site of a recovery and an immanent completion. There is something of a danger, however, in jumping too quickly from this generous spatial sense of poetic structure to defining the fragment as the central romantic genre. The Schlegelian logic that "Every poem is its own genre," "All Romantic poetry is the poetry of becoming," and "Romantic poetry is the art of poetry itself," suggests that every poem is its own fragment genre: each poem is individual and all poetry is incomplete.[29] This logic has recently taken hold of European and American interpreters of romanticism. Philippe Lacoue-Labarthe and Jean-Luc Nancy argue from within Schlegel and propose that "Romanticism will always be more than a period . . . in fact, it has not yet stopped in-completing the period it began."[30] Coleridge, McFarland's choice as the greatest English fragmentist, is translated into a representative emblem, and the incompletion and ruin of his work, "seen from the larger truths of existence, is nothing less than the final shape of every man's effort."[31] By situating the fragment more precisely as one strain within ruin poetry we are less likely to be overly romantic readers of ruin poems. So, in the final two essays of this study, I look at poems by Blake and Wordsworth to show the interrelationship of the structural claims of fragments and the thematic ones of ruin within a poetic aesthetic which was conforming to an apparent – that is, a romantic – split between the regions of the public and the private, the political and the aesthetic.[32]

An important historical link in the kinship between the ruin piece and the fragment and their connection with national myth-making can be found in the increasing eighteenth-century popularity of collections of those textual ruins called fragments and relics. Though the items in Percy's *Reliques* did not speak of ruin, anthologies of antiquities were evidence of ruin and decay through their very fragmented presentations. The "authenticity" was guaranteed by the inventory of incompletions. And much like the architectural ruins in the land-scape, textual ruins validated the antiquity of vernacular culture. It is not surprising to find the pieces "improved" upon by the zealous compiler.

If the ruin sentiment, allied to the antiquarian impulse, might give rise to sham ruins in the garden, then why should it not give rise to sham ruins in poetry as well? Here we can return to Levinson's argument and recognize that Macpherson's *Ossian* poems and Chatterton's Rowley texts are fine examples of this not merely literary, but broadly cultural fashion. So the romantic fragment poem might find a congenial readership in an already-formed audience of sham ruin readers. Certainly the Gothic elements in "Christabel" suggest that the poem belongs to one of Percy's collections; "The Giaour" and "Kubla Khan" might be fragments from an Orientalist's chresto-mathy; and Keats's first "Hyperion" fragment seems almost a piece of the Elgin Marbles.[33]

Yet compared with Macpherson's and Chatterton's efforts, none of the romantic fragments cited above so fully commit themselves to the past as to lose their flavor as contemporary, consciously created poems. The narrator of "The Giaour" is clearly an early nineteenth-century Englishman; the editorial apparatus that surrounds "Kubla Khan" insists on the poet's personal process of composition; and Keats's "Hyperion. A Fragment" is too crowded with Miltonisms and contemporary references to pose as an "authentic" Greek fragment. Though all these poems might be assimilated to the ruin sentiment, they also suggest that their incompletion may be more properly considered in visual or spatial, rather than historical or antiquarian, terms. This conforms, again, to the requirements of the naturalizing focus on ruin. The erosion of temporality, and the instantiation of permanence in an art made assimilable to nature, requires a poetic conceived in spatial terms. Just as antiquarianism provides the back-ground to the present but then, in the process of naturalization, opens up a wide moat between past and present, so the spatialization of ruin focuses attention on the non-historical, that is, the aesthetic dimen-sion of poetic events.

The romantic fragment was in one sense now *free* to include themes unconnected to the antiquarian interest in historical ruins, and in another sense *constrained* to avoid that antiquarian interest except insofar as it worked to substitute a mythic for an historical, a picturesque for a sublime, and a natural for a social version of the past.

Unmoored from an antiquarian grounding, the fragment opens itself up to a new poetic matter: the relation between its own incompletion and the greater whole to which it alludes, and which it both aspires to and struggles against. Insofar as the entire complex of poetic materials shifts towards the private and the autonomously aesthetic, this new matter takes the form of the problem of finding an adequation between what one wants to figure in language, and what one *can* figure in language.[34] So we may account for the significant transfer in attention from the *topos* of the immortality of poetry to that of the inexpressibility of poetry. The poetry of ruin in the eighteenth century gives place, in one form, to romanticism's ruined poetry.

IV

The fragment constitutes an important romantic poetic shape; the lyric is the characteristic vehicle for the romantic poetic voice. The alteration of the temporal-historical into the spatial-mythic form of ruin is contemporaneous with the opening up of a space for that inward meditation which had earlier in the eighteenth century been occupied by an objective and didactic voice cloistered in a poetic structure of permanence. The poetry which conspires with the imagining of Britain tends not to make *narrative* sense out of experience, but rather proposes in a *lyric* form a single, undifferentiated permanence. The notable exception to this is the great ruin poem *Jerusalem*, which insists upon narrative to assert temporality against the somnolence of naturalized poetry. Blake remembers the history whose atrocities make up an antithetical narrative to the mythic benignity of the lyric spoken in solitude in the landscape.

The loss entailed by this lyric proposition was presented in ruin poetry as longing for the days of the Bard, nostalgia for the figure of a central political, social poet who, sometime in an ever receding past, yoked poetry, prophecy, and political life. The compulsive recourse to the "lost bard" motif figures an anxiety over what would later come to be understood benignly as the lyric, private scope of poetry in general, but whose origins are found in the actual suppression of Celtic bardic voices. The evocation of poetic marginality, fixing the poet in a formulated phrase as the "lost bard", first theorizes the dispossessed poet and then allows for the recovery of poetic function in the role of the solitary singer. What we conceive of as modern poetry – the poetry which begins in the romantic period – is born by being defined against this "lost" poetic tradition. Such a lyric voice was to remain the dominant representation of the poet until recent political currents (the women's movement and cultural liberation struggles, minority cultures and other imagined communities) began the process of reclaiming poetry for group voices.

In addition to being a component in the mythology of a national past, the motif of the lost bard needs also to be thought of as a thematization of the decline of the immortality-of-poetry *topos*. If, as the "death of the bard" theme suggests, the poem can no longer present itself as the reparation of a broken world, then it will pasture a small green patch of subjective response. Poetry and the ideology of poetic autonomy thus produce, at the end of the eighteenth century, an aesthetic spa for the world-weary.

The representation of poetic marginality, the other side of poetic autonomy, is often presented in romantic writing as if it were an erosion of poetry itself. But as Stuart Curran's recent work on the genres of romantic poetry has demonstrated, the late eighteenth and early nineteenth centuries produced an extraordinary volume of published poetic texts: "the most eccentric feature of [the] entire culture [was] that it was simply mad for poetry."[35] The representation and the actuality of poetic marginality are quite distinct phenomena. The antiquarian researches which surrounded and also gave impetus to this massive group of poems are also closely linked to the production of a sense of cultural homogeneity. As Curran reminds us, it was through Percy's *Reliques* and Alexander Chalmers's 21-volume collection of English poets that "Great Britain recovered its national literature."[36] It was through such collections and histories that England produced for itself a version of a continuous poetic and hence, national, tradition. In this sense, even while the "lost bard" motif laments a diminished public poetic function, poetry continued to carry out a central ideological task, precisely through its "natural," private representations. The figure of the marginal poet is produced by and serves the larger hegemonic imagination of a community. The voice of that tradition, as it conforms to the ideological shape of nation-making, necessarily appears univocal and natural. Graham

Pechy makes a similar point in his discussion of Wordsworth's poetry: "In the space vacated by politics a transhistorical community is projected."[37] We can say more precisely that the lyric speaker speaks for this transhistorical community, and is identified with a British nation. Wordsworth's projection is grounded in earlier versions within the family of ruin poetry. The economy of the poetic produces both the contours of an ancient tradition of poetic activity as well as the figure of a transhistorical, solitary lyric voice as the latest version of the national poet.

Out of this complex of thematic and formal relations we can draw a genealogy of ruin poetry. We can isolate three major lines of filiation constitutive of ruin practice. First, beginning with "The Ruin," is the tradition of topographical poetry, one branch of which, the topographical building poem, works forward into the poetry of ruined castles and abbeys in the English countryside.

Second and closely related to the topographical line is the tradition of antiquarianism. This includes within its range textual fragments and relics, such as Percy's *Reliques of Ancient English Poetry*. It also presents the materials for the "lost bard" theme which is often found located within a ruined building poem. The antiquarian lineage is, in turn, closely linked to the tradition of the miscellany which, when it meets up with antiquarian fragments or textual ruins, lays the ground for the validation of poetic structure reduced to the shape of a brief lyric. From Tottel's *Miscellany* (1557), whose model was *The Greek Anthology*, and Goldsmith's *Beauties of English Poetry* (1767) up through Palgrave's *Golden Treasury* (1861), we move toward the anthologization of poetry, which means, in turn, the fragmentation of narrative poetry into lyric form. Francis Jeffrey, writing about 40 years earlier, suggests the same notion about lyricism that Edgar Allan Poe will express in "The Poetic Principle." Jeffrey describes the process of reading completed texts of long poems as one of fragmentation: "The truth is, we suspect, that after we once know what it contains, no long poem is ever read, but in fragments – and that the connecting passages, which are always skipped after the first reading, are often so tedious as to defer us from thinking of a second."[38]

So the anthology guides the fragment toward the condition of the lyric. The form itself is also closely linked with national fortunes: anthologies preserve the image of the nation as a set of lyric segments, as if the result of a collective literary effort. One nineteenth-century cousin of the anthology is *In Memoriam*, which Tennyson himself had originally planned to publish under the title "Fragments of an Elegy." And it was Tennyson who encouraged Palgrave to put together *The Golden Treasury*. In the preface to the volume, Palgrave invokes Tennyson's "high-hearted patriotism" as the muse of this "true national anthology." The original compilation ends with what Palgrave calls the "Book" of Wordsworth, the poet who gave the first half of the nineteenth century its "distinctive character." So Wordsworth is made to preside over lyric nationalism. The mission of coercing regional cultures into the shape of Great Britain having been, albeit imperfectly, completed, Palgrave can end his introductory remarks by turning patriotism out towards imperialism: the volume will be appreciated "wherever the Poets of England are honoured, wherever the dominant language of the world is spoken."[39] In the twentieth century, the poem itself has expanded into the category of the anthology: *The Cantos* and *The Waste Land* are in part compilations, and they exhibit as well the antiquarian desire to preserve relics.

The third major line of ruin poetry is what we can call the tradition of "accidental" ruins, poems that remained unfinished but found their way into the emergence of an aesthetic of incompletion that characterizes the romantic fragment and its modernist heir, the poem assembled out of the ruins of other poems and documents. So we can see, for example, that the interest in poets' posthumously published fragments is most illuminatingly investigated in the light of antiquarian interest in textual remains, as well as in the light of the supervention of lyric over narrative.

The ancestors of this branch of the ruin family are *The Faerie Queene* and *The Canterbury Tales*, and the most eloquent romantic example is Mary Shelley's editing into an *intentional* poetic structure of the "accidental" ruin / fragment of "The Triumph of Life," which Shelley had left unfinished at his death. In her preface to the 1824 *Posthumous Poems*, Mary Shelley writes that the poem "was his last work, and was left in so unfinished a state that I arranged it in its present form with great difficulty."[40] Her arrangement was deft, however, and responsive to the exigencies of the fragment fashion, for she omitted $3\frac{1}{2}$ lines which existed in Shelley's manuscript but which took the edge off a more suitably aposeopeic breaking-off point in the poem. These lines were not included in texts of the poem until Locock's 1911 edition.[41] The additional lines begin a new narrative cycle in the poem, and by adding them the portent of the question

"But what is life?", which is how Mary presented the ending, is altered from opening up onto an unspecifiable answer to being simply a pause in the narration. Our present-day fascination with the congruence of ruin and fragment is evidenced in the fact that the Blake poem which has garnered the most attention recently has been *Vala / The Four Zoas*, an internally fragmented, revised, crossed-out, and unpublished quasi-accidental-become-canonical fragmented ruin.

Each of the following four chapters explores an aspect of the ruin motif in English poetry. Together, they present episodes in the thematic and structural fortunes of ruin poetry from the Renaissance through romanticism. In each discussion, poetic and ideological intentions are interpreted as being intertwined. For the most part, this study records successes in the reparation of the meaning and shape of ruin in both poetic and ideological terms. With Blake's *Vala / The Four Zoas*, however, we are reminded that the subjective experience of ruin usually signifies defeat. But in between utter ruin and entire reparation runs another voice. The poetic of opposition to the official version of national victory over ruin is a faint but persistent sound. That oppositional voice is strongest in Blake's *Jerusalem*. His presentation of the idea of the nation as communitarian society links Blake back to the radical patriots of the seventeenth century. His ruin poem is an imagination of a poetic and a social wholeness whose constitution would be made by human variety and heterogeneity. Wordsworth's early embracing of republican ideals links him back also, to the traditions of the Real Whigs, the eighteenth-century Commonwealthmen.[42] The suffering human ruins which populate his early landscapes figure in their own bodies, though they can hardly speak, a refusal to be entirely assimilated into the picturesque terrain and a barely discernible demand to be represented.

The image of the ruin ceases to be poetically fecund once the secure grounding of national identity has been accomplished. Mythically stable, the equivalent poetry of the Victorian period enacts a pure idealization of the past: most significantly in Tennyson's *Idylls of the King*, but also in the general fashion for the chivalric and the medieval.[43] The image of ruin is not poetically central again until the poems of Rosenberg and Sassoon describe, and then Eliot attempts to repair, the crisis of European imperialism in the opening decades of the twentieth century.

2

Ruinists in Rome

The nation-making confirmed in later eighteenth-century ruin poetry both recapitulates and reverses Boadicea's native stand against Roman imperialism. The national images of both England and of Great Britain are built on Roman ruins, and so it is among the ruins of Rome that we can explore the context out of which the romantic ruin emerged. Important poems by Spenser, Dyer, and Byron return to this classical place of ruin sentiment, and it is here that the conditions are articulated for the poem as preservative of the nation. In his translation of Du Bellay's *Antiquitez de Rome*, Spenser maps out the criteria for the *topos* of poetic permanence, and enacts the building of an English sonnet sequence upon Roman ruin. In 1740, John Dyer turns to the ruins of Rome to locate the precedent for an English empire, but he must also find a way to present the distance and the difference between the fallen Roman empire and the intentions of the newly developing identity of an English empire. The doctrine of progress, so crucial to Enlightenment thought, comes athwart decay on the very ground of its own source of confidence – the artifacts and cultural heritage of antiquity. In *The Ruins of Rome*, it is finally the dependability of Dyer's own regulating and moralizing language that ensures the boundary between past and present. In Byron's version of Roman ruins, poetic structure cannot function as a rampart against the decay of architectural structure: self and ruin merge. Byron attempts to repair this ruin by elevating the category of the aesthetic above that of the temporal, and the inexpressibility *topos* over that of immortality. As he does this, Byron participates in that marginalizing of poetic voice which characterizes the romantic persona and distinguishes it from the public, moralizing voice of a poet such as Dyer. At the same time, however, Byron's position as outlaw and internationalist enables him to face the continuity of past into present unencumbered by the mythic mystifications which characterize much nationally-interested eighteenth-century ruin poetry. The cost of

Byron's rebel assertion, however, is the structural integrity of his poem.

I

In Spenser's rendering of Roman ruins we find the thematic cate-nation of poetic, political, and imperial fame. Three of Spenser's 1591 *Complaints* work with the theme of ruin: *Visions of Bellay*, first published in the *Theatre for Worldlings*, and revised for the 1591 volume; *The Ruins of Rome*, a translation of Du Bellay's *Antiquitez de Rome*; and *The Ruins of Time*, an elegy for the poet Sidney and ruined House of Dudley, set at the site of the ruins of the Roman British city of Verulam.[1] All three poems pose questions about and present solutions to the uncertain and interwoven relationships among ruins, poetry, and national identity. The lesson Spenser intends to teach by way of these three poems is that the image of the nation is made in poetry, and that poetry can ensure national immortality, repairing the ruins of previous empires and shifting the locus of the *translatio imperii* into the domain of poetic structure. From Rome to England, the three poems also convey us from a universal and classical poetic model to a native one, from the Roman poets buried beneath the city to the mourned poet Sidney, "In whom all bountie and all vertuous love / Appeared in their native propertis" (RT, ll. 283–4). Unlike the later native ruin of the eighteenth century, which will ground the spirits of the place in the comfortable locality of a benign nature, Spenser produces a Sidney who, escaping "earthlie slime" (RT, l. 290), is urban and courtly and associated with a classical cosmopol-itanism transferred from Italy to England through Verulam, British remnant of the Roman Empire. The ruins of Rome and of Verulam as the visible and material signs of the past introduce the problem which the immortality-of-poetry *topos* solves in a national key. The topic itself is ubiquitous in the period, offering the English poet not only a function for poetry, but, with sources in Horace, Ovid, and Proper-tius, the kind of classical lineage whose very existence and antiquity testifies to the validity of the assertion of immortality.[2] In addition to such literary value, the *topos* offers a privileged, though not entirely transcendent, place to preserve lovers and nations.

The foundation of a national poetry – that is, a poetry whose explicit mission is not only to join the classical tradition of fame, but also to integrate the nation into that order – belongs to the period when Tudor absolutism asserts England's coherence as a political unity. Sidney's *Apologie for Poetrie* both inaugurates and justifies English poetry as linguistically autonomous, and Spenser's elegy for Sidney in *The Ruins of Time* monumentalizes and recognizes that effort.

At the same time in which this Renaissance national poetry adumbrates the cultural nationalism necessary to the modern state, its values are yoked to the feudal polity. Margaret Ferguson makes the astute psycho-political point that the Renaissance "nationalist family romance," in which Troy and Rome are figured as the fathers of European states, portrays "the French and English monarchies as siblings, and potential rivals, to the empire founded by another son of Troy, Aeneas."[3] This is an aristocratic nationalism, in which nations are differentiated within a feudal family network which predates and whose representations continue through the establishment of absolutism. So, for example, in *The Ruins of Time*, Spenser prizes and attends to the strength of England's filial link to the Romans at the narrative expense of the link to the Saxons. In the period of the English Revolution, when the tensions arising in the absolutist period break open into a real challenge to monarchical power, the rebels will call upon a Northern and native ancestry, pitting the heritage of Saxon freedoms against the Norman Yoke in a seventeenth-century native patriotism that is both progressive and oppositional. Spenser's commitment to Protestantism links him to that later group which will challenge the Court, but such a religious dedication does not interrupt Spenser's own role as a poet aspiring to the Court and anxious for patrons to replace the ruins of the Dudley family.

Nonetheless, the pressures of Protestantism do provide a counterweight to the immortality-of-poetry *topos*. While *The Ruins of Rome* matches the immortality of poetry against the ephemerality of architecture, Spenser's earlier translation, *Visions of Bellay*, iterates a decay whose reparation is transcendent, not poetic: "Sith onely God surmounts all times decay, / In God alone my confidence do stay" (Sonnet 1). Through the course of the sequence Spenser hints at the power and possibility of a poetic solution to physical decay by building each sonnet as a verbal version of architectural triumph, which is then intentionally "ruined" by a closural couplet describing destruction. So, after an elaborate description of "A stately frame" decorated with "shining Christall" and "*Afrike* gold," with floors of "Jasp and Emeraude," Sonnet 2 concludes: "An earthequake shooke the hill from lowest seat, / And overthrew this frame with ruine great." *The Theatre for Worldlings*, the volume put together by the Dutch Protestant exile Jan Vander Noodt, is a likely site for a religious, transcendent solution to the problem of ruin. Yet the mastery of poetic structure over its subject–matter, implicit in the persistent pattern of building and ruination throughout the *Visions of Bellay*, is intimated as a mediate ground between heavenly and temporal power. In the later *The Ruins of Rome* and *The Ruins of Time*, Spenser will explicitly mobilize the immortality-of-poetry *topos* as a poetic resolution whose sway will extend over a political territory. The claim he will make for poetry then will be not only its endurance, but its capacity to make the nation itself endure. By nation, however, he will mean, not the territorial and cultural landscape of people and earth of the nineteenth–century nation, but the absolutist state administration that he serves.[4]

The Ruins of Rome, the central ruin text of the *Complaints* volume, establishes the structure that settles between heavenly permanence and imperial ephemerality. Like his *Visions of Bellay*, this sequence translates French into English, and participates in that nationalist "family romance," in which the vernacular is established, but securely linked to an aristocratic and classical ancestry. The issue of national power in this poem takes the form of imperial absolutism, and introduces the poet as the agent of imperial permanence. But Spenser also insists on the transfer of power from Rome to England by asserting the *difference* between his own situation and that of the Romans. Spenser writes that while ancient civilizations praised their own works, Crete boasting of the Labyrinth, the Rhodian recalling the "great Colosse," he is instead reaching out across time and space, to "sing above all moniments / Seven *Romane* Hils, the worlds 7. wondrements" (Sonnet 2). Of course this power transfer is as much religious as political, contemporary as ancient, and Spenser wishes to save the classical continuity while disestablishing the institutional link to the Roman Church. As spokesman from a later period and a westerly nation, Spenser attests to both the presence of the past and the power of the present. The vehicle of that presence and power is poetic structure, itself an ambiguous compromise between transcendent and political claims. *The Ruins of Rome* proves the immortality-of-poetry *topos* by showing how the voices of the Roman poets, those "ashie ghoasts" (Sonnet 15), call to the present poet to hear and respond to them from under the material ruins of the Roman Empire. The poet can monumentalize the Romans by extending their fame, which has been wrought by those writings which speak of empire:

> The corpes of *Rome* in ashes is entombed,
> And her great spirite rejoyned to the spirite
> Of this great masse, is in the same enwombed;
> But her brave writings, which her famous merite
> In spite of time, out of the dust doth reare,
> Doo make her Idole through the world appeare.
>   (Sonnet 5)

The allure of the architectural ruins comes to Spenser from the voices of the poets who thereby memorialize the empire whose decline is materialized in the objective decay. These ruins do not serve an aesthetic but a mytho–historical order. As the lineage of poets – Roman to Du Bellay to Spenser – is established through the relay of poems, so the fame of empire is also preserved. Thus the immortality of the nation is ensured by the *topos* of the immortality of poetry. The Protestant, Court nationalist is thus able to accommodate the requirements of the aristocratic mythology of origins without dislodging national aspirations.

The monument that Rome builds for herself is strengthened by the one the poet builds. The poet's explicit intention in *The Ruins of Rome* is to dig below the urban ruins, to "let those deep Abysses open rive" (Sonnet 1), and to make contact with the human spirit trapped there and release it through the newly made poetic structure. And there is no more secure shape to hand than the sonnet, whose triumphant closure admits no breach. As if to secure the poem's shape in the face of "these haughtie heapes" (Sonnet 27), Spenser transforms the Italian sonnet pattern used by Du Bellay, with its more fluid sestet, into the compact and local structure which we have come to call the "English" sonnet. Rather than meditating at length over a vast terrain as eighteenth–century ruinists will do, Spenser succinctly resolves each unit of his urban elegy. In this way the sonnet structure repairs the chaos of Rome's ruins.

Structurally buffered though he may be from the immediacy of ruin, the spectacle nonetheless appalls the poet: "why were not these Romane palaces / Made of some matter no less firme and strong" (Sonnet 9) than the earth itself? Of course the buildings *are* made of earth, but the stamp upon them, the shaping powers of the architect, cannot withstand the degenerative course of time. In Sonnets 25 and 27, the poet cannot with humility entirely affirm or deny the immortality of his own verse, but the examples within Sonnet 25 remake and reawaken Rome through the poetic "lofty style":

> O that I had the *Thracian* Poets harpe,
> For to awake out of th'infernall shade
> Those antique Caesars, sleeping long in darke,
> The which this ancient Citie whilome made:
>   Or that I had *Amphions* instrument,
> To quicken with his vitall notes accord,
> The stonie ioynts of these old walls now rent,
> By which th'*Ausonian* light might be restor'd:
>   Or that at least I could with pencill fine,
> Fashion the pourtraicts of these Palacis,
> By paterne of great *Virgils* spirit divine;
> I would assay with that which in me is,
>   To build, with leuell of my lofty style,
>   That which no hands can evermore compyle.

The fame of Orpheus and of Amphion, whose name abides even after the Theban walls have crumbled, provides the speaker with a link to the double tradition within which he places himself: on the one hand, his classical heritage anchored to a universal empire from which "Nought from the Roman Empire might be quight"(Sonnet 8); and, on the other, that of the supervention of architectural by poetic construction. The sonnet ends with an affirmation of the monumentalizing function of poetic structure as well as style. Though humility forbids the speaker to say that he has accomplished this ambition, the *topos* says it for him. In Sonnet 32, the last one of the sequence, the poet looks to Rome's ruins and complains:

> If under heaven anie endurance were,
> These moniments, which not in paper writ,

> But in Porphyre and Marble doo appear,
> Might well have hoped to have obtained it.

Spenser's distress here, like Wordsworth's later lament that words are
lodged in "shrines so frail," has already been ironized by the earlier
sonnets and so the poet persists: "Nath'less my Lute, whome Phoe-
bus deign'd to give, / Cease not to sound the olde antiquities."

In the same manner in which Du Bellay has revived "Olde Rome
out of her ashes," so has Spenser revived Du Bellay's text and given it
a "second life" (Envoy). "Needes must he all eternitie survive, / That
can to other give eternall days" (Envoy). These remarks compliment
Du Bellay, but also protect Spenser. The claims of temporality are
deflected to the field of fame, where Romans, Du Bellay, and Spenser
will all flourish, away from the mortal and decaying world in which all
buildings become detritus. This optimistic turn has penetrated the
rubble itself. In Sonnet 27, Spenser looks to a world in which even
ruins may be amended:

> Yet these olde fragments are for paternes borne:
>   Then also marke, how Rome from day to day,
> Repayring her decayed fashion,
> Renewes herselfe with buildings rich and gay.

Master of space and time, the Roman empire had contained all
empires within itself,

> All that which *Athens* ever brought forth wise,
> All that which *Afrike* ever brought forth strange,
> All that which *Asie* ever had of prise,
> Was here to see.
>   (Sonnet 29)

Now, through the Bellay-Spenser mediation, as Spenser intimates in
Sonnet 27, it may master the future also. The permanence of poetry
in the face of historical decline roots national permanence within
poetic continuity. Though the city had been sacked as recently as
1527, the resistance of Rome to utter obliteration is materialized in
her writers' words which wield their power even now:

And that though time doth Commonwealths devowre,
Yet no time should so low embase their hight,
   That [Rome's] head earth'd in her foundations deep,
   Should not her name and endles honour keep.

                            (Sonnet 8)

The poet does not finally make an opposition between poetry and empire, but maintains that they are interdependent: poetry keeps empire alive by memorializing it, and so makes memorable the ruins which are the apparent subject–matter of the poem.

In his discussion of Du Bellay's *Antiquitez*, Thomas Greene suggests that the sequence exemplifies the anxiety of influence: the gleaner of the relics of past poetry "will sow no new seed, make no new design. In the calm of this humility, the resignation of this sorrow, humanism found the strength to comprehend its tragedy and its solitude."[5] But while this may be true when Du Bellay responds to the classical model of poetic heritage, Spenser's version of continuity points his own nation and its poetry in the direction of futurity. His Protestantism moves him closer to domestic, national intentions and delivers a strength equal to the burden of the past.[6]

Spenser invites the future to memorialize his own work, drawing into the sonnets the image of the English nation. The poet's fame will result from his having been the first of his own "Nation" to have sung "Th' olde honour of the people gowned long" (Sonnet 32). Linked to the past, then, he produces poetry in the vernacular, in the tongue of the emerging nation. Du Bellay had made the point for himself explicitly: "D'avoir chanté le premier des François." Spenser sidesteps the problem of nationality by translating "des François" as the generic "Nation."

The "Envoy" of the sequence harnesses together the issues of nation, poetry, and ruin. Having poetically repaired the ruins of Rome, Spenser turns to his own master, Du Bellay, and acknowledges his precedence. Du Bellay earned his immortality through his feat of reviving "Olde *Rome* out of her ashes." Having repaired Rome, "Needes must he all eternite survive, / That can to other give eternall dayes." Spenser's generosity to Du Bellay will ensure his own permanence.

In *The Ruins of Time*, Spenser's elegy for the poet Sidney and the

Dudleys, the immortality-of-poetry *topos* is situated deeply in British soil. Though Verulam was defeated by the "hardie Saxons" (RT, l. 112), the kinship between the Roman and British empires organizes the poem. Troy, after all, belongs to the originary myths of both Rome and Britain. What Verlame – the woman spirit of the ruins – is most acutely aware of, however, is that the attacks of Pendragon, Boadicea, and the Saxons do not desolate her as much as her neglect by the poets. Only Camden has recounted the history of Verlame, and in her lines of praise to him, we feel the claims of national history jostling for position against Christian claims for transcendence: "Cambden, though Time all moniments obscure, / Yet thy just labours ever shall endure" (ll. 174–5). It is through poetry, however, that the most lasting monuments are built:

> Yet it is comfort in great languishment,
> To be bemoned with compassion kinde,
> And mitigates the anguish of the minde.
>   (ll. 159–61)

National antiquity in this poem is claimed via classical lineage, not through the autonomy of British earth, as the eighteenth–century ruinists will assert. In fact, the image of nature reclaiming culture in a benevolent return to nativity is utterly unlike Verlame's lament over the "moorish fennes" (l. 140) which now replace the course of the Thames by the side the ancient city. The earth is despised as "earthlie slime" (l. 290). After presenting Verlame's lament, the poem modulates into an elegy for the Dudleys, which structures most of the remaining parts of the poem. The point of linkage is that both Dudley, Earl of Leicester and Sidney, Leicester's nephew and the author of the *Apologie*, like Verlame, have no monument. Neither ancient city nor contemporary House has been the subject of poetry's labor of permanence: "Ne anie Poet seekes him to revive; / Yet manie Poets honour'd him alive" (ll. 222–3). The forgotten ruins of Verulam mourn the unremembered leader and poet and Verlame finds cause for her vocation in the fact that it has been the role of poets to monumentalize ruin, as exemplified in Spenser's own *Ruins of Rome*.

Sidney is not only an unmourned poet; he is figured as a national martyr. Again, the tension between transcendent and national intentions is felt as the dead poet is described politically and religiously:

he did devise
Unto his heavenlie maker to present
His bodie, as a spotles sacrifise;
And chose, that guiltie hands of enemies
Should powre forth th'offring of his guiltles blood:
So life exchanging for his countries good.

(ll. 296–301)

The deaths of Leicester, Walsingham, and Sidney propel the theme of the poem toward the issue of the relationship between power and poetry. The abstract problem of Fame is shown to be closely tied to a *realpolitik*, and Spenser makes a bid for his own usefulness in the same breath:

Provide therefore (ye Princes) whilst ye live,
That of the *Muses* ye may befriended bee,
Which unto men eternite do give;

(ll. 365–7)

Verlame then sings a song of the immortality of poetry, which alone can rise "Above the reach of ruinous decay" (l. 422): "wise wordes taught in numbers for the runne, / Recorded by the Muses, live for ay" (ll. 402–3). So the circle of Fame completes itself. Figured as the work's persona, Verlame perpetuates the poet Sidney and so brings fame to her own ruins, which will now be "memorized" (l. 364) for monumentalizing the lost statesman and the poet who died for his country's good – the poet whose own work promoted the nation *as* a good. Verulam's ruins are thus "English'd," become part of Britain. Since the Dudleys are associated with passionate Protestantism and Sidney with the claims of a vernacular poetry (in which Sidney seals the values of both courtier and Protestant), the Englishing of ruins is both an homage to the Dudleys' aspirations and a preparation for the nationalism of later generations of poets and statesmen, in which the language of religion will serve as the vehicle for the assertions of a material, not transcendental, community. In the final shuttle of fame, we hear the voice of Spenser in *propria persona*, who takes the image of ruin as a metaphor for his elegy: he calls *The Ruins of Time* "this broken verse" (l. 678). But the poem as monument repairs its own ruin, as Spenser centers himself as a national poet, repairing the ruins of empire through the *translatio imperii*.

II

Spenser's sonnet sequence turns on the axis of the immortality-of-poetry *topos* as the figure for the perpetuation of the nation. John Dyer's 1740 version of the theme is grounded in "liberty" as the principal concept linking England to Rome and past to present. Unlike Spenser's poem of aristocratic nationalism, Dyer's belongs to the world which had been built through the partial triumph of the seventeenth–century English revolution. Dyer lives in a nation which is aware of itself as distinct from other nations chiefly in its growth as a mercantile center of Europe and increasingly, with commercial expansion in America, the West Indies, and India, as a rival to France and The Netherlands. The ideological apparatus which encrusts this growth takes the form of the tradition of liberty: Britain as the protector of liberty embodied in the protection of property. Dyer produces an analogical relation between Rome and England, which he portrays as a concrete and economic similarity. The connection is no longer through the filial link of classical ties within the European aristocratic mythology of national origins, but through an analysis of the way in which Rome and its analogue, England, inhabit and control markets and trade. Hence the reiteration of the issue of trade throughout Dyer's *The Ruins of Rome*. Of course the decline of the Roman empire renders the analogy as terrifying as it is inviting as prospect and as history. Spenser uses poetic structure to organize the past mythologically, and perhaps, to supersede historical exigency. Dyer enlists poetry in an effort to forge an image of an autonomous nation aware of itself historically, and so able to defend itself from history's depredations. This confidence is the analytical ground of "Whig history," with both its poise and its posturing. Again we sense the necessity of a prior, Roman ruin, to the present nation–making enterprise.

Dyer's *The Ruins of Rome* thus serves as a central example of that eighteenth–century ruin poem whose provenance is in classical decay, but whose subject–matter is the moral ratio between pasts and presents: the past of Rome to its present; the past of Rome to

England's present. Laurence Goldstein describes Dyer's visit to Italy as his "first traumatic experience of history,"[7] and it is the character of both the breach and the defense constructed against it that draws our attention to the ruin motif. In the wake of the Settlement of 1688, it may have seemed that the threat of historical defeat had been adjusted to a new modernity, in which England could remove itself from the course of historical decline, having salvaged a British tradition to the victors' satisfaction from the opposite threats of communitarianism and Catholic absolutism. Dyer's optimism is salted with anxiety, however, and the image of Rome he calls upon is a model both to emulate and to avoid. Unlike Gibbon's reading of Rome's Augustan period, which he depicts as a dialectic of the bad and the not so bad,[8] Dyer contributes to that other framing of Augustinism which discovered in the Roman Empire the linking of the highest gains of imperial and cultural honor:

> Happy Augustus!
> . . .
> Thrice glorious Days,
> Auspicious to the Muses, Then rever'd,
> Then hallow'd was the Fount, or secret Shade,
> Or open Mountain or whatever Scene
> The poet chose to tune th' ennobling Rhyme
> Melodious; ev'n the rugged Sons of War;
> Ev'n the rude Hinds rever'd the Poet's name:
> (ll. 308, 383–9)[9]

A good part of what makes the Roman Imperial world so compelling to Dyer is that there poetry and empire go hand in hand. While Spenser attempts to prove poetry a superior good to empire, because capable of preserving it, for Dyer the flourishing of poetry is symptomatic of the health of empire.

Dyer performs poetically for the ruins of Rome what painters such as Hubert Robert and Pannini had done visually: he assembles the great ruined buildings of Rome into a grand and processional arrangement, rather than into a just representation of the early eighteenth–century disorder of the city. Jean Clay describes this anthologizing impulse in eighteenth–century ruin painting: "L'objectif est à la fois de rapprocher des bâtiments disperses dans la réalité et d'inventer un site coherent, une proposition urbanistique plausible qui les contienne."[10] The invention of a coherent site is crucial to Dyer's poetic enterprise. He wants to erect a poetic structure that will be both orderly and plausible; that is, to render a Rome both descriptively and historically coherent, and thereby redeem the ruins of empire. By reference to history Dyer can find the progress which is paralleled in his contemporary British expansionism, and by descriptive detail Dyer will find the elements of that aesthetic organization which is entering into the interpretation of Rome as the city rises as a museum out of the junkyard of history. In this way, Dyer adumbrates that separation out of the aesthetic from the political whose romantic shape we recognize in Byron's version of the ruins of Rome.

In paintings by Robert and Pannini, the ruins function as a kind of internal frame, a boundary in visual space.[11] Dyer enumerates the ruins of Rome in order to build a boundary or barrier between the temporal force which has ruined them, and the structure of his poetic text, whose very solidity is to be taken as an index of the health of his nation. In his confident descriptions, Dyer is of his age, "undertaking a meticulous examination of the things themselves for the first time, and then of transcribing what has [been] gathered in smooth, neutralized, and faithful words."[12] The poet's confidence in the transparency of the language he has to hand is symptomatic of how "greatness of empire and purity of diction have always gone together."[13] Dyer is poised on the cusp of a contradictory vision of antiquity, in which progress meets decay at the site of its birth. Dyer shifts his emphasis from the classical sources of thought to the economic and martial heritage which the same antiquity offers, and focuses on how England can escape the ruin which the Romans could not elude. In Dyer's poem the resolution accrues around the meaning and conduct of the term "Liberty," the Whig antidote to that Tyranny which, though it strangled the Romans, had been averted as a threat in Britain's case by the Settlement of 1688.

Dyer's interest in and attention to scales of organization amongst the debris of Rome is in keeping with his delight in taxonomy wherever it links up with empire and with trade. For example, here is how he explains to his patrons why he has delayed in finishing his corrections to the text of *The Ruins of Rome*:

I am about a Map of England, in which the courses of its rivers are described with the heights of their tides and navigations, and those places to which their navigations may and ought to be extended: and where communications should be made from river to river by good roads or canals, the latter to circulate our trade. Also at all manufacturing towns their manufactures expressed, and at the mouths of rivers and havens their chief exportations. And in which the courses of its hills and vales and of its lead, copper, tine, and coalmines are described; also the principal Roman roads, and the chiefest curiosities, ancient and modern.[14]

Once the poet has performed his classificatory and genealogical work on it, Dyer's Rome is as intelligible to him as England is, and the link between Roman and British empire is then literally mapped onto British soil as the "principal Roman roads" of antiquity. Liberty is the conceptual content of Empire before its ruin as Dyer finds it in the past as a guide to the present and the future, and Trade is the content which fills up the structure of liberty: it is on this basis that Rome both directs and warns the present:

> O *Liberty*.
> Parent of happiness, celestial born
> . . .Be *Britain's* Care;
> With her secure, prolong thy lov'd retreat;
>
> . . .
> But thou, thy nobler Britons teach to Rule;
> To check the Ravage of Tyrannic Sway;
> To quell the Proud; to spread the joys of Peace
> And various blessings of ingenious Trade.
>   (ll. 210–14; 224–7)

On the basis of this intelligibility, the poet is able to construct a poetic boundary between the ruins and himself, between the past and present, while preserving the analogy between Rome and Britain. The structure of the poem and its appropriateness as the site of moralization derives from the strength of this boundary, and it is from the constructed vantage point that Dyer is able to moralize in the transitive sense of the verb: that is, to alter the condition of the detritus by subjecting it to moral reflection.

Spenser's Rome is urban and classical; he never went to Rome, and the ruins he describes are derived from Du Bellay's poetic figures. But between the Renaissance and the eighteenth century, Rome had become a living museum, the site of aesthetic attention, where the melancholic look of ivy slowly began to compete with the thought of political event. The appearance of nature amidst these urban ruins as the vehicle of aesthetic meaning signals the coupling of aesthetic with historical distance by which it is possible to invoke the past *as* aesthetic and so deny its historical power.[15] This aesthetic response is littered throughout Dyer's poem: the stone is revealed to be alive with melancholy under the gaze of the poet. The fountains of Rome, in the shape of the Empire's conquered rivers, "with dripping locks / hang over their Urns, and mournfully among / The plaintive echoing Ruins pour their streams" (ll. 46–7). The dust of buildings rises with a "show of Sad Decay" (l. 131). Even the river "mournfully" rolls his "neglected wave" (ll. 12–3). The entire landscape is vital with affect, loading the urban detritus with a hint of the mollifying work of nature which is the mark of the later eighteenth–century British ruin poem. But Dyer does not submit entirely to the natural lure, and he makes his initial progress in the poem by sorting out the ruined prospect into a manageable walk, carving out a path amidst the ruins and then making the survey correspond to a chronology in relation to which the speaker can erect his historical and poetic analogy.

In the poet's initial survey, the ruins exert a counter–traction to the gravitational pull of history. The marbles are "Fall'n, Fall'n," "sunk," "Fall'n; obscured in dust" (ll. 16–18), but though they sink ever closer to each other and to the substratum of dust, they remain "ev'n yet Majestical" (l. 19). Though Dyer does not, as Byron will later in the century, conflate this pull towards similitude with the dust that *he* will someday become, he does capture the drag of the past upon the present, observing a monk who views

> The solitary, Silent, Solemn Scene,
> Where Caesars, Heroes, Peasants, Hermits lie,
> Blended in dust together.
>
> (ll.337–9)

But a spirit – the soul – moves *away from* the dusty prospect: while the speaker is looking at the "silent heap" of rubble,

> The solemn Scene
> Elates the soul, while now the rising Sun
> Flames on the Ruins, in the purer air
> Tow'ring aloft, upon the glittering plain,
> Like broken rocks, a vast circumfrence.
>
> (ll. 19–23)

As the eye moves down the ruin, the soul moves upwards, and the vertical oscillation becomes, abruptly, a horizontal one, as the speaker scans the vast terrain that makes up one "vast circumfrence" of the landscape's detritus. Dyer's depiction of the broken rocks suggests England's ancient stone circles, and the speaker goes immediately on in the poem to link the past of Rome to a present British glory. The buildings resolve themselves earthward while the imperial passage races into Whig modernity. Cicero's Cataline oratory invokes Liberty as the "parent of happiness," who is then implored to act as a power upon Britain. Through Liberty Dyer links the Roman names of martial and civil power with "The sacred Names / Of *Cecil, Raleigh, Walsingham* and *Drake*" (ll. 217–18), the empire builders of an earlier English generation.

In the course of the lines on Liberty, the imperial conquest and material prosperity of England's present enliven the ruins of the past. Through the transference we feel we are in the midst of triumph, not decay:

> [Liberty] whose hand benign
> Teaches unwearied Toil to cloath the Fields,
> And on his various Fruits inscribes the Name
> Of *Property*: ... th'heroic note
> (Smit with sublime delight) Ausonia caught
> And plann'd imperial *Rome.*
>
> (ll. 233–5; 240–2)

This two–way movement by which the soul moves upward while the ruins sink ever downward is later echoed by Georg Simmel, who writes of the architectural ruin that it is bounded by two impulses or instincts: on the one hand, the "brute, downward–dragging, corroding, crumbling power of nature," and, on the other, the advance or upward flight of the "human will."[16] For Dyer, the overcoming of the

mutually interfering drag of the two movements is made through a
complex poetic structure. Dyer invokes the immortality-of-poetry
topos, but in a melancholic key. "When Age descends with sorrows to
the grave," it generates a "kind Mood of melancholy" which "wings
the Soul and points her to the skies" (ll. 334–7). Melancholy is
boundary–making, its "diapason" producing a consonance out of the
"Winds and tempests" swept by "all–devouring Time" on "his
various lyre" (ll. 300–2). Fame as poetry now monumentalizes the
soul through an affective structure. At the same time, however, Dyer
calls upon a firm structure of moralization, which alters the ruins as it
reflects upon them. The poet summons up the past within the poem
and then cautions from his distance against the errors of the past.

> And there the *Temple*, where the summon'd State
> In deep of Night conven'd: Ev'n yet methinks
> The vehement Orator in rent attire
> Perswasion pours.
>
> (ll. 199–202)

> O Britons, O My Countrymen, beware,
> Gird, gird your Hearts; the Romans once were Free;
> Were brave, were virtuous – Tyranny howe'er
> Deigned to walk forth in pageant State.
>
> (ll. 510–12).

It is the power of making a moral sense out of the past that will
forestall the collapse of the present into the past. The dependability of
Dyer's boundary–making moralizing language derives, in turn, from
that assumed coherence of the vernacular within the tradition of
liberty and property materialized in Whig success. As a result, naming
and judging are inextricably interlaced:[17] Dyer's confidence in the
coextension of language and judgment generates the final moralizations of the poem:

> Vain end of human Strength, of human Skill,
> Conquest, and Triumph, and Domain and Pomp,
> And Ease, and Luxury. O Luxury,
> Bane of elated Life, of affluent States,
> What dreary Change, what Ruin is not thine?
>
> (ll. 531–6)

It is precisely this confidence which allows the poet to moralize in such a way that it appears to be a *particular* fault – Luxury or Ease or Pomp – that generates mortality, rather than what Keats's Oceanus will describe as a universal law of alteration: "We fall by course of Nature's law."[18] In fact, the charge of luxury was quite often invoked as what many Country Whigs felt was the danger of the Court Whig, Sir Robert Walpole. From the time Dyer went to Rome in 1724 until the publication of *The Ruins of Rome* in 1740, Walpole had both been in power and figured as the greatest internal threat to the moral prosperity of Britain. Just as tyranny and luxury were an internal threat to Roman supremacy, so might Walpole's luxury be figured analogically as the immanent menace to Britain.

Dyer's praise of empire extends into a sort of poetic imperialism, in which the poet makes a poetic structure that will outlast but also alter the character and meaning of the ruins, finally redeeming them through poetic permanence. "Enough of Grongar and the Shady Dales / Of winding Towy",

> Now the love of arts,
> And what in Metal or in Stone remains
> Of proud Antiquity, or through various Realms
> And various Languages and Ages fam'd
>
> (ll. 3–6)

becomes the compelling motive of the poem. The poet, beginning amidst the clutter of "Rent palaces, crush'd Columns, rifted Moles / Fanes roll'd on Fanes, and Tombs on buried Tombs" (ll. 24–5), reorganizes the snarl into a Panniniesque coherence. He first disarms the purely architectural and images it in natural terms, turning the city into a rustic landscape: "A solemn Wilderness! With error sweet / I wind the lingering step, where'er the Path / Mazy conducts me" (ll. 87–8).

Dyer names and gives historical ground to the material: Scipio, Marius, Pompey, Caesar, Brutus, Tully – each relic is associated with an individual and explained, rendering system out of chaos. The stones may crumble, but Dyer gives to each element its place along the horizon as he gazes from the Palatine Hill. And it is precisely this nominating and ordering which permits the altering capability of moralization, itself presaged in Rome by Cicero's Catiline orations.

After the taxonomic sorting out, Dyer addresses his analytical problem: to give England an imperial ancestry without carrying over that imperial decline. In the history that Dyer calls upon, his interests and sources are not in the poets but in the martial achievements of the Romans:

> Lo the bossy Piles
> The proud *Triumphal Arches*; all their Wars,
> Their Conquests, Honours, in the Sculptures live.
>
> (ll. 276–8)

But this genetic project is crossed by an intimation of mortality which produces as its poetic residue an anxiety inviting Neil Hertz's description of political "male hysteria," for the "trauma of history" – its inexorable character – is imaged by Dyer as threateningly sexual and female.[19]

Represented in terms that suggest that the Roman ruins will provide access to what Shelley later called "secrets of the birth of time," the remains of antiquity are tokens not only of the past but of the genesis of the present.[20] Hence the vaginal caverns that underlie the Roman landscape are double images: of Rome's birth as well as of its death:

> And frequent stopp'd
> The sunk ground startles me with dreadful Chasm,
> Breathing forth Darkness from the vast profound
> Of Isles and Halls, within the Mountain's womb.
>
> (ll. 56–9)

This downward movement does not, however, stop at the womb, for there is a site even more subterranean than the womb. Below the womb lie the sewers of Rome, its place of refuse and detritus:

> Nor these the Nether Works: All these beneath,
> And all beneath the Vales and Hills around,
> Extend the cavern'd Sewers, massy, firm,
> As the Sibylline Grot beside the dead
> Lake of Avernus.
>
> (ll. 60–5)

The Roman sewer system runs through the public areas of the city, and at the center of the system was the site where Romulus dug a ritual pit that inaugurated the very birth of Rome. As the marbles crumble into dust, they move towards their own points of origin, and by imaging the sewers within the womb, Dyer pictures waste as sharing the earth with fertility. The sewer image is here confused with the entrance to Hades, traditionally associated with Lake Avernus.[21] The anxiety of the imminent collapse of the present into the ruins of the past creates the representation of a temporal threat as if it were a sexual threat.[22] Yet as Dyer approaches the sewer system of Rome – the place of the most debased ruin and residue – he finds it to be also the source of the city itself. In his taxonomy of Rome, Dyer comes up against the city's history, and that history threatens to overwhelm the barrier between poet and observation, producing the anxiety that Dyer's poetic structure attempts to keep at bay.

Freud later formulated his own version of the ruins of Rome as a response to what he conceived to be a mystified understanding of the "oceanic feeling." When we turn to Byron's vision of the ruins of Rome in Canto IV of *Childe Harold*, we will see the "oceanic feeling" presented as an alternative to the ruins of history. In Dyer's case, we are given a negative image of the oceanic feeling. It is presented here as a subterranean and fetid gulf underlying and menacing the marbles of Rome and the articulations of the poet.

As descriptive detail is diminished in the second half of Dyer's poem, in order to trace Roman imperial history, the poem's speaker becomes increasingly alarmed. It is this anxiety which precipitates the closure of the poem, an ending which is brilliantly managed, for the alteration and moralization of the scene is at its strongest at the moment when the speaker is most alarmed. The source of Rome's decadence is situated in the vaginal territory that underlies the visible world of the ruins on the surfaces of the landscape: it is Luxury that turned Rome's brilliance into its death–sentence, and devouring Luxury invites us all:

> To the soft entrance of thy Rosy Cave
> How dost thou lure the Fortunate and Great,
> Dreadful attraction! while behind thee gapes
> Th' unfathomable Gulph where Ashur lies

> O'erwhelmed, forgotten; and high–boasting Cham;
> And Elam's haughty Pomp, and beauteous Greece;
> And the great Queen of Earth, Imperial Rome.
>   (ll. 537–43)

Dyer takes his image from an Ode of Horace, but alters it so it no longer merely suggests, but makes dangerously explicit Horace's pleasant attraction, which is now overtly figured as false.[23] The "pleasant grotto" strewn with rose petals now becomes a vortical lure annulling all temporal differentiation as the ruined empires lie in a heap of destruction.

The characteristic moralizing position of the speaker in the eighteenth-century ruin poem, whose eye constitutes a frame and the ruin the horizon, is that maintained by Dyer in his poetic ordering of Rome. The wrecked urban landscape is there – visible and to be moralized – producing meanings to the observing, educated eye. It is the impulse to moralize that is grounded in confidence, though compromised by the anxiety which attends the history of empire.

The transparency of ruins, insofar as they are visible, comforts the analytical method of the poet, who can extend outwards to investigate and make sense of the detritus. He can then enclose his interpretation in a bounded poetic structure. But the ruin, insistent and visible, challenges the poet by insisting on the question, "how did this come to be?" over and against the question, "what is this called?" When Dyer's analogical intention is threatened by a linear one, when the history of the past threatens to subvert the present, his voice prompts a comparison with Byron's anguished meditation amidst Roman ruins.

III

Dyer's voice conveys the tone of the almost satisfied Whig; Byron's, of the ironic radical aristocrat. In *Childe Harold*, Canto IV, Byron's radicalism is cosmopolitan and republican in character, and consequently the Rome he mourns is the Republic, not the Empire. Unlike Wordsworth, whose poetry moves comfortably in step with the process of homogenization that marks the opening period of English nationalism on its march toward jingoism, Byron is freed by his outlaw status to invoke an international republicanism and at the same time to deny its possibility in his contemporary world.

First in Spenser's, and then in Dyer's more attenuated manipulation of the immortality-of-poetry *topos*, the poet labors on ruins to make a structure of redemption which will serve the cause of both poetry and national identity. Disaffected aristocrat and exile, Byron is exempt from such labor and as a result, his stanzas on the ruins of Rome do not strain to maintain the boundary between past and present or between empire and empire. Byron does, however, point to a structure of aesthetic redemption, and he climbs out of the ruins he has massed around him on the back of the values of the autonomous artifact. Not that Byron eschews the claims of a homeland. In fact, he looks for fame and immortality in England: "I twine / My hopes of being remembered in my line / With my land's language"(9).[24] He also yokes Italy's to England's literary permanence. Shakespeare and Otway are the poets Byron cites as giving fame to Venice:

> Ours is a trophy which will not decay
> With the Rialto; Shylock and the Moor
> And Pierre, cannot be swept or worn away –
>
> (4)

But the character of the link between Italy and England that Byron suggests serves an aesthetic internationalism rather than the national interests of the theme of the *translatio imperii.*

Spenser historicizes the ruins of Rome mythologically; Dyer observes Rome analytically; and Byron restores Rome aesthetically. Dyer's Rome afforded an image of the past in which history and poetry might live as companionable structures, together protecting the present from the past's depredations, but also preserving the past as foundation and as moral reservoir. In Byron's poem of Roman ruin, the distance between past and present is significantly diminished, bridged by a labile self and by the contemporaneity of the history the poet invokes. In this dialectic of ruin, Byron is then authorized to emancipate aesthetic value from its historical order, and fix its form against historical decay. The terrible cost of that emancipation, however, as Byron presents it, is the power of poetic monumentality, which is collapsed into those historical wastes which face the speaker.

Though Byron will appeal to the permanent value of beauty, he is nonetheless much bolder than Dyer in making sense out of the contemporary political world around him. Because he is not significantly bound to the fortunes of empire or to serving the nation by making its image, he is capable of equanimously observing the continuity of the past into the present. He sees clearly that the Italy he tours in *Childe Harold* Canto IV has been the site of continual occupation, from the fall of the Empire to the most recent Austrian compromise. Byron evokes two Roman republics, the one of antiquity and the other of the last year and a half of the eighteenth century. In other words, Byron brings the issue of Rome and republicanism up to date, and by figuring the demise of the two republics as one event, collapses past into present.

Byron's reckless and sympathetic identification with the past weakens the stability of poetic monumentality. Early in Canto IV he takes on the issue of the encroachment of past upon present as he reproduces the travels of an earlier Roman. Just as Servius Sulpicius had toured the ruins of the Grecian world – Aegina, Piraeus, Megara, Corinth – so Byron also sees "all these unite / In ruin, even as he had seen the desolate sight" (44). The Roman, like the more modern Dyer, had moralized upon the scene, and "his yet surviving page / The moral lesson bears, drawn from such pilgrimage" (45). The comfort of such literary immortality is quickly turned back against itself, however, as Byron then looks to the ruins that Servius Sulpicius could not know of. To the "perish'd states he mourn'd in their decline" (46), Byron adds the ruined state of Rome. Byron cannot build any moralizing structure around this doubling of ruin, for he is himself "in desolation" (46), and Italy, which has recently passed through Austrian and Napoleonic hands, is in ruin again: "all that *was* / Of then destruction *is*" (46). Poet and city are alike prevented from benefiting from the work of a principle of progress, "and we pass / The skeleton of [Rome's] Titanic form, / Wrecks of another world, whose ashes still are warm" (46).

As past and present converge, the spatial boundary between the speaker's point of view and the wasted vision before him is as a chalk mark, not a wall. Without entirely identifying the self with the fabric of Rome, Byron does construct a persona made of dangerously perishable substance. The similitude of history predominates over its internal differences, and even as the poet's "soul wanders" from contemplating its architectural counterpart in ruin, "I demand [the soul] back / To meditate amongst decay, and stand / A ruin amidst ruins" (25). At the Colosseum also, the "wreck" of the building is identified with the self: "Among thy mightier offerings here are mine, / Ruins of years" (131). The external, focal perspective of Dyer's visual world is here interiorized as the perceiving self of *Childe Harold* collapses into its object of contemplation, and generates a visionary rather than a visual perspective. In Dyer's poem, the speaker and the ruins are each propped up by their opposition: the poet and his poem are mutually constructive. In Byron's poem, the plastic self conforms to the shape of its observation: "We thus dilate / Our spirits to the size of that they contemplate" (158). In these protean conformations, the difference between personal and public history also is extinguished. The insubstantiality of the persona of the poem alerts us to a qualified conception of the role of the poet in building monuments. Literary permanence, the immortality-of-poetry *topos*, is challenged here by historical contingency, and as the monument crumbles, so does its architect–builder. The poetic theme which arises from such ruin is that of poetry's insufficiency, what Curtius calls the "inexpressibility" *topos*. In the tradition of inexpressibility *topoi*, however, the inadequation of object and poem is a humble reflex of the superlative qualities of the object of praise.[25] In the form it takes for Byron, inexpressibility results instead from the frailty of the poet and his structure. The form of the ruined world and that of the human form also become congruent: so, as he picks through the debris of the battlefield of Waterloo in Canto II, Byron figures an abandoned skull as an architectural ruin:

> Look on its broken arch, its ruin'd wall,
> Its chambers desolate, and portals foul.
>
> (6)

Byron approaches Rome by way of Venice and here he touches on the means to redeem decay: by substituting the value of beauty for that of power. Italy is "a land / which *was* the mightiest in its old command, / And *is* the loveliest" (25). The substance of Venice's value is translated from its history as a republic to its present as an aesthetic object. The privilege of such aesthetic appreciation derives as much from Byron's own eccentric, that is disengaged, relation to the demands of

a nationalist poetic in England as from the political inconsequence of
Italy after 1815 to the European powers.

Byron's speaker approaches the gigantic ruins of Rome, "stum-
bling on recollections" (81) which, Bernard Blackstone reminds us,
"are recollections as much of his own internal defeat" as of the
collapse of Roman power.[26] The speaker's difficulty in making orderly
sense out of either his own or Rome's past, his difficulty in distin-
guishing the monumental from the trivial, either in himself or in the
landscape, is evidence that he does not view Rome as an analogy for
Britain or as an easily charted map: "now we clap / Our hands, and
cry 'Eureka!' it is clear – / When but some false mirage of ruin rises
near" (81). Dyer's competent sorting out of statuary confusion is
quite unlike Byron's ambiguously luxuriant sense of the Roman
"chaos of ruin!"

> who shall trace the void,
> O'er the dim fragments cast a lunar light,
> And say 'here was, or is,' where all is doubly night?
>   (80)

The vortical pull of historical differentiation into sameness makes a
taxonomy of Rome all but impossible. The ruins on the Palatine are
entirely "obscure." The confusion of the material is, however, what
will allow for the extraction of atemporal art from the historical
structure of architecture:

> Temples, baths or halls?
> Pronounce who can; for all that Learning reap'd
> From her research hath been, that these are walls –
> Behold the Imperial Mount! 'Tis thus the mighty falls.
>   (107)

The collapse of temporality produces only one lesson, that "History,
with all her volumes vast, / Hath but *one* page" (108).

In the set of devastations which structure Canto IV the ruins of
Rome and the present politically ruined Rome, that remnant of
Napoleonic ruin, merge into one another. Byron's lament is a present
anguish over and hope for Italy:

Europe, repentant of her parricide,
Shall yet redeem thee, and, all backward driven,
Roll the barbarian tide, and sue to be forgiven.

(47)

The Rome Byron proposes to recover, and despairs of recovering, is
the republic:

Alas, for Earth, for never shall we see
That brightness in her eye she bore when Rome was free.

(82)

John Hobhouse, Byron's friend and author of *Historical Illustrations of
the Fourth Canto of Childe Harold*, annotates stanza 82 to bring out this
point:

The Rome which the republican Florentine regretted and which an
Englishman must wish to find, is not that of Augustus and his
successors, but of those greater and better men, of whose heroic
actions his earliest impressions are composed.[27]

Hobhouse then goes on to make a point linking the aesthetic point of
view with the republican one: "We have heard too much of the
turbulence of the Roman democracy and of the Augustan virtues."[28]
Order is the handmaiden of tyranny, and the disorder of fragments
and relics is a sign of a vital turbulence. While Dyer's strength in the
face of historical passage came from the security of his Whig morality
and language, both of which prop up the immortality-of-poetry *topos*,
Byron has no firm station from which to make his classification and
order out of ruins. What *was* and what *is* are indistinguishable in the
debris, and the immortality-of-poetry *topos* gives way under pressure
to that of poetic inexpressibility. The marmoreal jumble produces the
conditions for a supralinguistic beauty, and the Palatine Hill, which
under Dyer's eye had organized itself into language, is in Byron's
view a stimulating and disorderly mass of cultural remains and natural
encroachments:

Cypress and ivy, weed and wallflower grown,
Matted and mass'd together, hillocks heap'd

On what were chambers, arch crush'd, column strown
In fragments, chok'd up vaults, and frescos steep'd
. . .
        Away with words! draw near,
Admire, exult – despise, laugh, weep – for here
There is such matter for all feeling.

                                        (107–9)

In the poetic pessimism that accompanies Byron's historical pessimism, the boundary between written monuments and architectural
ones is diminished, since monumentality itself has become ephemeral. In recompense, immediate sensory apprehension supervenes
upon all monuments. The lines of an eighteenth-century ruinist
confirm the endurance of the poetic monument over the physical one:
"These mould'ring walls confirm the moral verse."[29] But in Byron's
case, poetic structure can no longer function as an assurance against
the decay of architectural structures, and since the self and the object
of observation have also become one thing, the poem simply records
the desolate, visual fact: "Tully was not so eloquent as thou, / Thou
nameless column with the buried base" (110).

As Byron surveys the rubble of Rome, from which historical
content is being evacuated – times and places falling into one another
– the character of what he views undergoes an alteration. The
pleasures of the eye and of aesthetic intuition are focused on the
atemporal notion of "sculpture." Byron provides a refuge from
historical and national monumentality in aesthetic atemporality.

According to anthropologist Henri Lefebvre, architectural monuments perform a central social function, offering "to each member of
a society the image of his/her appurtenances and social face; it is the
collective mirror 'more real' than an individual one."[30] The monument, in its own shape as well as in its claim to futurity, "permet la
transition perpetuelle de la parole privée à la parole publique."
Importantly, "chaque espace monumental devient le support
métaphorique et quasiment métaphysique d'une société."[31] The
passage from private to public speech promotes the identification of
the individual with the nation. Spenser and Dyer use the image of
Rome to open up or to explore the identity of Britain. Byron is
radically subjective, turning the direction of flow around, from public
into private speech, and moreover, assuming that the poem cannot

adequate itself to what it seeks to take on thematically. So he eschews altogether the problem of the poem as the image of the nation. As he faces the crumbling memorials, what Byron watches is the demystification of monumentality itself.

It is at the Colosseum that Byron fully discovers an aesthetic permanence that will compensate for the impossibility of republicanism in the ruined world. The Colosseum is endlessly rich, "the long-explored but still exhaustless mine / Of contemplation" (128). Byron visited the site not long after the Pope's return to the city in 1814, at which time the Pope refused to let Touron's excavations of the site continue, filling in the archaeological work and restoring "the stations of the Cross first placed there by Benedict XIV, thus reclaiming the Colosseum as a strictly religious symbol and site consecrated to the Christian martyrs."[32] That the emblem of both imperial decadence and now papal anti-republicanism should stand while other pieces of ruin lie unrecognized is a charged fact for Byron. The building stands as a monument to the worst of human impulses, embodying what in *Manfred* Byron calls the "gladiators' bloody circus" (III, 27). In *Manfred* the hideousness of historical event is altered by the aesthetic resonance caused by a "rolling moon" (III, 31) that transforms the gory monument:

> Which soften'd down the hoar austerity
> Of rugged desolation, and fill'd up,
> As 'twere, anew, the gap of centuries;
> Leaving that beautiful which still was so,
> And making that which was not.
>
> (ll. 33–7)

In Canto IV of *Childe Harold*, Byron separates human history *in* time from the aesthetic power *of* Time as a suprahuman principle: "Oh Time! the beautifier of the dead, / Adorner of the ruin" (130).

Dyer had been concerned to enumerate the statuary of Rome in order to organize and then re-present the city's history and shape. Byron turns to isolated elements of the museum city in order to situate them in timeless, aesthetic terms. The poet turns to that which refuses history, and away from that which history torments. The movement he goes through is from the contemplation of individually bounded moments of beauty – most notably the Apollo Belvedere and the Laöcoon – to that which promises an absolute atemporality: the ocean and the "oceanic feeling." By the end of Canto IV, the boundary has collapsed between the worlds of culture and nature. In 1821, Byron wrote of sculpture that it was:

> The noblest of arts because the noblest imitation of Man's own nature with a view to perfection – being a higher resemblance of man so approaching in its ideal to God who distantly made him in his *own* image – that the Jehovah of the Jews forbade the worship of Images – because he was a "jealous God" – that is, jealous of man's embodied conception of deity.[33]

In his contemplation of the Laöcoon and the Apollo Belvedere, Byron does not see immortality as the effect of public monumentality – of grand building and design – but rather, as private agony and beauty extracted from time. Both statues had themselves been physically lifted out of time and space, carried off as loot to Paris by the Napoleonic forces and only returned in 1816.[34] In the Laöcoon, the "father's love and mortal's agony" merges with "an immortal's patience" (160); the struggle is in vain but it is perpetual, canceling out any alterations time would work. Similarly, Byron's stanzas on the Apollo reverberate against Winckelman's interpretation of the statue as supra-historical: "there is nothing mortal here, nothing which human necessities require."[35]

> All that ideal beauty ever bless'd
> The mind within its most unearthly mood,
> When each conception was a heavenly guest –
> A ray on immortality – and stood
> Starlike, around, until they gather'd to a god!
>
> And if it be Prometheus stole from Heaven
> The fire which we endure, it was repaid
> By him to whom the energy was given
> Which this poetic marble hath array'd
> With an eternal glory – which, if made
> By human hands, is not of human thought;
> And Time himself hath hallow'd it, nor laid
> One ringlet in the dust – nor hath it caught
> A tinge of years, but breathes the flame with which 'twas wrought.
>
> (162–3)

This separation of the aesthetic – immune to ruin – out from the historical prepares the ground for Byron's final recourse to the Ocean:

> The Ocean hath his chart, the stars their map,
> And knowledge spreads them on her ample lap;
> But Rome is as the desert.
>
> (71)

The Ocean, with its repetitive, cyclic action, and its atemporal and undifferentiated substance persisting over time and space, affords the only natural counterpart to the persistence of sculpture.

By choosing Ocean over Rome, Byron opts for affect over intellect, for sameness over difference, for rest over struggle. In Rome, the human constantly struggles against nature, and the results, though decayed, insist on a difference between matter and humanity. The Canto regresses from historical struggle to an aesthetic permanence in which pain is preserved and transmuted to the profoundly inhuman comfort of the "deep and dark blue Ocean" (179). Unlike Dyer, who fears the deeps, Byron is drawn to them, "to mingle with the Universe, and feel / What I can ne'er express – yet can not all conceal" (178). The persistence of oceanic life admonishes the poet. If Rome is, like Tithonus, always aging, never fully dead nor alive, "Time writes no wrinkle on [the] azure brow' (182) of the ocean. The oceanic feeling is utterly alien to the struggles of men; it is "boundless, endless and sublime – / The image of eternity" (183).

Byron's journey from republicanism to subjectivism amidst the ruins of Rome imprisons him within that strain of romantic ideology which pursues aesthetic autonomy as it represses or escapes historical claims. For Byron, however, such a position is less a mystified denial of history than a petition for a necessary retreat from its ruins.

The three discussions which follow take us to England and its provinces and explore the ruin theme in English poetry as it does take on the historical problem of making the nation's image in poetry. Disengaged from the aristocratic nationalism which yokes Rome to England culturally, this tradition of ruin poetry confronts the anxiety of decay by looking back through a native ancestry rather than a classical one. And, as opposed to Byron's distance, these poems face the nation directly. But Byron's closing stanzas of oceanic feeling

invite us to consider briefly in Freud one twentieth-century variation
on the subjectivity that Byron discovered in Rome.

Note: *Freud in Rome*

Now let us, by a flight of imagination, suppose that Rome is not a
human habitation but a physical entity . . .

When, in *Civilization and its Discontents*, Freud sought an appropriate analogy for the persistence of the unbounded "oceanic feeling"
alongside the "narrower and more sharply demarcated ego-feeling of
maturity," he chose the ruins of Rome as the vehicle of comparison.[36]
He was looking for an example with which he might represent the
simultaneous operation of both historical and taxonomic principles.
That is, and he was aware of the implicit problem, Freud was looking
for a metaphor that was capable of imaging at once both time and
space, yet would still be readily understood by the reader. The
analogy would then reveal the psyche to be built from elements of
entirely different origin, vertically juxtaposed, as if occupying a single
site. The Roman analogy, Freud decided, is finally insufficient, and
testimony to "How far we are from mastering the characteristics of
mental life by representing them in pictorial terms" (p. 19).[37] The
insufficiency, as Freud presents it, derives from the impossibility of
presenting in one image Rome at different historical stages: "the
same space cannot have two different contents" (p. 19).[38] Yet, as
often occurs in Freud's works as well as in the psyche, the insufficient
is not necessarily to be discarded, nor can it easily be discarded, and
Freud's representation of the mind as the imaginatively reconstructed
ruins of Rome remains a striking as well as an intelligible analogy. In
this analogy, we find the reparation of Roman ruin to be identified
with a permanence whose contours are congruent with subjectivity.
The inverse of Byron's depiction of the soul expanding to the shape
of what it observes, here the world of ruin is shrunk to the size of an
individual, but cured and completed at the same time.

Freud elaborates the similarity between mind and Rome in two
movements. In the first, he provides us with a cross-sectioned archaeological "map" of Rome. Perhaps because what motivates him is
the paradoxical problem of assigning a determinate origin and structure to an "unbounded" feeling, in his analogy Freud is drawn to the

image of physical boundaries of city walls. The observant visitor to
Rome will be able to see, in spatial juxtaposition, remains of Roman
walls of different periods (the Aurelian Wall, the Servian Wall), and
perhaps even "trace out the plan of the whole course of [the Servian
Wall], and the outline of the *Roma Quadrata*" (p. 17). Within these
boundaries designating the different places and moments at which
Rome separated itself from the outlying areas, the buildings present a
chaotic muddle of bits and pieces from different historical epochs, in
addition to which confusion it "is hardly necessary to remark that all
these remains of ancient Rome are found dovetailed into the jumble
of a great metropolis which has grown up in the last few centuries
since the Renaissance" (p. 18). In some unintended manner, the
city's remains obscure their own historical differentiation, and in their
spatial adjacency they erode temporal succession. The contents – the
material for a taxonomy of ruins – are in place, but the possibility of
deriving from them a genetics of ruins becomes more difficult. The
elements of modern "jumble" are of a piece with the republican and
imperial ruins.

In this collapse of past into present we hear reverberations of
Byron's confrontation with history's "one page," and can see how
much closer to one another these two versions of ruin are than either
is to Dyer's "ruin sentiment." The source of the discrepancy may be
hinted at by juxtaposing Freud's temporally leveling clutter to Dyer's
Rome, in which the vision of a ruined past encourages the speaker to
secure the boundary between present and past. After surveying the
remains of various stages of the Roman state, Dyer is assured of the
distance between himself and the marble dust:

> Me now, of these
> Deep-musing, high ambitious Thoughts inflame
> Greatly to serve my Country, distant land;
> And build me virtuous Fame; nor shall the Dust
> Of these fall'n Piles with shew of sad Decay
> Avert the good Resolve, mean Argument,
> The Fate alone of Matter.
>
> (ll. 128–33)

As an Englishman and a "modern," Dyer believes himself capable of
rendering the ruins of Rome legible and moral, analyzing the visible

landscape by means of a capable and transparent language. Importantly also, Dyer's traveler makes a distinction between the materials of marble and of mind – "sad Decay" being "the Fate alone of Matter." Finally, Dyer differentiates among types of monumentality: buildings are ephemeral, while the conduit of Fame is not.

Freud, in the extension of the line of the romantic ruinist Byron, shows the identity of observer and observation, and this requires an internalization of the external observation through a "flight of imagination" (p. 18). The Freudian analogy then, is not simply *about* the similitude of psyche and city, but is also dependent, for its use as an analogy, upon an activity *of* the psyche, which is presented in the second part of Freud's reconstruction.

To fit the mind to the contours of Rome, he argues, the analogist must make architectural alterations which strain at the boundaries of pictorialism: "There is clearly no point in spinning our phantasy any further, for it leads to things that are unimaginable and even absurd" (p. 19). This reconceived Rome "is not a human habitation but a psychical entity . . . in which nothing that has come into existence will have passed away and all the earlier phases of development continue to exist alongside the latest one" (p. 18). By a process of imaginative superimposition, each Roman building would be replaced, in its complete state, in its appropriate setting: "In the place occupied by the Palazzo Caffarelli would once more stand – without the Palazzo having to be removed – the temple of Jupiter Capitolinus" (p. 18). The buildings themselves would be present in every stage of their own history: "and this [Temple of Jupiter] not only in its latest shape, as the Romans of the Empire saw it, but also in its earliest one, when it showed Etruscan forms and was ornamented with terra-cotta antefixes" (p. 18).[39] In this model of the psyche Freud is able to resurrect history on the site of taxonomy, apparently without disturbing either model. This Rome is internally unbounded, just like the boundless "oceanic feeling" of both Freud's initial interlocutor and Byron's poetic persona. This imagined Rome is as permeable as the psyche, a human rather than marmoreal site, and the center of a "nation" whose provenance and direction is the sole self.

In Freud's version of Rome the preservation of the psychic city is bounded, given that the mind is bounded, by the vicissitudes of mortality. Inward rather than public, Fame for the individual psyche can only be won by the subject for and to himself, within his own psychic apparatus or in the consulting room. The poet's access to Fame had linked him to the nation as both agent and guarantor, while the psychoanalytic patient's immortality is collapsed to the shape of his own, albeit Roman, mind.

3

History into Landscape: Vernacular Ruin Poetry

I

When we turn to ruinists in Britain, we approach the familiar area of eighteenth-century "ruin sentiment," which ambiguously refers to both a range of objects and the human response to those objects. Sanderson Millar's garden follies; Samuel and Nathaniel Buck's encyclopedic series of all the "Views of the Most Remarkable Ruins of Abbeys and Castles Now Remaining";[1] Percy's assemblage of the relics or ruins of Border poetry; watercolors made by Turner during his tours of England and Wales as well as Batty Langley's designs: all these generate or are infused by the ruin sentiment. Though ruin sensibility inhabits a vast range of visual and literary practices in the eighteenth century, ruin poems have not been examined with the kind of critical attention that art historians have given to ruin painting and garden ornamentation nor that literary critics have given to the presence of antique structures in Gothic novels.[2] Yet the ruin was a staple amongst eighteenth-century poetic themes, and the ruin poem is ubiquitous in the periodical literature.[3] In magazines of ruling-class taste like *The Gentleman's Magazine* (an eighteenth-century version of *Reader's Digest* aimed at the audience of *The New Yorker*) the cultural landscape can be observed. In the representation of ruins in poetry, moreover, is to be found a symbol of the difficult emergence of the idea of the unified British nation. The ruin serves as the visible guarantor of the antiquity of the nation, but as ivy climbs up and claims the stonework, it also binds culture to nature, presenting the nation under the aspect of nature, and so suggesting national permanence. The poet can manipulate the image of ruin to turn the threat of the encroachment of nature upon culture into the proof of the authenticity of the nation itself. One can interpret the growing taste for the picturesque as part of the literal groundwork of building a nationalist consciousness which paradoxically presents itself as being natural, not cultural.

Though the vernacular ruin poem follows neither the function nor intention of the Claudean landscape scene in both the poetry and painting of the eighteenth century, its central feature can be more easily understood by comparison with that convention. John Barrell's acute discussion of landscape painting here informs my own.[4] The ruin in a Claude landscape is structurally useful since it forms part of the painting's interior frame, and a parallel poetic frame can be read in the English prospect poem, as for example, "Here, half conceal'd in trees, a cottage stands; / A Castle there the opening plain commands."[5] In the following example, a late eighteenth-century ruined castle poem calls attention to the moral rhetoric of the painted landscape convention:

> An eye that beauty in the landscape views
> May catch from life the Painter's glowing hues;
> But cold the charm that *Claude* or *Gaspar* find,
> If to the *moral picture* we are blind.
>
> In many a scene, thus view'd, a *local tale*
> Bids Time on his inverted pinions sail;
> And, of past ages by a charm possess'd,
> The moralizing vision can arrest.
>
> In this majestic range are themes combin'd,
> That glance on the reflecting Poet's mind;
> The forms appear – the living shadows play,
> As if the ruins breath'd in their decay.[6]

The "moral picture" here becomes an attribute of the landscape, but by virtue of the arresting action of the "moralizing vision." Like Dyer's transitively transformative moralization, the world's horizon is made intelligible by the person of culture and the transparent language in which he speaks.

In the Claudean frame, the ruin is neutral and general, bearing more of a formal than a thematic function. But when the optic is centered upon the ruined structure itself, the relationship between natural and cultural intentions alters. The decay of the castle now becomes primary and the problem of how the ruin came to be as it is –

the theme of its origins – is of greater importance than its physical position on the horizon. As John Barrell has argued, the localization of topographical poetry challenged the generality of the Claudean prospect: we can further specify this insight by noting the meaning and effect of the particularity of the ruin. The ruined castle poem, then, is linked to but is not identical with the landscape poem.

The ruined structure at the center of the poem suggests the close connection between land and history, and marks how deeply the natural world is imbued with cultural values. But insofar as the castle is in decay, it also suggests an opposing movement, the "naturalizing" of culture by time. While the ruin poem in general carries this theme, its eighteenth-century version serves a focused end: suggesting that what time approves and draws to its bosom is the nation, and so giving mythic status to historical events. This appears to be time's benign, not devastating, action. The myth of British origins, a myth for the eighteenth-century world to live by, requires that nature be substituted for culture, and we can observe these poems move from their generic niche among building poems to that among landscape poems.[7] Figured first as a cultural *memento mori*, the ruined castle is subsequently represented as a piece of the natural environment.

A most striking version of the naturalizing of culture can be visually understood by comparing the two engravings of the ruins of Pontefract Castle which appear at the front of this volume.[8] The difference in aesthetic taste between the two illustrations is, of course, the fashion for the picturesque, but what we often overlook in picturesque taste is the price exacted: what had to be given up to achieve it, and what ends it serves beyond the formally aesthetic. In the poetry of the period, the alteration of the presentation of the ruined castle as the site of historical event and succession into its presentation as a piece of nature conforms to a desire to master the content of the past while unfettering its form. In this process of myth-making, the castle is rendered less an historical site, anchored in the past and changing over time, than a permanent feature of a presence situated in the stability of the countryside.[9]

The newly presented castles are meaningful insofar as they merge with the natural features of the landscape and are so disposed in space as to elicit subjective sentiments rather than articulated, objective moralizations. The chronicling ruinist who preserves the image of the nation by enlisting the immortality-of-poetry *topos* offers himself as a link between the domains of community and of poetry. The subjective ruinist responds personally to the pathos of decay, which he takes to correspond to either (in the melancholic strain) a decay within the self, often associated in romantic poetry with the loss of youth, or (in the more optimistic strain) to the animation of the natural world. In neither strain of subjectivism does the claim of the reparative powers of poetry take priority. Often, in fact, such poetry is presented as assimilable to and not distinct from nature, and the poet figuratively displaces his authority from bard to bird. With respect to landscape ruins, then, the picturesque, rather than framing the natural in the image of a painting, masks the historical, producing it *as* natural.

The transformation of the historical building poem into the land-scape poem consists as much of a psycho-aesthetic as an ideological undertaking. The ruined castle history poem belongs to the aesthetic of sublimity linked with the sublime affect of terror, while the picturesque ruined castle poem offers a poetic mediation of mel-ancholy. So, a chronicling poet sustains the terror of ruin even into the present:

> Hark! the loud engines tear the trembling walls,
> And from its base the massive fabrick falls,
> And all at once these ancient honours fade;
> This princely pile, with all its splendid spoils,
> Sinks midst the havock of intestine broils,
> In prostrate ruins lost, and dark oblivion laid.[10]

The mythicizing poet subdues terror, however, and circumscribes sublimity within the contours of the picturesque. Sublimity provokes anxiety; picturesqueness, a more mild, at times even vacant mel-ancholy:

> For thy knights have approv'd their knighthood well,
> And returned with trophies home;
> But minstrels their deeds have forgot to tell,
> And snow-white breasts have ceas'd to swell –
> All are crumbling in the tomb.[11]

In its alternate form, as historical chronicle, the ruin poem enu-merates the events of the castle's past. In this way it is reparative,

bringing human history back in to bear on materials which otherwise
sink into obscurity. So, for example, observing the ruins of Pontefract
Castle in 1756, John Langhorne specifies a particular death among
the field of many:

> He pensive oft reviews the mighty Dead,
> That erst have trod this desolated Ground;
> Reflects how here unhappy *Sal'sbury* bled,
> Nor Refuge from the Pop'lar fury found
>
> . . .
>
> For what avail'd that thy victorious queen
> Repair'd the ruins of that dreadful day?
> That vanquish'd YORK, on Wakefield's purple green,
> Prostrate amidst the common slaughter lay?[12]

Though the ruin of defeat might be reversed politically, the evacuation of historical meaning from the building's remains can only be
repaired by Langhorne's poetic effort. In this variety of ruin poetry,
the internecine quarrels and battles that constitute the history of the
emergent nation are central thematic materials. Britain is thus seen as
born out of a set of struggles and the particularity of reference
responds to the complexity and difficulty of political history. This is
the poetry of a nation authenticating itself by describing its pre-
history to itself.

To construct this image of the nation, the chronicle ruin poem first
simply asserts the fact of the ruin's antiquity. Langhorne's poem
presents a detailed record of the castle and the succession of events
that comprise its history. The poem parades a temporal pageant
through the past, to which a general moral is attached:

> Right sung the bard, that all-involving age,
> With hand impartial deals the ruthless blow;
> That war, wide-wasting, with impetuous rage,
> Lays the tall spire, and sky-crown'd turret low.
>
> (ll. 1–4)

While sluttish time may smear the ruins of Pontefract, poetry's
monument hands back to the stones the force of human action, event
by event and name by name.

Langhorne preserves the castle through his poem, instantiating the immortality-of-poetry *topos*, but danger accompanies the return to the ruin of historical particularity and differentiation. So, says the anonymous poet-speaker of the 1776 "Spontaneous Thoughts, written in the Ruins of Winchelsea Castle," "Forsaken walls and ruins I despise":

> To balls and banquets unmolested stray,
> Let me in peace my wayward path pursue;
> In viewing these I see my own decay;
> If walls thus perish – I must perish too.[13]

This tangible anxiety over the transience of the historical community and its artifacts is the psycho-political impetus to a distinctly benign ruin poem. As the course of the eighteenth century increasingly involved Britain in a set of international interests and needs demanding the presentation of a unified nation, while the Acts of Union with first Scotland and then, in 1800, with Ireland into "The United Kingdom of Great Britain and Ireland" also demanded images of a coherent British polity, the chronicle history poem was superseded by a ruin poem whose focus was the ideological homogenization of the nation, prompting a coincident mythologization of the past.

The threat of the encroachment of time upon the present is avoided in Ovidian fashion by metamorphosing the castle from a piece of culture into a piece of nature. For example, by 1808, the range of the historical power of Kenilworth Castle has been benignly, but forcefully, reduced:

> Many a ruined tower
> Gives kindly shelter to the struggling flower,
> And many a child, escaped from school to play,
> Pursues its gambols in the sunny ray.[14]

The process of assimilating the castle into nature conforms to the usurpation of a mythic over a particularized historical conception of the past. This, in turn, answers the demands of an increasingly homogeneous society, and the supervention of industrial over agricultural social organization.[15] In mythic or homogeneous history there is an advocacy of an idealized "pastness" which submits the circumstances of history to a flawless and mild uniformity. The permanence of the contemporary world and its landscape is jeopardized by reminders of the discrete moments of the past, while it is reinforced by a myth of an indefinite past.

The ruined castle offers an image of an emptying out of social function, a result of unexpected as well as predictable turns of historical change, and would have formed a terrorizingly sublime contrast to the balanced and beautiful country houses through which English political power circulated in the eighteenth century.[16] The process of naturalizing the castle would be a way of controlling, by representing, the specter of transience and the fall of power. So, for example, at the great house of Saltram, Zucchi's and Angelica Kauffman's paintings of ruin are carefully managed within the decorating scheme in such a way as to contain them within the country house itself and make them safe within an environment rather more beautiful than picturesque.

Lawrence and Jeanne Stone have called attention to the symbolic meaning of the country house as "a return to law and order in the countryside after a long period of social chaos and aristocratic factional violence,"[17] and we can understand the power of the empty and ruined castle as a reminder of the specific historical threats of political transience as well as the vehicle for the more general and poetically traditional moral reflection on transience. As the English ruin poem disengages from aristocratic nationalism and classical literary heritage and attaches itself to the needs of a capitalist and then imperialist ideology, the Britishness of place is foregrounded. If, to cite the Stones' play on Corbusier, the country house was a "machine for living the life of an English country gentleman,"[18] then the ruined castle was the visible remnant of a broken machine. Certainly, evidence of ruin that might be mastered by being converted into an ornament in the estate park would be far less politically threatening than a ruin bearing the traces of actual and local conflict and domination. As part of the eighteenth-century landscaping euphoria, in which the realities of agricultural capitalism were distanced from country house life by way of grand views and designed prospects, the reality of temporal ruin was offset not only by making sham ruins, but also by moving real ones. So, for example, Netley Abbey, near Southampton, which was the subject of many a ruminative ruin poem, was dismantled and reassembled under the benign protective "permanence" of Thomas Dummer at Cranbury Park.[19] Placed in a "safe" landscape, the ruins alter from being historical debris into being a cultural trope designed to present the image of a "natural" nation.

While historical precedent, the fact of having been stationed on the land from early on, was an important component in the representation of the origins of the nation, that precedent was more useful as nostalgic myth than as historical reality. The image of a coherent nation might be generalized out of the ruling class's probe into its ancestry by finding in the historicity of ruins a general emblem of origins, but the actuality of historical transience, materialized in the facts of architectural decay, was repressed as real ruins became benign simulacra in the landscaped estate park. In fact, between 1920 and 1955, over 450 country houses were torn down – confirming the historical permeability of that myth of permanence.[20] The desire to locate an ancestry in the past was not only useful to establishing the coherence of post-1688 Britain. It was also yoked firmly to the presentation of commercial Britain to the larger world. The development of nationalist consciousness within the polity focuses on increasing the degrees of identity within an otherwise highly stratified society.[21] A central cultural need, then, is that symbols of origin be generalized beyond their local derivation so that they might be attributed to and then recognized by "Britons" in general.

As an image of the past, the ruined castle of the landscaped park exemplifies also the erosion of a public or common world as concretely realized in the privatization of the landscape through enclosure.[22] The myth of general provenance stands in for the facts of individual agricultural ownership, and here we can see how the emptying out of history from the ruined structure might generate that mild melancholia which saturates the "naturalized" castle poem:

> scattered lie
> The wrecks of the proud pile, 'mid arches gray,
> Whilst hollow winds through mantling ivy sigh.

The aesthetic category of the sublime, attended by terror, is a counterpart to the vertigo of historical implication: sublimity is anxiety-producing, and the anxiety is dialectically reformulated into the de-historicizing – the making picturesque – of the past. But a loss has been suffered, registered, and displaced as nature's "sigh."

The ruined castle is invested with a sensibility that is companion-able also with the "naturalizing" of the role of the poet, his shift from a public to a private occupation. In the example just cited, the sigh belongs to the wind, displaced from the self who witnesses the ruin. This floating melancholia is kin to the mourning impulse described by Walter Benjamin as "the state of mind in which feeling revives the empty world in the form of a mask, and derives an enigmatic satisfac-tion in contemplating it."[23] Certainly, as the castle becomes landscape its social function is evacuated, it becomes an empty world and private functions and feelings can then fill it up. For example, in an 1805 poem on the remains of Clackmannan, the poet counterpoises the gloomy meaning of deserted and broken walls to the pleasures of growing up nearby:

> Though mute thy bell, and drear thy empty halls,
> Long I've rever'd thee and will love thee still . . .
> For here I've saunter'd at the peep of dawn
> With fond companions of my earlier years,[24]

The reduction of the past to Byron's "one page," and to the dimen-sions of a single personality, can be understood as a poetic reaction-formation to the actuality of historical events, which include the assimilation of Scotland into Britain. While the chronicling castle poem had been shot through with the horror of particular death and damage, the homogenization of disparate histories into a mythic past alters the anxious affect into a melancholic one. The poet reacts to loss by identifying with that loss and then internalizing it.

As the repression of history cuts the poet off from the past, it both reminds him of and then cuts him off from an idealized notion of an earlier public role. This idealization unites the function and the name of the poet with the immortality-of-poetry *topos* itself. The identifi-cation of the poet with that lost role – which will be explored here as the theme of the lost bard – becomes a solipsistic feeding on the self. The movement from public terror to private melancholy, external anxiety to unhappy consciousness, matches the reduction of poetic scope from recording the objects of monumentality to expressing subjective reactions. Yet in the dialectic of ruin poetry, as the poetic text appears to move further away from preserving the image of the nation, the thematizing of just such a loss substantiates the nation's seamless mythic antiquity. As history becomes myth, as ruin becomes nature, so does the political origin of the nation merge, as if immemorially, with the soil itself.

The desire to experience the heterogeneity of the past as a homogeneous featureless past is written into these fairly late lines on Kelbourne Castle:

> Like a dream,
> Fitful and fair, yet clouded with a haze,
> As if of doubt, to memory awakes
> The bright heart-stirring past, when human life
> Was half-romance; and were it not that yet,
> In stream, and crag, and isle, and crumbling wall
> Of keep and castle, still remain to us
> Physical proof, that History is no mere
> Hallucination, oftentimes the mind –
> So different is the present from the past –
> Would deem the pageant an illusion all.[25]

Here we read the utter distancing of the past from the present, with a corollary collapse of the past from "real" to illusory status. Though the poet asserts that "history is no mere / Hallucination," the temper of the passage suggests otherwise, since by "history" what the speaker means is not an ongoing historical actuality, but a reified, romanticized past. We read also the complete naturalization of the castle, as if as unconstructed as "stream, and crag, and isle."

The ubiquity of the ruined castle poem reflects a cultural need to present the unity of the nation to itself. The marked eighteenth-century interest in things antiquarian opens up the heterogeneity of the past in order to sanction the historical provenance of the nation, but then mystifies it and separates it from the present to ensure the stability of the Now. That historical heterogeneity is interesting not only insofar as it corresponds to the sense that the nation's past is built out of the linkage of disparate and successive events, but also as it corresponds to the euphoric experience of simply accumulating peculiar and ancient objects and texts which is the characteristic stance of antiquarianism, a kind of "primitive accumulation" of the nation's historical data.

The ruined castle poem belongs, of course, to the larger pervasive ruin sentiment, the general mourning for lost culture – for example, in Chinese and Anglo-Saxon poetry – and a more particularized Christian program to "repair the ruins of our first parents." But the eighteenth-century variant poetically compliments specific anxieties which seem to be at least partially resolved by turning the historical ruined castle into a "natural" one, the sublimity of terror into the more benign melancholy of the picturesque.

When Kenneth Clark wrote his important study of the Gothic Revival, interpretive thought about the eighteenth century clustered around ideas of order and balance. Accordingly, Clark attributed the growth of ruin sentiment in the eighteenth century to political tranquillity: "When life is fierce and uncertain the imagination craves for classical repose. But as society becomes tranquil, the imagination is starved of action and the immensely secure society of the eighteenth century indulged in daydreams of incredible violence."[26] As our understanding of historical and cultural knowledge of the period has deepened, such a benign view can no longer be easily held. Not only was the eighteenth century as contentious in its way as the seventeenth and the nineteenth, but eighteenth-century literature is as fraught as that of the early twentieth century. In her distinguished book, *The Daring Muse: Augustan Poetry Reconsidered*, Margaret Anne Doody has convincingly disrupted an overly orderly vision of eighteenth-century poetry.[27] She shows a universal machine thrown carnivalesquely out of whack well before the onset of canonical "sensibility," with excesses of affect and intellect which reach well beyond decorous norms. Social historians such as Roy Porter have offered a society itself excessive and contradictory, and post-Namierian historians portray a nation of real and politically invested interests, not the least of which was the formation of a nation state in an international context and the organization of political and economic resources for a coherent capitalist enterprise.[28] Rather than seeing the ruin obsession as a perverse reflex of living a soft life, we might better see it as a response to the insecurity of the period, a response to a sense of society being so fragile that it cannot bear to remember that is has a history, although at the same time, the coherence of the polity demands the backing of a native antiquity.

The parasitism of nature upon history, in other words, can be figured as comforting as well as threatening. Country Whig society, in particular, prefers to look obliquely at the countryside which it is transforming by agricultural reform and enclosure. In this transformation the agricultural proletariat will be fully formed, a group which will later require shaping into an industrial proletariat. This industrial proletariat will be marked by a sense of identification with the nation as a whole, not simply a local habitation.

The shape of the ruined castle poem shifts from being terrible and sublime to being melancholic and picturesque as the poem moves from representing the historical specificity of the past to generating the image of an essential, indefinite, and uniform past. By homogenizing all pasts into one, the poet views history over an unbridgeable gap between that now vague history and his own present, and that gap provides a temporal barrier against the devastation that time wreaks upon power.

The price the poet pays for that distance between past and present is a sense of the loss, along with history, of poetry's own historical and social functions, which are figured as the "primitive" oral function of the ancient British "bard." This sense of loss does not necessarily correspond to an historical truth, but it does correspond to a sense of a growing gap between political and poetic functions. And the poet will find, in his isolation, some recompense: the self supervenes upon the community and the structure of poetry appears to no longer require a public or traditional sanction. The poetry may thus be more critical and personal than before, but at the cost of a great reduction in range. But here it is worth pausing to examine more closely the motif of the "death of the bard" in that moment before the egotistical sublime was codified.

II

Taking Gray's "The Bard" (1757) as one boundary and Scott's "Lay of the Last Minstrel" (1805) as the other (while allowing for the uneven appearances of similar topics before and after), we can follow the idealized representation of a poet, the bard, whose hypothesized centrality to ancient social and political experience testifies not only to his personal power but also to poetry's power as a shaping force in history.[29] The formulation of the lost bard can be construed as an eighteenth-century native antiquarian instantiation of the immortality-of-poetry *topos* as it engages with national aspirations, since this predicated bard is the preserver of the nation's story. The fictionality of the theme of the loss of the bard – the unverifiability of his historical status – is itself evidence of the growing importance of the national theme in the period. But it may also be true that the "death of the bard" theme responds to, by distancing and mystifying, an increasingly more concrete fact about both poet and poetry: the diminution of public, social forums for poetry, and more particularly, the emptying out of what are retrospectively identified as "bardic" functions.

To the eighteenth-century ruinist, the "bard" was an altogether different creature from the more familiar and modern "poet." By the very use of the word "bard," Gray and the antiquarian cohort were making clear their historical allegiances, for the term "bard" is Celtic, and until the seventeenth century it had been used only as a foreign word, associated with the vernacular of Scotland, Ireland, and Wales. For a long time, then, the term did not shake its local geographical origin, and by referring to the bard, one was noticing that the function belonged to a separate, distinct culture. The domestication of the term should be understood, then, in the light of the Acts of Union of 1707 and 1801, in which the political merging of the boundaries between England and Scotland, and England and Ireland, demanded the incorporation of disparate, and potentially disruptively national-istic, cultures into an overarching British culture.

In his *Dissertation on the Rise, Union, and Power, the Progressions, Separations, and Corruptions of Poetry and Music* (1763), John Brown traces the development of the bard from an original role as legislator and historian. Describing the bards of Northern Europe, Brown lists among their characteristics that "their Songs were of a *legislative* cast; that they sung the great Actions of their Ancestors, were themselves renowned Warriors, and kindled the Valour of their Armies by their Songs."[30] In "An Essay on the Ancient English Minstrels," those singers who "seem to have been the genuine successors of the ancient Bards," Thomas Percy remarks on the bardic skill as "something divine; their persons were deemed sacred; their attendance was solicited by Kings; and they were every where loaded with honours and rewards."[31] Percy argues that the rise of Christianity lowered the status of the British bard, and then points to the superiority of the Danish bard, "in whom the characters of historian, genealogist, poet and musician were all united."[32] The functions of poet, historian, and jurist were all fused in the most ancient order of bards, but then the legislative was separated out from the bardic role, which nevertheless retained both "Power and Dignity in Full Union."[33] Brown argues, however, that the gap which had opened between legislator and poet was irreparable: "The *Legislator's* and *Bard's* Character cannot again be *generally* or *fully united.* We have seen they naturally separate in an early Period of Civilization: And the Departments become so distinct, as to create a General Incompatibility and Repugnance too clear to need an Illustration."[34] Brown's sense of that "Incompatibility" is an expression of a movement within a later eighteenth-century "division of knowledge" itself: poetry and political life appear to be parting company.[35] This division diminishes the authority of poet, poem, and the immortality-of-poetry *topos*, for it circumscribes the social power of the poetic monument. Though the separation of legislator from bard might be good for the autonomous development and intrication of both knowledge and power, it would certainly diminish the status of the bards themselves, and the presumed centrality of the bard to ancient social life would have been both part of an attractive image of the past and a lamentable absence from the present: "The natural Flame of savage Music and Poetry is now almost entirely quenched in the Several Parts of this Island."[36]

At the same time, however, the separation of legislator from poet *increased* the authority of poetry, though in a different sphere. As poetry approaches the nineteenth century, the secularization of spirit takes the shape of poetry's authority in the affective domain. Brown maps this shift from external to internal influence by suggesting that on the one hand "the legislator may still incidentally retain a Part of the Poet's dignity" while the poet, "though no longer a Legislator, may still occasionally exert his Salutary Power, by his Influence on the Passions of the Soul."[37] We have not to go very far to find the role of the poet as an "unacknowledged legislator," and the historian of the self and the world it half-creates.

The nationalization of the term and image of the ancient bard is a cultural variant upon what Christopher Hill has described as "Norman Yoke" ideology, feeding both revolutionary and Whig arguments that English Constitutional rights predated the Norman Conquest: "the continuity of English law and institutions, as a peculiar and peculiarly admirable feature of English development, became a dogma of Whig historians."[38] Debate about royal prerogative versus parliamentary privilege spoken in the metaphor of the "Norman

Yoke" remained part of English political rhetoric, even after its heyday in the period around the English Revolution. The debates about the Norman Yoke, like that explored by J. A. Pocock on the antiquity of the Constitution, were in intent originally movements within juridical and constitutional theory.[39] However, the terms of the argument continued to resonate throughout the eighteenth century in more generally cultural terms. The bard, as a critical figure for a mythically ancient, indigenous, and free culture could be given a niche as ancestor of the modern poet as the modern world claimed a national past not only through political institutions but through poetic inspirations. Though Gray expresses a melancholic rupture with the past in "The Bard," he relies also on that thread of continuity by which to measure present poetic diminution.

As an added mark of poetic distinction, the domestication and "Britishing" of the bard was assisted by its assimilation to Greek and to the Latin form, *bardus*, thereby endowing Celtic pre-history with a status attractive to Enlightenment classicists. The pre-history of Britain thus recovers its kinship to the classical world. Brown's *Dissertation* begins with a long investigation of the Greek bards whose works "contained the essential Parts of their *religious, political, and moral* systems."[40] But this sense of family connection is rather different from that of the Renaissance, which asserted aristocratic filial connections with the classical world through literary lineage. Here the thrust of the argument is towards the progress of a commercial nation's poetry. Brown concludes that by founding a national institute of poetry and music, the nation would temper the excesses resulting from Empire and "refine the Taste, inforce the Religion, purify the Morals, strengthen the Policy, of the most prosperous Kingdom; in a Word, would give a proper and Salutary Direction to that Overflow of Wealth, which must either *adorn* or *overwhelm* it."[41]

In Gray's "The Bard" the bardic image was poetically fixed for a generation and the poem, in turn, became a source for other, popular versions of the bardic function. The numerous direct imitations spawned by the poem have been examined and documented by Edward Snyder.[42] Though not explicitly a ruined castle poem, "The Bard" provided the background for many poems which use the image of a ruined castle as the site for an anxious or a melancholic nostalgia for mythic pastness. "The Bard" is complex and interesting in part because it enacts the problem of the relationship between heterogeneous and homogeneous accounts of the past without resolving that problem. John Sitter, exploring *Literary Loneliness in Mid-Eighteenth-Century England*, calls "The Bard," "the best example of ... a collision between the speaker-poet and the hostile force of history."[43]

In the poem, Edward I attempts to secure his conquest of Wales by having all the native bards killed, his fear testimony to their political power. The status of the event as actual history is uncertain, and it is true that all historical accounting is story-telling, but what is important here is the way Gray seals the matter of British history firmly to poetic history. Though Edward succeeds with his massacre, the song of the sole surviving Bard rouses a chorus of those who have been murdered, and they collectively ventriloquize the last living one. The song translates music into prophetic spell. The bards are transformed from retrospective and objective historians into prospective seers, and they are liberated into agency as historical actors. This new song survives the literal and temporal death of the bards and transforms historical, differentiated time – the linear advance of disasters which will befall the Norman house – into mythic, homogeneous time. The prophets foretell that the institution of the house of Tudor and the authority of Elizabeth will reanimate the voice of the chief of the ancient bards: "Here from the grave, great Taliessen, hear; / They breathe a soul to animate thy clay" (ll. 121–2).

What Sitter calls a "collision" between poetry and history in Gray's poem does not result in an explosion, but in a compromise. The bardic chorus "adjusts" Edward's action (itself evidence of the bards' original power), altering the historical meaning of the massacre, even though it could not alter the fact. Edward's murder of the bards is transfigured into the suicide of the last bard, who thereby appropriates Edward's power. The "last song" becomes a recurrent one, and in a continuing dialectic, the linearity of history becomes recursive in the Tudor transformation, as the ancient bards are called forth from their graves. Finally, then, the bards redeem themselves through the voice of their prophetic projections.

The incantatory quality to the opening movement of Gray's Ode performs this oscillation between historical particularity and mythic generality: Cambria, Hoel, Llewellyn, Cadwallo, Urien, Modred, Plinlimmon, Arvon are as much music as meaning: grouped together, they sound like the non-referential words of a charm, but on its own each is replete with Welsh reference: reference that is now to be assimilated to the culturally incorporative violent mission of British-ness in the mid-eighteenth century.

The atmosphere of the poem is imbued with a floating anxiety that oscillates between attaching itself to the experience of the Bard and to that of the Normans. The Bard curses Edward: "Ruin seize thee, ruthless king" (l. 1); the King is unable to mediate the "wild dismay" (l. 10) thus generated among his men, and the Lord-Marcher Gloucester stands "aghast in speechless trance" (l. 13). As the contest between bardic and martial power is established, the bardic exhausts military force. Importantly also, the bardic power is *collective* as it confronts the Norman adversary.

Unmediated by print or page, these ancestral poems/prophecies act directly upon their public. The vision of the future proposed by the bardic group is poignantly transpersonal, actual, and powerful. Yet when left by his comrades, the last bard adumbrates the solitude of the romantic poet: "Stay, oh stay! nor thus forlorn / Leave me unblessed, unpitied, here to mourn" (ll. 101–2). The community of bardic voices evaporates. "In yon bright track, that fires the Western skies, / They melt, they vanish from my eyes" (ll. 103–4). The external world of massacre, which infuses the site with bloodshed, does not mitigate the internalization of the loss and identification which characterizes the last bard's plangent song. Thus the transfer from terror to melancholy is given a national genealogy.

When Gray's antiquarian researches led him into the history of Wales, he found the apocryphal story of Edward's massacre compel-ling as much for what it reminded him about the present as what it told about the past. Gray argued that the persistence of Welsh poetry in spite of these original extinctions was proof of the potential durability of poetic matter as well as proof of the political importance of poetry. Edward's intention had been to extinguish the native rebellion incited by the bards, but, Gray wrote in his article *Cambri*, "their works (we see) still remain, the Language (tho' decaying) still lives, and the art of their versification is still known, and practiced to this day among them."[44] In fact, though there has been a suggestion that Gray did use elements of Welsh prosody in the poem, his choice of a Pindaric ode for the form of the piece rather links this anti-quarian world to the classical one.[45] As J. B. Leishman points out, the Pindaric ode played the double function of bestowing immortality on both its public beneficiaries and the ode-maker himself.[46] Gray's poem may then be viewed as participating in the immortality of poetry *topos* as both a native theme and a classical form, in such a way further dignifying the status of both "bard" and nation. Consequently, the poem acts to monumentalize the author, including him in the tradition he describes.

As a good Whig, Gray's adoption of Norman Yoke ideology to ground his narrative is not surprising, and in his commonplace book "argument" for the poem, he brings together an alliance of native anti-Normanism and poetic strength. Describing the prophecy that will be sung by the bardic chorus, Gray writes:

> [it] foretells the misfortunes of the Norman race, and with prophetic spirit declares, that all his cruelty shall never extinguish the noble ardour of poetic genius in this island; and that men shall never be wanting to celebrate true virtue and valour in immortal strains, to expose vice and infamous pleasure, and boldly censure tyranny and oppression.[47]

Yet it was precisely this desired alliance, in which poets marched as agents in history and publicly censured tyranny and oppression, that Gray could not find in the reality of poetic and/or contemporary history. His impulse is an idealizing one, working up a nostalgia for a poetic agency to which he is unable to engage himself in the present. It was Gray's sense of the rift between the ideal poetic mission and actuality that, according to his friend William Mason, accounted for the long hiatus in the composition of the poem:

> Milton, of all our great Poets, was the only one *who boldly censured Tyranny and Oppression*; but he chose to deliver this censure, not in poetry, but in prose. Dryden was a mere court parasite to the most infamous of all courts. Pope, with all his laudable detestation of corruption and bribery, was a Tory; and Addison, though a Whig, and a fine writer, was unluckily not enough of a poet for his purpose.[48]

Gray was dismayed by an obvious gap between the functions of an ideal political poet, and the actual tradition he was part of. The notion of there having been some other time in which poets were really central to social and political life was given a nostalgic grounding for him in melancholic identification. A variant strain of the anxiety of the "burden of the past" as Walter Jackson Bate has illuminated it, Gray's anxiety/melancholy was rather less about the subject matter of poetry than about the social and political *function* of the poet.[49] Rather than turning to the writing of local political poetry or the censuring of tyranny himself, Gray was reinspired by finding himself in touch with a bardic source itself of a presumably uninterrupted ancient lineage. Mason explains: "I hardly believe [the Ode] would have had his last hand but for the circumstance of his hearing Parry play on the Welch Harp at a concert at Cambridge, which he often declared inspired him with the conclusion."[50] John Parry, a blind harpist and collector of Welsh antiquities, had been a sensation amongst antiquarians when he went to London in 1746, and when Gray heard him in 1757, he wrote that Parry had "scratch'd out such ravishing blind harmony, such tunes of a thousand years old with names enough to choak you, as have set all this learned body a'dancing . . . Mr. Parry (you must know this) it was, that has put *odikle* in motion again."[51]

Gray himself is thus prompted to become the latest in the chorus of bards, Parry's "authentic" connection with antiquity providing the concrete link between Taliessen and Gray, between the ancient bards and contemporary poets.

Overall, in "The Bard" Gray equivocates the standard of what constitutes bardic success. The Bard dies, but the bards survive; the poetic line no longer speaks against tyranny, but by assimilation it has the potential to do so again; the Bard kills himself and in so doing ensures his perpetuation. Linear history becomes recursive and so ensures its permanence. This is a Whiggish mythic solution to the crisis of the immortality-of-poetry *topos*. The authority of the Bard is diminished, but the dignity of national history, though shrouded in mist, is heroic. Though the contemporary world does not offer to Gray a new version of or a substitute for the lost bard, the possibility of progress, as in Brown's *Dissertation*, is offered. Though the intimation of the romantic isolate can be felt at the poem's close, the poem also struggles to maintain the links between poetry and politics, and to affirm the poem as the monument preserving a nation conceived as vernacular, British, and ancient.

The seepage of historical referentiality from the sublime ruin poem in the 50 years after "The Bard" (which conforms to Pocock's depiction of the loosening of the bonds between past and present in constitutional debate – "the past tended to lose its immediate and controversial relevance to the present"[52]) can be gauged by turning to the anonymous "Conway Castle," an 1809 successor poem to Gray's poem. Here we no longer find any question of either a collision or a collaboration between poets and history. The death of the bards is presented as utterly final, unmodifiable, and tragic:

> No sacred Bard surviv'd, the last
> Of all the slaughter'd band, to tell
> That in their country's cause they fell;
> To heav'n's high throne for vengeance cried,
> Then grasp'd their tuneless harps, and died![53]

The castle itself is reared as a monument to the silencing of the indigenous "all-inspiring strain" of "Freedom":

> Conway! then thy tow'rs arose
> 'Mid thy bleeding country's woes!
> It was not pride, it was not state,
> That rais'd thee high and made thee great;
> But fell ambition, to control
> Cambria's brave and stubborn Soul!
>
> (ll. 13–18)

The castle becomes the crypt of the bardic song. The presentation of Welsh nationalism is here entirely antiquarian and unthreatening to the growth of a British sense of nation, for the position of the tyrannic oppressor is occupied by the contemporary France of the Napoleonic wars and then dressed in medieval Normanism.

As the poet-speaker hastens to assure the reader, Cambria *is* now Britain and the Empire is firmly situated and unthreatened by the defeat of the bards. Significantly also, the poet-speaker does not make claims for his poem beyond its ancillary relation to Empire. The breach between poetic and political agency is presented as complete, as the icon of military power-as-oppression inhabits the place of earlier poetic power-as-freedom. At the same time, the poem shows how completely Conway Castle has been transformed from an historical world to a temporally undifferentiated natural site. In the first part of the poem the poet is seen, historically, as political, and is matched against Norman power. In the second stanza, the castle as the symbol of that power is naturalized, and melts into the landscape:

> But many an age has pass'd away,
> Conway! since thy halls were gay;
> Since, within thy courtly bow'rs,
> Pleasure wak'd the laughing hours;
> But the ling'ring hand of Time
> Still leaves the awful form sublime,
> To charm th'exploring eye;
> While woods bedeck the mountain's side,
> Impending o'er th'impetuous tide,
> In wild variety.
>
> (ll. 27–36)

Against the temporal gulf that protects present from past, the spatial blending of humanly modified rock and natural rock produces a "charm" out of "the awful form."

In the final stanza, the external world of politics and history has now been fully interiorized and poeticized: as the castle is made part of nature, the nation itself is seen as natural and personal:

> Britain, now with freedom crown'd,
> Leaves these proud turrets to decay;
> She wants no castle's strength, or high-rais'd mound,
> To check the battle's stern array,
> Secure in his benignant sway,
> Whose scepter'd virtues guard the throne,
> Who feels his people's happiness his own;
> And, when for war she doth prepare,
> Looks in each British heart, and sees a fortress there.
>
> (ll. 37–45)

There appears, in fact, to be *no* public world at all, only the sympathetic and subjective intuitive connection between individual and nation metaphorized as a "fortress," the effect of which is externalized as Empire.

In Scott's "Lay of the Last Minstrel" (1805), the threat of the curse, "Ruins seize thee, ruthless king," has been softened into the melancholic measure of an ailing bard whose enervated voice fails him as he sings. Ancientness in this poem is the token of degeneration, not pedigree; nor does it signal any capacity for perpetuity. The wearing down or out of the central bard is figured most nostalgically. The active, defiant jump of Gray's Welsh Bard is a "triumph," while Scott's Borderer minstrel is "infirm and old" (Introduction, l. 2). While Gray's Bard carries the burden and privilege of history, Scott's is absolutely cut off from the past: "The harp, his sole remaining joy, / Was carried by an orphan boy" (Introduction, ll. 5–6) – that is, carried by a child whose own history has been obliterated. The attenuated decomposition of the last minstrel is striking: "for, when to tune his harp he tried / His trembling hand had lost the ease . . . / He tried to tune his harp in vain" (Introduction, ll. 66–718). With an orphan as companion, Scott's bard is himself childless, his own son dead, further evidence of the end of the central bardic line. The pride of minstrelsy is sapped also, as the collective breaks up: "For, with my minstrel brethren fled, / My jealousy of song is dead" (Canto IV, stanza 35). The death of the ancient minstrels signals the end of an historical continuity, and the end of fame: "All mourn the Minstrel's harp unstrung, / The name unknown, the praise unsung" (Canto V, stanza 2). Gray's Bard triumphs in his suicide, while Scott's becomes a domestic pet singing for the local youth.

The Whig Gray could bear easily the actual violence of the incorporation of Welsh culture into British: the anti-Norman heritage was quite distinct from Whig pride in the organized Britain of the Settlement world. But Scott had a more ambivalent sense of the Act of Union of 1707. Paul Henderson Scott argues that Scott's acceptance of the Union was always "reluctant, grudging and conditional."[54] The depiction of the ruined bard corresponds to the loss of a local culture, and in his "Introduction" to *The Minstrelsy of the Scottish Border*, Scott laments that "the peculiar features [of Scotland] are daily melting and dissolving into those of her sister and ally," that loss being "of a kingdom once proud and independent."[55] Though Scott was a British patriot when faced with the wars with France, he was torn on the question of Scottish cultural identity.

But if "The Lay of the Last Minstrel" grieves that the prophetic, political power of the bard has gone, the poem presents a replacement for that power in the individual by way of the transformative power of Fancy: "But when he caught the measure wild, / The old man raised

his face . . . in poet's ecstasy" (Introduction, ll. 88–91). Scott's bard
has lost touch with the historical continuity he was to preserve, but
Fancy intervenes in memory's interstices: "Each blank, in faithless
memory void, / The poet's glowing thought supplied" (Introduction,
ll. 98–9). So the poem shifts away from the drama of history to
the pleasure of the autonomously poetic. In fact, in the poem's
opening prose paragraph Scott points out to the reader that "the
description of scenery and manners was more the object of the
Author, than a combined and regular narrative." The poem also often
mixes the worlds of culture and nature by distributing the attributes of
poets among the elements of the landscape. So he presents the
overtaking of culture by nature:

> the stream, the wood, the gale,
> Is vocal with the plaintive wail
> Of those, who, else forgotten long,
> Lived in the poet's faithful song.
> (Canto V, stanza 2)

In the diminishment of poetic purview and authority from the political
world to the self, from history to fancy, the castle as the site of bardic
song (which appears ubiquitously as a motif in ruined castled poems)
is also reduced to the space of the domestic – the old man is moved
from castle to domestic hut:

> A simple hut; but there was seen
> The little garden hedged with green,
> The cheerful hearth, and lattice clean.
> (187)

The process of deculturation is completed when we learn that the
inspiration for the minstrel's song has been nature itself, not historical
event:

> When the throstles sung in Harehead-shaw,
> And corn was green on Carterhaugh,
> And flourished, broad, Blackandro's oak,
> The aged harper's soul awoke!
> (188)

Turning culture into nature, history into myth, and bards into birds, the ruin poem swivels on its axis, now facing a picturesque present strewn with melancholic reminders of an immemorial past, and away from direct attention to the frightening sublimity of actual historical event.

III

Insofar as he adjusts his range to the limits of the picturesque, the poetic ruinist naturalizes his own function, and images poetry as lost to its public monumentalizing role. In this way, the poet is himself "privatized," and the immortality-of-poetry *topos* diminished.

The poet's paradoxically "abundant recompense" for his imagined loss can be considered in terms of the liberation of generic convention into idiosyncratic and immanent poetic "kinds" which allots to the poet a kind of power answering to the desires of the private self. The utopian reversal of the nostalgia for the lost bard is, at its compensatory best, the declaration of the poet as a solitary "unacknowledged legislator," and the conception of the poem as the "growth of the poet's mind." The reliance upon poetic closure for monumentalization is reduced as the work conforms to the shape of poetic process itself rather than to a commemorating structure, Shelley's "winged words" take on the characteristics of "chains of lead," and so the inexpressibility *topos* comes to replace that of immortality.

The picturesque ruinist encourages the mythic gap between past and present but he consequently experiences himself as cut off from a continuous tradition. The demands of an ideological necessity become the source of both poetry's deprivation and subsequent rededication to a different set of issues. The expressive model of poetry is formed by the shift away from an explicitly monumentalizing function.

From diminished function to diminished structure is no large leap, and looking at the death-of-the-bard theme in tandem with the problem of ruined structures, both issues woven into the fabric of the venerable and immemorial origin of the nation, we can see how the shrinking of the poet's compass carries with it a reduction of the preservation of the image and memory of the nation to the preservation of the self. Poems begin to seem as transient as ruins, and the horizon of monumentalization shrinks to the dimensions of an individual memory. As the past closes down, the presence of the self opens up: privatization eschews history and invites psychology.

As the historical capacity of the poet as bard is imaged as limited, and relegated to an unapproachable place on the other side of this temporal moat, as well as reformulated within an innocent, stable past, his poetic function is increasingly transferred to the landscape: the voices of bird, stream, and wind follow after that of bard, natural sounds take over from human ones. In Gray's "The Bard," nature has been subject to human power: "Cold is Cadwallo's tongue, / That hushed the stormy main" (ll. 29–30). By 1832, however, at Kelburne Castle, Ayrshire, the power of voice belongs to the bird, who "from out the thicket sends a gush / Of song that heralds summer." In "The Nightingale," Coleridge designs a bird superior to the poet, and suggests that the "poet who hath been building up the rhyme" (l. 24) would be better off listening to the nightingale, "Surrendering his whole Spirit, of his song / And of his fame forgetful" (ll. 29–30). To be immortal, Coleridge asserts, the poet's "fame / Should share in Nature's immortality" (ll. 30–1), fusing the traditionally opposed permanences of nature and culture.[56] To find a highly mediated version of the overcoming of the poet's voice by nature's, we have only to settle near Keats's "Ode to a Nightingale." The stanza which pines after that bird which "was not born for death," transforms the distance between the incapacitated, mortal poet and the capabilities of the eternal bird into an absolute and tragic break. As a result, the subject matter of poetry becomes, not how the poem endures, but rather, at least in the case of Keats's poem, how triumphantly insufficient it is.

In her essay on "Tintern Abbey," Marjorie Levinson has interestingly reconstructed the social meaning of abbey ruins in the romantic period as Catholic and Protestant emblems,[57] and we can pause at this central locale of romantic ruin to add something of a prehistory to Wordsworth's poem, allowing a glimpse into the process by which the ruined abbey poem is de-historicized and naturalized. Sneyd Davies's *A Voyage to Tintern Abbey* (1742) exemplifies many of the characteristics of the objectively moralizing and poetically secure ruin poem.

> Tintern her venerable fabric rears,
> While the sun, mildly glancing in decline,

With his last gilding beautifies the shrine:
Enter with reverence her hallowed gate,
And trace the glorious relics of her state;
The meeting arches, pillared walks admire,
Or, musing, hearken to the silenced choir.
Encircling groves diffuse a solemn grace,
And dimly fill th'historic window's place;
While pitying shrubs on the bare summit try
To give the roofless pile a canopy.

Here, O my friends, along the mossy dome
In pleasurable sadness let me roam;
Look back upon the world in haven safe,
Weep o'er its ruins, at its follies laugh.[58]

Nature here is antithetical to culture: the shrubs can't manage to make a roof for the roofless pile, while the traces of historical event assert themselves against the "encircling groves." Nature attends this ruin without overwhelming it, the sun augmenting and complementing the "glorious relics." The status of the poet is affirmed also as the abbey as a physical structure is supplanted by a monumentalizing poem which can make a whole out of a ruin; its structure becomes a haven from which the poet can fashion his own moralizing structure, secure in both a social and a transcendental guarantee of his reparative voice.

But the ruin in Wordsworth's "Tintern Abbey" is superseded by a memory which is itself the limit of monumentality. In Wordsworth's poem, the building as ruin stands outside the field of vision (we are now a few miles upstream from the ruins of Tintern Abbey) and it functions as a marker for the real poetic monument which is located in Wordsworth's memory as well as in Dorothy's mind (the edifice to be built as a "mansion for all lovely forms" [l. 140]) and in her memorializing memory, "a dwelling-place / For all sweet sounds and harmonies" (ll. 141–2). The contraction from built structure to poem-monument to the self is part of a set of parallel shifts: from public to private thematic compass, from historical to individual history, from history to memory, from the poetic structure of memorialization to a postponed longing for a realizable poetic structure.

With the expansion of the self as a balance to the closing down of history, the "collective mirror" of monumental space now affords a glass in which community is reflected back as privacy and subjectivity. In his nostalgia for the bard, the speaker of this 1790 picturesque ruin poem recollects and invents the public speech that Lefebvre links to monumental space:

> Here, at the gorgeous tournament,
> When warriors cherished martial fire,
> Oft would the Bard, to pleasure bent
> Wake the soft magic of the lyre.
>
> Struck by whose notes, at evening hour,
> The shepherd as he hied him home,
> Charmed with the Minstrel's thrilling pow'r
> Would hasten to the high-arc'd dome.
>
> Oft would the fretted roofs resound,
> With praise of glorious chivalry,
> Till every hero caught the sound,
> And bade their numbers float on high.[59]

In his poetic, however, the castle ruinist participates in the reversal of the public function: as privateness fills up the husk of the destroyed public martial or religious building, the ruin is figured as the playground for children or the site of poetic apprenticeship, instead of the place of successive historical events. So, for example, Wordsworth hears a harbinger of his own poetic career as he stands, a child, within the ruins of a "fractured arch":

> The earth was comfortless, and touched by faint
> Internal breezes, from the roofless walls
> The shuddering ivy dripped large drops, yet still
> So sweetly mid the gloom the invisible bird
> Sang to itself that there I could have made
> My dwelling-place, and lived for ever there,
> To hear such music.[60]

The poet here places his origin in the natural world, where he appears to be unencumbered by the society whose public values his very being now implicitly criticizes. This poet, whose voice resonates with the bird's, is part of the development of the representation of a marginal poet – what we think of, by way of the work of Jerome McGann, as the poet of romantic ideology.[61] Through this figure were created new categories which have given rise to our own ideas about the alienation of the poet and the autonomy of aesthetic life. We are mistaken, however, if we conclude from the privatizing and naturalizing of the poet that his word and work is thus eccentric to the persuasive ideology of nationalism in the period of its formulation. The private may be displayed or represented as marginal when it is, in fact, a concept central to the ideological formation, particularly as the formula of solitude is reiterated in a countryside which is becoming, on the one hand, ever more concentrated into private hands and ever more codified into productive agricultural practices, and on the other, ever more homogenized and seen as one nation rather than as a set of localities. So the solitary speaker in the landscape, the man speaking to men, is an abstraction of those men, an enabling image of the nation now formulated as personal, individual, and non-historical. The success of this natural nationalism can be measured by the combination of its apparent inevitability and its almost invisible intentionality.

In concert with what John Sitter calls the mid-eighteenth-century poet's "flight from history," the idea of a marginal poet is echoed in a poetry which thematizes the demise of public poets and images this theme amidst the ruins of what should be the sturdiest of structures: the castle. The death-of-the-bard theme dovetails with the ruin sentiment in the abandoned halls of decaying castles.

The castle was for eighteenth-century people a figure of complex and often contradictory meanings. Examples of the continuity of England's past, castles were also painful and anxiety-producing reminders of civil strife, rebellion, and the possibility of invasion. As the project of national unity became ever more connected to the self-image of Britain as permanent power in the larger imperial world, with internal cohesion an ever more necessary prerequisite for external interventions, so the aestheticization of the castle as an artifact intensified. Benjamin Boothroyd's *History of Pontefract* (1807) articulates a romantic endorsement of this impulse. Boothroyd, echoing Norman Yoke ideology, begins by referring to castles as emblems of tyranny: "Castles in the bosom of a country clearly indicate, either that the people are about to lose, or have already lost their freedom." He then proceeds to suggest the dangers of occupations of castles, as in the Civil War: "The disaffected have availed themselves of [the castles'] strength to raise the standard of rebellion." He concludes: "We may therefore consider it as one good resulting from the civil war, that the many castles and fortresses in the interior of this country, the remains of the Norman conquest and feudal oppressions, were reduced, dismantled and destroyed."[62] The reduction of the political usefulness of the castle to the status of debris paves the way for its reappropriation as romance and as art, which have their own ideological use – that is, the shoring up of an ideal of permanence of a countryside which in fact was always subject to alteration and change.[63] For what is most strikingly false about poetically casting England's ruins as the effects of moldering time – "Thy stones to dust are daily moldering down" ("Clackmannan Tower," l. 4) is a recurrent refrain – is that the castles were, for the most part, destroyed all at once, and by fiat. Though it was an integral part of the national history that the Catholic abbeys had been dissolved and demolished by order of Henry VIII, the fact that numbers of native castles were destroyed by parliamentary decree shortly after the Civil War did not enter into, and in fact was obscured by, the picturesque aesthetic.

The castle poem displaces the source of ruination from human history to natural inevitability. Disarmed of their martial meaning, the relics of the castle can become part of the landscape and so a stimulus to the individual fancy. This transformation turns the temporal distinctions between past and present into an enduring presence, and modulates what had been a temporal into a spatial effect. As Christopher Mulvey notes, nineteenth-century visitors to Kenilworth Castle went "not to see a place where the acts of history had really happened long ago but to see a place where deeds of fancy were fictionally recurring forever."[64] In this momentum, we catch something of the shift from linear, historical narrative to circular, uniform imaging, the ruined castle passing from the chronicling of explicitly political moments of the past (the Wars of the Roses, Tudor Ascendancy, Civil War) to misty and imagined moments and places,

> Where many a maiden fair, with smiling brow,
> Moved o'er the trembling harp her arms of snow;
> Where shell and song their genial powr's employ,
> And awful chiefs unbend their brow to joy.
> And many a grey-hair'd bard, with rapt'rous fire
> Sung Fingal's lines and Oscar's hallow'd lyre.

In a note to this 1804 poem of the Scottish tower Dornadilla, the author cautions the reader against expecting historical veracity:

> It may appear an anachronism to suppose the songs of Ossian to be sung in the halls of Dornadilla, whom Buchanan and our other Scotch historians made to commence his reign 261 years before the Christian aera. To the poetical reader, and the admirer of the venerable Ossian, I need not mention this. Let others see, that they are not the first in detecting the apparent inconsistency, though perhaps the dispute which that could bear might give sufficient grounds for poetical faith.[65]

Scotland's local cultural autonomy is subordinated to the national needs of Britishness, which this poem paradoxically promotes by presenting itself as grounded in yet distanced from historical events, and by giving priority to the demands and claims of poetic faith.

Francis Drake's poem, "On the Ruins of Pomfret Castle" (1750), provides a good example of the heterogeneously historical ruin poem. This text is overtly public, moralizing, social, and of the character of a chronicle. Drake was the son of a Royalist family, his great-grandfather, Nathan Drake, having taken part in and then written a manuscript history of the sieges at Pomfret (Pontefract) during the Civil War. Drake's father had been rewarded by Charles II with the Pontefract living. Written when Francis Drake was 29, his poem presents us with a poet-speaker figured as historian-bard: the embodied social memory of the nation as history, legend, and genealogy.

Drake opens his poem by claiming a double heritage: his personal ancestry links him to the Civil War, and the poetic ancestry he claims through the epigraph to his poem is to Shakespeare:

> Fatal and ominous to noble Peers,
> Within the guilty closure of thy walls,
> Richard the Second, here, was hack'd to death;
> And, for more slander to thy dismal feat,
> We give to thee our guiltless blood to drink.
> —Earl Rivers' Speech in Shakespeare's
> Richard the Third. Scene, Pomfret Castle.

The epigraph from *Richard III* signals a political lineage of poetic power and historical movement. As Swift wrote and Boothroyd takes for the epigraph of his volume on Pontefract, "I love Pomfret. Why? 'Tis in all our histories. They are full of Pomfret Castle." In Shakespeare's lines Woodville, Earl Rivers, compares himself to Richard II, and by analogy Drake puts himself in a lineage that also links him to Shakespeare. In fact, the historical Rivers was himself also a poet, and it was within the halls of Pontefract that he wrote the poem, "Sumwhat musyng, And more mornyng," a poem which was subsequently published for the first time by Percy in the *Reliques*, another place where ruins were reconstructed.[66] Finally, to complete this tally of Pontefract ruin images, the castle itself was built upon the ruins of the Roman British town of Legeolium, and the name Pontefract – "broken bridge" by folk etymology – recorded the ruination of a bridge in 1070, as William I chased after some Northumbrian insurgents.[67]

Drake suggests that the continuity of poetic structure had given Pontefract a place well before his own poem's entry into poetic heritage. The reparation of the castle is accomplished in the poem as a defiant, monarchical and transformative gesture against the Parliamentarian order to have the fortress demolished. As the poet links his poetic function to Shakespeare, he also links past to present. From the moment of the original de Lacy acquisition of the estate from William the Conqueror until the demolition by General Lambert in 1648, Drake traces a line of historical continuity and, in effect, uses his monumentalizing text to rescue Pomfret for posterity.

As a response to the anti-Royalist attack, Drake's poem builds an alternative structure for what had been destroyed. The actual destruction of the castle occurred in a way which ironically inverts the plot of Gray's "The Bard," in which Edward tries to eradicate historical memory by killing the bards. In this case, the anti-historical project is associated by Drake with Parliament's destruction of a monarchical tradition. The thwarted Royalist wishes to restore the history of the castle, the history of non-republican England.

Throughout the poem Drake offers data from the past in verse, and then marginally authorizes the historical veracity of the lines. For example, the following lines,

> See yonder tower, still blush with crimson stains
> That flowed in plenteous streams from noble veins
> Where Vaughan and Gray by Gloucester's arts expired,
>
> (ll. 49–51)

are annotated by a full paragraph of historical explanation.

In addition to its position as a piece of reparative poetic architecture, the historical chronicling ruin poem "On the Ruins of Pomfret Castle" produces its voice as objective and transitively moralizing. The poet reconstructs through the aid of his confident morality. While the castle itself "now in undistinguished chaos lies," the speaker's historical conscience can make sense out of this detritus, investigate it, and give it shape in the orderly consecutiveness of the poetic narrative. But though the poet maintains his distance from the ruin, and upholds his poem's immortality, the language of destruction, horror, and bloodshed that wells up in the narrative speaks to the historical anxiety which challenges the present and threatens to eradicate the gulf between observer and ruin. The poet wishes to revive the past, but he is dogged by the threat of it as well. Not only do we experience the "hostile" and "brutal rage" and "crimson stain" of "intestine broils" (ll. 16, 35, 49), but we must gaze over and again at the destruction wrought by "civil discord," "wreck of ruthless wars and hostile rage" (l. 11) and the "dire effects" of "more than civil arms" (l. 6). The moralizing voice of the poet speaks out against ambition and self-aggrandizement as it attempts to build a wall against future incivility.

Drake's poem does engage with history, however anxiously, and supports the continuity of public poetic function and the overt memorializing of the internal complexity of the political nation. By contrast, in the 1804 lines on Dornadilla, the voice of the past is as frail as the powers of its unaccommodated poet: "A secret voice comes / whisp'ring to my ear, / 'Avaunt frail worm! the mighty once were here'" (ll. 11–12). Meaning has been drained from the ruin, emptied out "Without a trace thy founder's name to show" (l. 20). The grey towers, resonant with potential moralization, "mock the transient race of man, / And look sublime beyond his narrow span" (ll. 15–16). At this point in the poem the fancy intervenes and transforms the sorrowful locale into an imagined earlier landscape, in which a feudal hunt inspires an anachronistic love of nature. In this peculiar passage, redolent more of the attitudes of 1804 than anything medieval, "the assembled bands," after the hunt,

> with rising rapture stop,
> And pause on nature's charms from high Benhope:
> From high Benhope, whose awful summit soars

> In midway sky, and looks on distant shores;
> Exalted there, they bend with fond amaze,
> Wide o'er the subject world, a wilder'd gaze;
>
> (ll. 41–6)

Borne aloft through this contemplation of nature, the "expanding soul"

> soars above the pole,
> And swells, on wings of inspiration driven,
> As Angels brighten on the bourne of heaven
>
> (ll. 51–4)

The homogenization of the past here produces the conflation of past and present, as the soul seems to be shared out amongst huntsmen and poet-speaker. The reverie is broken as the poet now returns to the present and notes that "tho' the years have hushed the harp, tho' song has failed" (l. 69), the ruins still animate the passer-by with "wild desire thy mystic tale to hear" (l. 73). The action of fancy has redeemed the tower's name, and the poet now takes over from the reduced function of the bard. The longing to rescue the bard from physical ruin appears again in "Donnington Castle": "And where is the Bard who so sweetly could sing, / And tell of the warriors of Britain of old?"[68] An exchange is enacted between the idealized version of an historical bard and the poet's own private imaginative processes. The poet who addresses Dornadilla substitutes his imaginative reconstruction for the historical materials of a past, which is then moralized for the present. Antiquarianism shows itself to be anti-historical, although employing the counters of native antiquity.

In the Scottish "Clackmannan Tower" of 1805, the built object has become entirely subject to the prospect it surveys, as well as subject to the individual memory of the voice which observes that prospect. An earlier, moralizing ruin site might have linked the speaker to a world of shared values as well as shared doom, as in Cunningham's "Elegy on a Pile of Ruins" (1761):

> Then what avails Ambition's wide-stretched wing,
> The schoolman's page, or pride of Beauty's bloom?
> The crape-clad hermit, and the rich rob'd kind,
> Levell'd, lie mix'd promiscuous in the tomb.[69]

But "Clackmannan Tower" testifies to an individuated, personalized poetic vision. The poem begins by reference to a mystified, general and homogeneous past: the tower was "Once the gay seat of Kings / And warlike Heroes of most high renown" (ll. 1–2). The poet inserts the debris into the tradition of the ruin theme, but then quickly goes on to focus, *not* on the ineluctable pull of time and transience, but on his private love of the site and his memory of his youth, the compensation of growing up while the building declines. The horror of historical succession is mitigated by this private meditation. At the same time, moreover, the structure of the tower itself, though ruined, is softened and made part of the landscape by being interpreted as if it were growing, not a built thing.

Georg Simmel describes that moment of ruin when "the balance between nature and spirit, which the building manifested, shifts in favor of nature."[70] A significant trajectory of the ruin poem leads us precisely from history into nature. But whereas the intransigent movement of time has been seen as an anxiety-producing threat to the present, the ruin as it becomes part of a stable nature affords comfort to the poet. The speaker of "Clackmannan Tower" performs this naturalizing function of the structure, rendering the human construction as if it were a fecund element of the non-human world: "Oft too at eve we've / Climbed thine ascent to pluck wild blooming flow'rs" (ll. 11–12). Here "thine" assimilates the wall of the tower to the land around into one organic form. The larger past of Clackmannan's history, part of David I's domains and later given over to the Bruce family estate, is reduced to the speaker's own past, and he walks across the site tracing his own progress rather than the castle's decline. It is the continuity of a natural, unbounded present that becomes the center of the poem. And here, too, the voice of the bard is superseded by the creatures of the surround, the sight of the ruined building disarmed by the benign power of the open prospect before it:

> How pleasant 'tis to view the plain below,
>   Where plenty waves her treasures in the breeze;
> How cheerful 'tis to hear the cattle low,
>   And lovely songsters warble 'mongst the trees:

> The sprightly lark in tuneful pipe doth raise
>   And sings in heavn'ly notes its morning lay;

> In sweetest melody his Maker's praise
> The blackbird chaunteth from the dewy spray.
> (ll. 21–8)

The poet's cultural role has receded into the landscape. By the end of the poem, the speaker tells us that the most important lesson he has learned at this sight comes not from the ruin itself, earlier the site of the lesson of temporality, but from the river, "Where first I learn'd great nature's gifts to prize" (l. 32). The piece of culture in nature is now ancillary to the poem's new focus: the natural world. The nature in the prospect of Clackmannan is peaceful, persistent, and permanent – the emblem of the persistence of a natural nation.

While many eighteenth-century castle poems had reacted in terror to both "intestine broil" and the relentless movement of time, at the nineteenth-century ruins of Kelburne the atmosphere is Wordsworthianly soft and still: less a sadness originating in the sense of the passing of the day than an ease at natural recurrence:

> While overhead the elm, and oak, and ash,
> Weave, for the hundredth time, their annual boughs,
> Bright with their varied leaflets.
> (ll. 14–16)

An oceanic feeling, the "sea murmur ceaseless" (p. 26) pervades the atmosphere. If the cultural world is no longer figured as opposed to nature, then the threat of decay has been either sidestepped or overcome. In the first part of the poem, a process takes place in which the poet naturalizes the castle by verging on metaphorizing it as a mountain:

> up between
> The green secluding hills that hem it round
> As 'twere their favourite, Kelburne Castle stands.
> (ll. 26–8)

The castle is in dialogue with the mountain, and it is the sameness of nature that prevails over historical differentiation. We sense, too, an enormous breach between the quieted, permanently present nature and some violent distant past, "when, on each peak, / Startling black midnight, flared the beacon fires" (ll. 75–6). The slow regulated iambic pentameter, the foregrounding of a "natural" rhythm against the iterated formality of ballad organization, aids in this transformation, and effectively makes the immortality-of-poetry *topos* redundant, because the poem itself does not distinguish itself from nature.

In another late ruined castle poem, the 1825 "Crookstoun Castle," the gap between heterogeneous and homogeneous history is explicitly cited on analogy to that between culture and nature.[71] Nature is again sufficient unto itself and is uncoded: that is, what the poet remarks upon is the non-communicative function of the castle and its surroundings:

> And vainly may rave the winter wind
> Through thy loop-holes piping shrill,
> For it chills no blood, it damps no mind.
>
> (ll. 26–8)

The folding of history into itself, as a circular, non-differentiated present, is shaped into the repetitive duration of animal and environmental life: "Still sounds the hare . . . / Still wheels the crow . . . / Still Levern sweeps" (ll. 31, 33, 41). And it is this which "makes it sweet" (l. 1) to linger near the ruins. The castle's remains are represented as surrounded by these natural effects but the structure itself is a negation of social event, and the erosion of the building is accompanied by a total evanescence of the past. The temporal location of pastness is abstract and general, some "days that have passed away" (l. 4). The past is reduced to a blank space, and history, in turn, is generalized into a set of chivalric/romantic commonplaces in which a self-identical event continually re-enacts itself. Or, more precisely, this event *negates* itself, since the poet pictures a set of occurrences which do *not* take place:

> And no lovely maid o'er thy drawbridge strays,
> When the western sky is bright,
> To tread alone the greenwood maze,
> On her own sweet form in the stream to gaze
> And sigh for some absent knight.
>
> (ll. 51–5)

The reduction of the castle to those phantasmal, mythic shapes is attributed to a poetic as well as an architectural collapse. The dead of the castle are "long-forgotten" (l. 5) and the continuity of their stories has been broken. Here the poem quotes Shakespeare to index its own distance from him: "Like a tale that has been told" (l. 12), the castle no longer signifies human communication, linear, narrative, temporal, but instead nature, stone, returning to itself. Natural languages fill up the terrain: the winter wind, "piping shrill" (l. 32), the crow, "with as wild a scream as when warfare was nigh" (l. 34), the river as it "sweeps and sings / O'er his pebbles as of yore" (ll. 41–2); but human language, poetic language, has collapsed:

> but minstrels their deeds have forgot to tell,
> And snow-white breasts have ceased to swell –
> All are crumbling in the tomb.
>
> (ll. 58–60).

The landscape of Britain has come to be entirely identified with the culture of Britishness.[72] This assimilation of culture to nature serves nationalism in that it makes it impossible to extricate the purposes of the polity from the soil itself. The greatest poet of such an assimilation is Wordsworth, whose nationalist ruin poetry is the subject of the next chapter. His poetry also offers an appropriate conclusion to this survey of ruin. In *The Prelude* he provides a startling image of the human intervention which characterizes the moment when the ruin has been so naturalized as to disappear from the landscape. "Et in Arcadia Ego," the ruin is a *memento mori*, but in the presence of the egotistical sublime, even the ruin is integrated. Earlier in this chapter, we noted that passage in *The Prelude* in which Wordsworth meets an omen of his poetic calling among ruins, and in the voice of a bird. Later in his childhood he has another ruin experience which alters the promise of temporal doom into a spatial prospect, naturalizing the building, and rendering it a benign part of nature and a site for poetic prospect. Byron, we recall, despairingly collapses himself into decay when he looks at the ruins of Rome. Wordsworth, on the other hand, incorporates the ruined building by gazing from it, not at it, erasing it from his field of vision yet using it as a prop to his imagination. We can end the view of vernacular ruins with Wordsworth brother and sister as they wander along the banks of the Ermont,

that river and those mouldering towers
Have seen us side by side, when, having clomb
The darksome windings of a broken stair,
And crept along a ridge of fractured wall,
Not without trembling, we in safety looked
Forth, through some Gothic window's open space,
And gathered with one mind a rich reward
From the far-stretching landscape.

(1850, VI, 211–8)

4

Out of the Wasteland: Wordsworth's Repair of Ruins

The picturesque ruin poem substitutes nature for culture: it is a poetically short, but a notionally significant step to find Wordsworth presenting a ruined *nature* when he intends to describe a cultural crisis. Playing against those conventions of the picturesque poetic vocabulary of the country which have been imbued with the values of national antiquity, in his early poem, "A Night on Salisbury Plain," Wordsworth is able to take naturalized ruin and foreground its political meaning. In this dialectical reversal of the achievement of naturalized ruin poetry, Wordsworth interrogates the landscape politically. From the ruin of Stonehenge in the waste of the chalk Downs to the rich sanctuary of the "last spot of earth where Freedom now / Stands single" (*The Prelude*, 1805, X, 981–2),[1] Wordsworth travels along a changing physical and political route. In his poems of human suffering he shifts natural ruin onto the bodies of the poor and displaced, clearing ground for the recovery of vernal life. In "The Ruined Cottage," he offers his own poetic subjectivity as the mediate space for healing the wreckages of human and vegetative existence. And in the harmonizing of his subjectivity with, to him, an increasingly natural nation, Wordsworth performs an adumbrative version of Arnold's declaration of the nation as the "best self." As a representative man, Wordsworth presents his poem of personal poetic growth equally as an epic of national redemption.

I

When England declared war on France in February, 1793, and once again the props of his affections were removed, Wordsworth imaged his alienation at home in the language of wooded greens and peaceful breezes:

I, who with the breeze
Had played, a green leaf on the blessed tree
Of my beloved country – nor had wished
For happier fortune than to wither there –
Now from my pleasant station was cut off,
And tossed about in whirlwinds.

(1805, X, 253–8)

"A Night on Salisbury Plain" is Wordsworth's poetic version of his fugitive experience in Wiltshire in the summer of 1793, and the poem records his sense of being repatriated only to find that home has become unlike itself.[2] He was unable to arrange a meeting with Dorothy until well into the winter, as well as being in difficulty with his Uncle Cookson over money and Annette Vallon, and perhaps suffering a combination of anxiety and post-partum depression after the birth of his daughter. It is hardly surprising that the "naked," "wasted," "fruitless" landscape near Stonehenge looked as ruined as it did to Wordsworth.

In "A Night on Salisbury Plain," it is not only a sere prospect that claims the senses of the poem's "Weary Traveller," but an atmosphere of uncanniness as well. The peculiarity of tone derives from its use of what F. W. Bateson criticized as an "unco-ordinated collocation of supernatural horror and sober eye-on-the-object realism."[3] Voices emerge from crannies amongst boulders; the dead seem to rise up under the hooves of a prescient horse; Druid elders engage in bloody rites in some liminal time between past and present, some shadowy space between hallucination and event. At the same time, however, the poem catalogues the concrete privations occasioned by colonial war and its effects on the economy and the people at home. These effects are both competing and contradictory, but in exploring and vindicating them, we can see how the uncanny climate of "A Night on Salisbury Plain" focuses and illustrates the difficult return of the native to a country which, by apparently betraying its own principles, has become foreign, unfamiliar, and at enmity with itself. Freud's observation that "the uncanny is that class of the frightening which leads back to what is known of old and long familiar" provides a good motto for such a vindication.[4] Unlike Freud's traveler, however, what Wordsworth's experiences is not the psychological but the political source of the uncanny.

The issues central to this early poem are ones which make visible to us the elements of Wordsworth's sense of the junction of political and national crisis; the problems he poses by rendering images from the aftermath of the American War as mirrors to the War with France include: can colonialism and domestic harmony be reconciled? Is England's history that of tyranny or wisdom? While the forward march of ruin poetry equated the two meanings of the word, in this early oppositional poem, Wordsworth probes the question, Is the "country," in the sense of the nation, a synonym as well as a homonym to the "country" as natural countryside? When Wordsworth rewrote "A Night on Salisbury Plain," first as "Adventures on Salisbury Plain" and then as "Guilt and Sorrow," he made the narrative more psychologically intricate. The first version – our concern here – tells the story of a midnight meeting between an exhausted anonymous traveler and a destitute woman who has been defeated, her husband killed after being pressed into service in America, and her family destroyed. The revised versions focus on psychological rather than political realism. "Adventures on Salisbury Plain" and "Guilt and Sorrow" introduce a murder story, a case of disguised and discovered identity, and completion by an experience of self-recognition and excoriation. In the later versions, the uncanniness of atmosphere is resolved as a reflex of plotting, in which peculiarly familiar strangers turn out really to be relatives. Such plotting in turn binds the narrative machinery to a narrow moralism, and reduces its resonances to the private, domestic realm. In the 1793 poem, however, uncanniness functions as a poetic representation of the contradictions at the core of a policy of oppression instituted by and upheld through the actions of a government violating what Wordsworth takes to be the foundations of its own stability. If nature is conflated with nation, then a ruined nature is a sure symptom of national corruption.

In Book XII of *The Prelude*, Wordsworth would remember his 1793 experience on Old Sarum as one in which he "saw / Our dim ancestral Past in vision clear," a vision with which he "was gently charmed, / Albeit with an antiquarian's dream,"

> And saw the bearded teachers, with white wands
> Uplifted, pointing to the starry sky,
> Alternately, and plain below, while breath

Of music seemed to guide them, and the waste
Was cheared with stillness and a pleasant sound.
(1805, XII, 347–53)

He recollects a powerful hallucination in which he saw a "single Briton in his wolf-skin vest," the ancient nation's warrior evocative of what Wordsworth calls "barbaric majesty" (1805, XII, 322, 326). Significantly, he records the events as evidence of his domination over nature: "I called upon Darkness, and it took" (1805, XII, 328), whereupon he then elaborates a vision of Druidic sacrifice on the Plain. The growing power of the poet is such that he is able to revalue his visiọn, which transmutes into one of benevolent Druids waving wands and gazing upon the heavens. Exemplary of the animating power of the poet, the episode is immediately followed in *The Prelude* by the narration of Wordsworth's exultant experience atop Mount Snowdon.

If we begin with this revision of the memory of Salisbury Plain, it is to make more palpable the distance between the confident appropriation and recapitulation of his experience and the unnatural, blighted atmosphere in the 1793 rendering, in which we find a landscape of utter dreariness: empty, bleak, blasted. In that first poem, the plain calls forth in the traveler only a "feeble voice" (l. 51), a voice answered by the whistling which sweeps "the thin grass" (l. 53) and the "wasted strain" of a "desert lark" (l. 54). As in the world of Browning's "Childe Roland to the Dark Tower Came," here nothing is recognizable, nothing is *homely*. The 1793 text of "A Night on Salisbury Plain" provides a good gloss to that later description in *The Excursion* in which the Solitary points out that antiquarian remains can be pleasing if one is in the right sort of mood, "pleased / To skim along the surfaces of things, / Beguiling harmlessly the listless hours."

But if the spirit be oppressed by sense
Of instability, revolt, decay,
And change, and emptiness, these freaks of Nature
And her blind helper Chance, do then suffice
To quicken, and to aggravate – to feed
Pity and scorn, and melancholy pride,
Not less than that huge Pile (from some abyss

Of mortal power unquestionably sprung)
Whose hoary diadem of pendent roçks
Confines the shrill-voiced whirlwind round and round
Eddying within its vast circumference,
On Sarum's naked plain.

(PW, III, 137–48)[5]

In July 1793, it was certainly the case that Wordsworth was enduring feelings of instability, revolt, and decay. Later, describing his poetico-philosophical emergency on the model of a walk out in the countryside, Wordsworth called this shock to his "moral nature" a "stride at once into another region" (*The Prelude*, 1805, X, 234, 240–1). For a man suffering what he later called his first real "revolution" (*The Prelude*, 1805, X, 237) – the political self-betrayal of his nation – what makes Salisbury Plain an apt place for Wordsworth to lose his way and have to wander for a few days is that this "other region," this terrain most unlike the fruitful country of nature's benevolence, is also England most *like* itself, since the monument Stonehenge is the marker of England's own antiquity. The birth of the nation is here mapped onto the same "spot" as the blasting of the nation. The setting also appears ironic, since Old Sarum, the borough where Salisbury Plain lies, was one of the rottenest of the pre-reformed rotten boroughs, as well as having become something of a tourist spot in the antiquarian rage.

Images of home as found and as lost eerily crowd the emptiness of Salisbury Plain, from the "unhoused" (l. 1) savage of antiquity whose plight opens the poem and adumbrates the brutality of Wordsworth's contemporary Britain, through the closural images of a "lowly cot" in which the Traveller and the Vagrant will receive their adventitious "homely bread." The loss and apparent irrecoverability of a permanent local habitation is voiced by the republican narrator, the nameless Traveller, and the nomad Female.

This reiteration of homelessness finds its most pressing antithetical image in the inhospitality of a ruined shelter in which Traveller and Vagrant meet, set nearby the relics of Stonehenge. Wordsworth calls this place the "dead house," his words resonating with his contemporary William Gilpin's description of Salisbury Plain in *Observations of Western England* as "one vast cemetery," and of the barrows in the area as " the mansions of the dead."[6] Against this human dislocation

Wordsworth sets the evacuation and ruin of nature itself. The conflation of nature and nation provides the etiology of the Traveller's
sickly vision on the Plain – a vision of "comfortless," "wan dead,"
"decayed" "ruin."

Until the declaration of war, the moment at which the complex
character of English nationalism decisively shifted its balance towards
a defensive, reactionary force when faced with the rivalry of a competing French nationalism, Wordsworth had relied politically on the
premise that England provided a distinguished model for liberty, a
model grounded in the republican, oppositional patriotism of the
seventeenth century. Embodied and intuited by Wordsworth himself
through the emotions he experienced as a child, when, from "feeling,
humble though intense, / To patriotic and domestic love / Analo-
gous, the moon was dear to me" (*The Prelude*, 1805, II, 194–96), he
conceived of this model as available as well to others. In particular, he
was anxious to press English liberty upon those whose version of
nationalism would shortly react most dangerously against England,
the French. When the poet and Robert Jones had arrived in France in
1790, they were celebrated as Englishmen:

> We bore a name
> Honour'd in France, the name of Englishmen,
> And hospitably did they give us hail
> As their forerunners in a glorious course.
>   (*The Prelude*, 1805, VI, 409–12)

When Wordsworth verbally echoes the gloriousness of 1688, we are
invited to recognize that by 1805 Wordsworth's notion of Liberty had
migrated from its grounding in a Miltonic model of free common-
wealth to a Burkean version of the British Constitution.[7] In this sense,
changes in Wordsworth's own perspective are representative of a
changing valuation of nationalism. In the period of the English
Revolution, republicanism was linked to a predominantly progressive
version of nationalism which brought about, in the following centuries, the capitalization of agriculture and trade, and by the end of
the eighteenth century, had worked to blend the heterogeneous
elements of geographical terrain into a British national identity. The
shift of that national impulse into its more reactionary form, in which
nationalism yoked to the state was able to carry out the vast project of

nineteenth-century imperialism, may be said to have taken place between the Settlement of 1688 and the opening of the war with France in 1793.

But to Wordsworth both in 1790 and when he returned to France the following year, this foreign country must itself have seemed happily familiar. Though there has been dispute over Wordsworth's sympathies while in Paris, whether in 1792 he was closer to the Girondins or the Jacobins, it has been demonstrated by Z. S. Fink that there *were* significant links between Girondin theory and seventeenth-century English political theory which would have afforded Wordsworth the kind of material to exemplify the congruence he and others trusted between the French and the English ideals of liberty: "Now it is to be observed that the poet's stay in Paris coincided exactly with the period at which the influence of English republicanism on the Girondins was at its height."[8]

Yet the home to which he returned in the late winter of 1792 was hardly behaving like the political forerunner of enlightened French ideals of liberty and equality. The Royal Proclamation against Seditious Publications had itself been issued in May; there were food riots in Cornwall and South Wales brought on at least in part by agricultural protectionism; Grey's motion for Reform had been defeated, while Pitt's campaign of what David Erdman rightly calls "disinformation" was succeeding nicely,[9] and Tom Paine had been tried and convicted, *in absentia*, for seditious libel. The famine and bad harvests of that year suggested that nature itself was ruined by such tyranny. Pitt would soon suspend Habeas Corpus and the government issued press-warrants in February. It may have been quite prudent for Wordsworth to recast the Female Vagrant's talk of the press-gang back some years, for a man had been tried earlier in 1793 for calling the pressers "A set of Oppressors."[10] The necessity for press-warrants suggests something of the distance still to go in the accomplishment of a coherent national identity in Britain, in which the laboring poor would think of themselves in national rather than local terms. Faced with the national identity implied by the French calls for liberty, equality and fraternity, in which "the people" were identified with "the nation," the unfinished character of British nationalism in 1793 can be marked.[11] It is within this defensive atmosphere that we can gauge the necessity of the rise of a "governmental patriotism," that Burkean nationalist ideology, which C. B. Macpherson argues is not so much aristocratic and conservative as it is exemplary of capitalist ideology moving into a more uncompromising phase: what Burke cherished "was not simply any hierarchical order but a capitalist one." Burke's ability to fuse the values of traditionalism with those of capitalism, Macpherson argues, was a function of the fact that "the capitalist order *had in fact been* the traditional order in England for a whole century."[12]

In the context of the complex relation between French and English ideals of liberty, Stonehenge and the double vision of Druids at the center of "A Night on Salisbury Plain" seem poetically appropriate to Wordsworth's purpose. The Female Vagrant tells the Traveller that a local shepherd has seen "the sacrificial altar fed / With living men" (ll. 184–5) by the Druids on the Plain; but she says that the shepherd has also seen them benevolently giving astronomy lessons "To Vast assemblies" (l. 192), demonstrating how "the living fires that bright and slow / Rounding th' aetherial field in order go" (ll. 193–4). This is substantially the same double vision that Wordsworth will later record in *The Prelude*; in the earlier rendering, however, the vision is not yoked to the powers of the imagination of the poet, but rather, it is an ambiguously real and hallucinatory part of the generally eerie quality of the Plain.

In the period between 1688 and 1793, the patriotism of the republican movement is slowly taken over by a hegemonic, or governmental, language of patriotism, whose purposes are both internal – the homogenization of people into a totality – and external – the competition with other newly emergent nationalisms. So, it is not surprising that the image of the Druid might be called upon to serve competing purposes, and here Wordsworth participates in a long and controversial debate about the meaning of Druidism to the nation. In the next chapter, we will see how Blake takes on the Druid image to produce a poem of a communitarian nation, but Wordsworth is more ambiguously implicated in nationalistic intentions.

In his study *The Famous Druids*, A. L. Owen makes the important point that as the eighteenth century proceeded, the image of the wise Druid had come to predominate over that of the cruel and sanguinary Druid, and was increasingly associated with imperial projects and the destiny of the English Nation.[13] In his work *Patriotisms*, J. H. Grainger gives a sketch of the varying claims of what he calls "oppositional" and "governmental" patriotism, which we can specify more precisely

by their links with progressive and reactionary nationalism. Oppositional patriotism, rooted in that version of progressive nationalism
which promoted Norman Yoke ideology of the seventeenth century,
later formed part of the campaign against "Old Corruption," which
had begun amongst country Tories and, transmuted, was one source
of Wilkes's presentation of public liberty.[14] It was Burke who was
most effective at the transitional moment at taking control of the
imagery of patriotism and adjusting it to state needs. When descriptions of liberty and agitation for reform were popularly linked with
the fortunes of French republicanism, which itself began to seem a
rival to, rather than a comrade of, English liberty, Burke was more
easily able to appropriate the language of oppositional patriotism,
which had served the moment of progressive nationalism in the
seventeenth century, making it now serve state interests.[15] The
identity of nation and state, accomplished between 1688 and 1793,
was the ground in which nineteenth-century chauvinistic nationalism
would flourish.

   The assimilation of the Druid figure to governmental, reactionary
patriotism was aided by that strain of antiquarian research which
argued that the Druids had been a help to the rise of British
Christianity. What makes Wordsworth's presentation so interesting is
that it looks in two directions and the double vision of the Druids
images the poet's own 1793 confusion about the character of the
nation. His Druids are tyrants as well as teachers, his England a site
of liberty, a "beloved country," *and* an imperial "Monster tyrant"
(l. 462).

   The double vision of the Druids corresponds to the ambiguous
meaning of "liberty" itself for Wordsworth. The republican tradition
in England, that tradition which influenced the Girondins through
the writings of, among others, Harrington and Milton, presented
Wordsworth with a description of liberty which predated the Settlement of 1688 and so also predated the accommodatory theme of
some sections of the ruling class that the goals of the Republicans *had*
in fact been attained in 1688. It is at the moment of the Settlement
that the balance begins to shift towards the hegemonic nationalism
whose fulfillment can be dated to 1793, when English and French
nationalism precipitate 26 years of war. But it is the earlier republican
category of liberty, associated with both progressive nationalism and
oppositional patriotism, to which Wordsworth alludes when, re-

counting meetings in London calling for abolition of slavery in the spring of 1793, he applauds the effort which though baffled, "nevertheless / had called back old forgotten principles / Dismissed from service" (*The Prelude*, 1805, X, 206–8). This principle of liberty, invoked in the *Letter to Bishop Llandaff*, refuses Burke's description of the English Constitution, and derives as much from English political tradition as from Rousseau.[16]

But the nation Wordsworth was living in was a nation which had not actually grounded its constitutionality in 1688 in democratic soil, as Tom Nairn has recently reiterated in his engaging essay, "The burial of popular sovereignty." Nairn's argument, an extension of his earlier work (along with Perry Anderson) on the incomplete character of the bourgeois revolution in England, suggests that the state Settlement of 1688, while it might serve capitalism, was early diverted from the principle of popular sovereignty associated with constitutionalism elsewhere. "However defective in practice, [both the American and the French version of constitutionalism] and the standard fare of modern polity derived from them rest on the principle of popular sovereignty. The British Constitution, a mass of common-law judgments, rituals, time-honored customs and sanctified procedures" was patrician in origin and intent, and provided the grounding to the existence of a Parliament which, under the Settlement, was to be considered the invested power of "the crown in Parliament."[17]

Though the republican narrator speaks an internationalist rhetoric in "A Night on Salisbury Plain," drawing India and empire generally into its condemnatory sway, we can nonetheless sense Wordsworth's own reluctance to abjure contemporary Britain, and his desire to recover the tradition of progressive nationalism in its form as oppositional patriotism. So, he creates both an anti-Burkean image of English history in his barbaric Druids as well as an alternate version of the benevolent state Druids. It will be out of this alternate history that Wordsworth will find his way back to a recovered nature and nation. The presaging of that alternative history is evinced in the last lines of "A Night on Salisbury Plain," in which the narrator calls for the abolition of all traces of "Superstition's reign, / Save for that eternal pile which frowns on Sarum's plain" (ll. 548–9). The admonitory power of Stonehenge may remind the nation of both its barbarity and its civility.

But while Wordsworth would retrospectively analyze and understand

1793 as an aberrant period of national distortion, his rendering of these stone ruins of national origin may analytically appear to twentieth-century readers to respond to a more fundamental incongruence between two competing descriptions of liberty: a distinction between a democratic and a patrician orientation. Wordsworth accepts the values of the Glorious Revolution as congruent with those of both 1642 and the French Revolution, but they were not. By late 1818, Wordsworth himself will explicitly rely on the conservative point of view: "The Constitution of the Country," he wrote in one of his addresses to the Westmorlanders, "is a mellowed feudality."[18]

In one of his 1988 Charles Eliot Norton Lectures, Harold Bloom made the point that irony and sublimity are incompatible,[19] and it makes sense to acknowledge the republican Wordsworth of "A Night on Salisbury Plain" as a poet who takes aesthetic categories and, by making them politcal, produces irony in the place of sublimity. In what we might think of as a companion text to "A Night on Salisbury Plain," Gilpin's *Observations on Western England*, the author characterizes Stonehenge as "totally void, though in a ruinous state, of every idea of picturesque beauty." Rather, he suggests, the most useful way to apprehend it is through the class of the sublime. Gilpin writes: "it is not the elegance of the work, but the grandeur of the idea, that strikes us." The terrain is strikingly empty and fearsome: "Our ancestors worshipped the God of Nature, in those boundless scenes, which gave them the highest conception of eternity."[20] Burke had found fear constitutive of sublimity, and Wordsworth deftly politicizes the aesthetic category by taking both fear and privation (another affect associated with the Burkean sublime), and turning the aesthetic quality linked to the sublime landscape into the material conditions suffered by the Female Vagrant.

The Female Vagrant has most poignantly suffered the contradictions and the privations of the colonial system: for she grew up in the fruitful homely world of Keswick, that "nook of English land" (*The Prelude*, 1805, IX, 221) which Wordsworth will later synecdochically substitute for the whole of the terrain of Britain and represent as the essence of the nation. The Female Vagrant recalls her fall from the abundance of a natural England:

Can I forget my seat beneath the thorn,

My garden stored with peas and mint and thyme,
. . .
The cowslip gathering at the morning prime,
The hazel copse with teeming clusters brown . . .

(ll. 235–6, 241–2)

One of the sharpest evocations of uneasiness in the poem comes
when, amidst the strangeness and discomfort of the tumbledown
spital at the center of the wasted Plain, and after the narration of the
Druid vision, the Female Vagrant produces her language of pure
coziness: she introduces her vision of country life, and allows the
Traveller to intuit its fecundity, a domestic country life with "merri-
ment and song at shearing time" (l. 239), with "dance" (l. 249) and
"ballad" (l. 250). Wordsworth's careful enumeration of the gifts of
Keswick is not a jarring confusion of style, but a significant counterpoint which makes ever more evident that this homely – in the sense
of ugly and stark – barren plain is, nonetheless, the source of and
harbor for the possibility of a truly homely – in the sense of cozy and
comfortable – home.

Freud suggests that repression lies at the center of uncanny
experience. Here, it is the bounty of England that has been repressed
by the unnatural and so un-national actions of the state. In later work
Wordsworth will psychologize this bounty as the "fructifying virtue"
attending "spots of time," and as he iterates "visionary dreariness" he
will replace the political with the psychological uncanny. In the later
reversal, the uncanny does indeed function as Harold Bloom suggested as "the conceptual limit to the sublime,"[21] for the weird
landscapes of "spots of time" act as a foil to the singularity of self by
dramatically refusing as well as inviting the self to identify with an
inhuman surrounding.

In "A Night on Salisbury Plain," however, Wordsworth's poem of
the political uncanny, the Female Vagrant invokes the fecund alternative to the human and natural ruin by speaking of the hidden home
at the center of this frightening and 'ambiguous gloom," after which
she goes on to narrate a story which tracks her life from that lost
fruitfulness to present decay. Her tale moves from the sad but
inevitable alienation of youth from nature into labor and then into an
aberrant alienation of labor through war. Not only does humankind
fall away from nature, but the recompense of culture is insufficient to

itself: "the loom stood still" (l. 296). As Wordsworth presents it, the American War had rendered England inhospitable to its own inhabitants, pressing them into service against their brothers. As a parent nation, England acts unnaturally also by refusing the autonomy of its child, America, to grow and be free in the best tradition of what Wordsworth understands as British liberty. Wordsworth gives us as symptomatic of this family perversion the disease of colonialism:

> The nations, though at home in bonds they drink
> The dregs of wholesomeness, for empire strain,
> And crushed by their own fetters helpless sink.
> (ll. 448–50).

Forced to go to America where her husband is killed in combat and her children by disease, the Female Vagrant is finally left alone at sea, having suffered the pure unnaturalness of the War, the "brood / That lap, their very nourishment, their brother's blood" (ll. 314–15). We can sense the desolation of the earlier event when she compares the bleakness of Sarum to the enervated tranquillity of her oceanic experience, "Peaceful as this immeasurable plain." But the peace she describes here is that which follows complete privation; it is not the peace of satiety. Here again Wordsworth materially grounds the aesthetic description. Dyer and Gilpin both compare Salisbury Plain to the ocean, evoking its boundlessness. Gilpin writes: "If you approach within two or three miles of the edge of the plain, you see, like the mariner within soundings, land at a distance, houses, trees, and villages; but all around is waste."[22] The frisson of sublime experience can only take place as an aesthetic experience if it is a simulacrum of lived fear. Sublime infinitude in "A Night on Salisbury Plain," however, is materially anchored in the physical exhaustion of the abject nomad. Landing back in England, the Vagrant finds a nation that can afford her no home at all: "And homeless near a thousand homes I stood, / And near a thousand tables pined and wanted food" (ll. 386–7).

The story the Female Vagrant tells comes not as a revelation to the Traveller so much as a confirmation of what he has already known and not known on his frightening passage through the dreary landscape. When she presents the double vision of the Druids, the event hovers between reality and vision. This hovering is confirmed by the

Traveller's own experience of Salisbury Plain's voices – the speaking tomb which warns him to flee might equally well be that of one of the few inhabitants of the terrain or a voice from another world.

The Female Vagrant travels from West to East; the Traveller, perhaps following Wordsworth from France to England, from Wiltshire to Wales, moves from East to West and journeys backwards in time as he advances in space. He goes from a cultivated world to an uncultivated one, from home to vacancy, from the present into the past. Expecting a cottage to appear which never does, the sole residue of homeliness is the antithetical image of "crows in blackening eddies homeward borne" (l. 58).

The poem had opened with a contrast between the unhoused savage of antiquity and the man of 1793, but as the stanzas track the Traveller, Wordsworth doubles his description of the savage so that the "wet cold ground" (l. 64) that the Traveller must sleep on cannot be distinguished from the savage's "fenceless bed" (l. 9). Through such identifications, we come to see the Druids as both the mirrors and the begetters of the Pittites. The narrator had begun the poem by suggesting that the houseless savage had an easier lot to bear than the anonymous Traveller, because to be savage was to know only savagery. The Traveller and the Vagrant, he argues, suffer more because their suffering comes from a "sad reverse of fate" (l. 22). As the Traveller alters his bearings, shifting from Salisbury Cathedral to Stonehenge for his visual landmark, Wordsworth materializes this metaphor, for the wanderer embarks on a literal "reverse of fate," walking backwards into the nation's prehistory and finding there the evidence of its present barbarism as well as, in the Vagrant's memory, the materials for national regeneration.

At first the Traveller mistakes Stonehenge for a ruined castle, but here there is no mantling ivy – the figure for culture returning to nature so often presented in eighteenth-century poetry – but naked prehistoric walls. While the conventional ruin poem presses culture toward nature's warm and soothing embrace, here it is culture that infects nature. The light of "reddening stones" (l. 92) of human sacrifice is followed by the rise of a sickly unnatural sun, "a dismal light its farthest bounds illumes" (l. 96). This is certainly not the enlightenment, invoked near the end of the poem as "reason's ray" (l. 429). In fact, all light is blotted out except for a momentary "pale abortive beam" (l. 106) of lightning which reveals a "naked guide-

post's double head" (l. 107). This post marks two opposing directions: a warning perhaps of the possible paths ahead of England and a
symptom of Wordsworth's ambiguous situation between republican
and 1688 versions of revolution. From the post the wanderer reaches
the gloom of the shelter. This "decayed retreat" (l. 146) for the
indigent and the sick is itself infected, a site where "no human being
could remain" (l. 125). But it is in this inhospitable hospital that the
homely and the uncanny coincide: here the Traveller and the Vagrant
meet, exchange stories and comfort, and prepare to venture toward
the dawn.

Unlike "Tintern Abbey," the poem which covers the tracks laid out
across the Wiltshire Downs, "A Night on Salisbury Plain" does not
end with an "abundant recompense." Though there *will* be a place to
take the wanderers in, it is an isolated cottage, surrounded by the
"melancholy lowings" from the pasture. The Traveller and the
Vagrant will be treated well: "For you yon milkmaid bears her
brimming load / For you the board is piled with homely bread"
(ll. 419–20), but we are not to miss the point that England is Two
Nations: in the "lowly cot," they will share "comforts by prouder
mansions unbestowed" (l. 418). Such moments of community are
perhaps the closest Wordsworth comes to formulating political "spots
of time." The accompanying imagery is, of course, the reverse of the
"bleak music" and "blasted tree[s] of the later psychological "spots,"
because community requires the priority of the external over the
internal world: "And think that life is like this desart broad, / Where
all the happiest find is but a shed / And a green spot 'mid wastes
interminably spread" (ll. 421–3).

From 1793 to 1805 Wordsworth reconsidered the extent of that
oasis: it grew gradually greater until it became the whole of Britain. In
a sonnet of 1802, Wordsworth repudiates any historical and organic
link between English and French republicanism by severing the
connection between Milton and the Girondins:

> Great men have been among us, hands that penned
> And tongues that uttered wisdom – better none;
> The later Sidney, Marvel, Harrington,
> Young Vane, and others who called Milton friend.
>   . . . France, 'tis strange,
> Hath brought forth no such souls as we had then.
>   (PW, III, 116)

By 1805, revising *The Prelude* after Napoleon's coronation, and his English nationalism overtaking his social criticism, Wordsworth finds the whole of Britain to be "this last spot of earth where Freedom now / Stands single in her only sanctuary" (1805, X, 981–2).

The summer expedition through Salisbury Plain ended with Wordsworth's trip to Tintern Abbey, a trip which five years later would be memorialized in a very different tone. The plenitude of the landscape of Tintern Abbey could not produce a poem in Wordsworth during the summer of 1793, not because "nature then to [him] was all in all" but because the unnatural nature of Salisbury Plain was at that time more present to him, a nature and a nation both alluring and dreadful, and he crossed the Plain "more like a man / Flying from something that he dreads, than one / Who sought the thing he loved." "Tintern Abbey" could only be written after the political uncanny had given way to the psychological uncanny and irony had given way to sublimity. What was gained by such transformations is palpable in Wordsworth's great poetry; what was lost can only be imagined.

II

Suffering is permanent, obscure and dark,
And shares the nature of infinity.
The Borderers, III, 1543–1544

In the period between composing "A Night on Salisbury Plain" and "Tintern Abbey," boundaries of poetic waste and fecundity, Wordsworth wrote a series of poems and fragments which have come to be classed as his poems of "human suffering."[23] These poems filter out the contingent from the essential characteristics of humanness and assign to the distilled essence the value *natural* and the property *permanence*. Thus Geoffrey Hartman praises the poet for approaching poetic settings "always as a man dealing with what is permanent in man," and so achieving an archetypal rather than an archaic poetry.[24] Though Wordsworth overtly links permanence and suffering, thereby acknowledging the cost to persons of their intimations of infinity, these poems of 1796–8 also trace out a more complicated and for Wordsworth more troubling economy of ruin and repair. From the natural ruin of "A Night on Salisbury Plain" to the fecundity which overcomes cultural waste in the Wye Valley, green to the very door, Wordsworth travels an obstrusively peopled landscape. The old man traveling to his wounded son in Falmouth, the Cumberland beggar, and the discharged soldier are all humans in states of mental or physical decay, and in the case of Margaret of "The Ruined Cottage," bearing the mental affliction brought on by physical and social deterioration. The natural/national ruin of "A Night on Salisbury Plain" pitted suffering humans against both state and landscape. In those poems which treat of human ruins, Wordsworth introduces a partial amelioration of the countryside by blending the paupers into safe surroundings, letting them live and die in "the eye of nature" ("The Old Cumberland Beggar," l. 196). The naturalizing of ruined people, turning them into features of the terrain, suggests Wordsworth's desire to reconcile himself to his own country and has much in common with the naturalizing of ruined buildings, whose achievement finds form in "Tintern Abbey." But this desire is equally matched by the anxiety aroused by the very humanness of these ruins, and which prevents the represented ruin from subsiding easily into the topography. In his book *Wordsworth and The Recluse*, Kenneth R. Johnston provides a reading of these poems which focuses on Wordsworth's psychological ambivalence towards the characters he writes about. My discussion here is indebted to Johnston's perceptive framing of these texts.[25]

As we have seen in the previous chapter, cultural ruins in the landscape – castles, abbeys, follies – provide, by the end of the eighteenth century, a picturesque redeployment of humanly built structures. These ruins repress disturbance and soothingly fold the social into the native world. But human ruins necessarily invoke a sense of dread, the dread of regression to pre-consciousness and a world without speech. Wordsworth offers us people who, by their apparent integration into nature, paradoxically evince how very wide the gap is between nature and culture. For example, the dismay the narrator initially experiences in his encounter with the discharged soldier may be attributed to that sense of the uncanny which derives from the frightening edge between the inert and the living.[26] Mary Shelley will later explore the transition from matter to life; but here Wordsworth suggests a frightening reversion to matter. Wordsworth's charge then is not only to "landscape" these human ruins, but to master the dread that human ruin motivates. As in "A Night on Salisbury Plain," the autonomy of aesthetic categories and judgments is put into question by being obviously derived from material and political conditions. The imagery of bodily and mental ruin in these poems plays against the charm of the picturesque and though Wordsworth vigorously forges a metaphorical language of natural purposes, the suffering indigents are unavoidably the refuse of social, not natural, processes: the expenditures of poverty and war. These human ruins embody a principle of resistance to decay which Wordsworth will translate, over time, into the permanence of nature. That principle of resistance is the human in its contingent, historical, and articulate action rather than in its natural essence. Beginning with the stark fact of decay, whose source is found in social deprivation, Wordsworth promotes an ecological rather than a social point of view. Imperturbable and impassive, the vagrants and bereaved women of the poems of human suffering occupy a border zone between the living and the dead: they adumbrate the stone-like disposition of the leech-gatherer and the "diurnal course" linking Lucy with "rocks, and stones, and trees."

Though Wordsworth functionally participates in the poetic program of pruning the countryside of any disturbing political history by landscaping the human ruin and shifting the effects of culture into metaphors drawn from nature, the old man and the beggar and Margaret continue to exceed their naturalization. This is what provokes our complaint that the benign natural moral of "The Ruined Cottage" is something of a let-down. The figures continue to make claims on us precisely as humans, and on the basis of their experience of privation. While "A Night on Salisbury Plain" works against the trope of landscaped ruin by attending to decay of nature itself, the human ruin poems mark out something of a brambled path for Wordsworth's later apprehension of the countryside as not only recovered but identical with the nation as a political and cultural entity.

The compositional layers of "The Old Cumberland Beggar" presage the progress of the poet's domination of ruin. The first section Wordsworth composed, corresponding to lines 44–66 of the version published in *Lyrical Ballads*, is not yet plotted in the familiarity and nurture of Cumberland. But in the course of his revision and expansion of the fragment Wordsworth ties the beggar ever more closely to a particularity of place, finally specifying him as one whom the young Wordsworth had "Observed, and with great benefit to my heart, when

I was a child."²⁷ In its form in 1796 as a purely descriptive passage, however, the "solitary man" belongs to no welcome or homely landscape, nor does he safely belong to the past. More like the Wandering Jew than a neighborhood beggar, "his age has no companion" (l. 45). A circumstance that Wordsworth will repeat is inaugurated here as the old man looks at the ground, "Instead of common and habitual sight / Of fields with rural works, of hill and dale" (ll. 48–9). In "A Night Piece," composed two years after these manuscript fragments, Wordsworth revised into benignity this desolate scene of staring earthward, as a shaft of moonlight "Startles the musing man whose eyes are bent / To earth."²⁸ The "pensive traveller" (1815) of "A Night Piece" is moved by this apparent beckoning from nature. "He looks around, the clouds are split / Asunder, and above his head he views / The clear moon & the glory of the heaven" (ll. 8–10). The most significant recurrence of this scene is Wordsworth's 1805 description in *The Prelude* of his ascent of Mount Snowdon. In this variation Wordsworth himself is the traveler who, "with forehead bent / Earthward," is startled by a brightening of the night ground which "with a step or two seem'd brighter still." Shifting his gaze upwards, Wordsworth is faced with his most profound vision of the integration of mind and nature, where moonlight and imagination converge, there where "Nature lodg'd / The Soul, the Imagination of the whole" (1805, XIII, 29, 37, 64–5).

Wordsworth's experience on Mount Snowdon serves him well as a national as well as a natural climax to his epic. When he had visited the Alps with Robert Jones in 1791 the disappointing reality of Mont Blanc had compounded its visual disadvantage by diminishing the very faculty of the imagination, usurping "upon a living thought / That never more could be" (1805, VI, 455–6). The climax of *The Prelude* produces at once the recovery of national, natural, and psychic integrity, and while distorting the sequence of lived experience, fixes the British Snowdon episode as the last consequential event of *The Prelude*, and the ultimate redemption of the beggar's glance.

These three versions of the ground-bent regard disclose Wordsworth's changing sense of nature's responsiveness. Nature appears to signal the traveler-speaker in "A Night-Piece" in a manner withheld from the anonymous beggar, and atop Mount Snowdon actually rewards Wordsworth *in propria persona*. But in the original manuscript fragments of "The Old Cumberland Beggar" and "Animal Tranquillity and Decay," we are closer to the wasted landscape of "A Night on Salisbury Plain." The "little span of earth" (l. 50) the nameless man surveys is dry and scattered with nature's own detritus: straw, a scattered leaf, rut-marks, summer dust. Once he has been given his niche as the individual Cumberland beggar of Wordsworth's childhood, the old man will fit more securely into a category which will not threaten by intimating an identity between beggar and traveler-Wordsworth. Presented as an anonymous man, however, the beggar is dreadful because he is both a stand-in for the narrator and in danger of being no one at all: a bit of trash on the highway, bypassed by "Boys and girls, / the vacant and the busy, maids and youth, / And urchins newly breeched" (ll. 64–6).

Written not long after the fragment, Wordsworth's "Inscription for a Seat by the Road-side Halfway Up a Steep Hill Facing South" presents a world in which nature persists in that punishment of humankind, associated in "A Night on Salisbury Plain" with the national self-betrayal of the war. Here the passer-by is exhorted to identify with "the weary homeless vagrants of the earth" and the rustic artisans" who are "chafed and fretted by December's blasts." In both of these texts Wordsworth has in part displaced ruin from nature to the human frame. What he gains by the displacement is a partial recovery of nature itself, while continuing to offer a criticism of the social relations fostered by an oppressive state. Nature is not yet entirely benign, and it was a punishing nature indeed that the coastal populace had observed on the shore near Spithead in 1795 after a terrific hurricane had ravaged a muster of forces being prepared for the West Indian campaign. Wordsworth himself visited the fleet shortly before, and it must not have been lost on him that the very house he was staying in at Racedown was owned by a Colonial merchant family, with massive properties to be protected in the Caribbean.[29]

The overflow material from "The Old Cumberland Beggar" that was published in *Lyrical Ballads* as "Old Man Travelling: Animal Tranquillity and Decay" rotates slightly the concerns of the Beggar fragment. In this poem nature itself is composed, if not kind, and the old man is ordered and "led" (l. 12) by the native environment. This intimation of an identity between beggar and nature invites two quite distinct interpretations. The impassiveness the old man embodies has all the seductiveness and ease of regression. But that ease is abruptly damaged when we hear this human ruin speak, explaining to the narrator that he is walking a great distance for a last visit with his sailor son, who is dying in a Falmouth hospital.

We are shocked out of identifying with the lure of natural regression by this intrusive presentation of death as the result of a violent culture rather than an ineluctable nature. Immediately the pace of the old man's journey begins to *matter*. His slow deliberate movement now presents his terrible incapacity, which is perhaps as much an incapacity of mind as of body. It is most disturbing that this thing-like old man is capable of speech. His humanness is thus thrust upon us and the dulling lull of "mild composure" (l. 10) is suddenly exposed. The suggestion of "settled quiet" (l. 8) is shaken and we feel, as in "A Night on Salisbury Plain," that Wordsworth has once again sketched in the political origin of an aesthetic experience. But Wordsworth soon revised his reading of the intention of the poem, in keeping with changes in his political intentions, and unfortunately, though not surprisingly, he decided to omit the final six lines from all versions subsequent to 1805. The political importance of the poem was foregrounded in a 1799 review of *Lyrical Ballads* in *The Monthly Review*: "The termination seems pointed against the war from which, however, we are now no more able to separate ourselves, than Hercules was to free himself from the shirt of Nessus." The reviewer adds hopefully that "the old traveller's son might have died by disease," rather than by warfare.[30] This was a view that Wordsworth himself had come to share by 1798, and it is probable that Wordsworth took this public comment as reason to make the deletions.

That the figure in the published version of "The Old Cumberland Beggar" is the instrument of ends he cannot know is presented in the opening verse paragraph of the completed poem: the man's shaking hands loose crumbs that he tries to control but which, reaching the ground, become the "destin'd meal" (l. 20) of local birds. The ecological balance of the opening scene immediately suggests that this condition of poverty is, if not necessary, at least integral.[31] The poet, however, in order to produce this economy of ends, must trade away the beggar's subjectivity. Those actions which we suppose to be the end product of human intentions turn out to be the function of some structure of circulation entirely outside the reach of purposive activity. Insofar as "habit does the work of reason" (l. 100) in their almsgiving, this is as true for the locals who help him as it is for the beggar himself. The network of natural connectedness is then reworked within a human world whose balances are also maintained through intuition rather than through reason. These filiative links pull human relations into the forms determined by a Shelleyan blank nature. In these opening mirror passages Wordsworth alters the social consequences of the original fragment, in which various village folk had callously passed by the beggar. Now it appears less that the old man is being designedly ignored than that his function does not depend upon social recognition. Wordsworth then counterpoises this benevolent ecology to the interfering ministrations of statesmen. Wordsworth presents his beggar as an endangered species whose human use is to offer himself as a marker of the continuity of past and present.[32] This version of the "one life," however, is disturbingly unmindful of connectedness as intersubjectivity. Kenneth Johnston has interpreted the halo which "the benignant law of heaven / Has hung around [the beggar]" (160–1) as emblematic of a significant moment in Wordsworth's adjustment to the dangerous power of the people in the landscape, a moment in which Wordsworth curatively "redirects [that power] back into normal human community." This, Johnston argues, is "the triumph of the first *Recluse* poems."[33]

While Johnston's is a generous as well as profound reading of the poem, "The Old Cumberland Beggar" also invites a more skeptical consideration of its ruin figure. Harold Bloom praises the poem for presenting a human as a "mode of consciousness"; but it may be more accurate to find in the beggar a cultural fetish or talisman. Not only does the beggar promote the separate good of each neighborhood almsgiver and the general good of the natural economy, but he draws off onto himself the general threat and anxiety of poverty.[34] The poem offers a natural circuit in which the beggar is enriched and augmented, threatened only by the social intervention of those "who have a broom ready in [their] hands / To rid the world of nuisances" (ll. 69–70). Yet he functions also to collect on his person the chaos and conflict of the social world. A vehicle of continuity, binding the larger social group together, he is also the magnet which attracts to his body the stuff of contemporary chaos. The beggar is the site of an image produced out of concrete anxiety and the fear of privation. The polemic against the statesmen converts into speech the fear that the loss of the beggar entails a loss of community. Wordsworth here identifies nature and community without yet incorporating the state into his equation. At the same time, however, the beggar is evidence of a socially insufficient community. Here Wordsworth substitutes the sufficiency of nature for the inadequacy of social practice.

But insofar as the beggar preserves the community, he also presents to Wordsworth the shadow of the cost of integration, the shadow of selfhood. The Cumberland beggar is frighteningly a mode of unconsciousness. Geoffrey Hartman has persuasively argued that the Boy of Winander in *The Prelude* is a stand-in for a Wordsworth who has never experienced an alienation from nature: the boy is both securely at home in the natural world, but just as surely bound to extinction. In a similar manner, the Cumberland beggar ensures the poet's own consciousness even as he embodies a natural state of unconsciousness, alarmingly close to death.[35]

By looking at one other example of a human ruin poem, we can locate another modulation in Wordsworth's recuperation of ruined nature. The fragment on the discharged soldier opens with a version of stasis that is quite unlike the regressive passivity of the old Cumberland beggar. The poem begins with an extended presentation of the narrator's inner calm and achieved relation to his environment, providing the standard for any later deviations. The active subjectivity of the speaker is thus set up around the human ruin as an interior boundary or frame. In this episode Wordsworth composes his poem against ruin, and becomes an inhabitant of the structures which his poem makes. Theodor Adorno writes: "For a man who no longer has a homeland, writing becomes a place to live."[36] As Wordsworth comes to revalue his homeland after its apparent self-betrayal, he constructs a parallel countryside in poetry which he inhabits as narrator. This home is the countryside itself. The "Discharged Soldier" fragment offers a narrator who at the very height of an equanimous relation to the environment comes upon the human wreck of a soldier: bare hands, wasted face, sunken cheeks. The vision appears as a personal admonishment and as evidence of some larger natural and human imbalance. The edge between the speaker's outward pity and his interior terror is registered by the word "ghastly": ghostly and pale, the man both inspires fear and radiates it. Most distressing, and athwart the narrator's full sense of well-being, the soldier is so painfully thin that "You might almost think / That his bones wounded him" (ll. 44–5). This discharged soldier, whose very body is imaged as the site of an internecine war, is a reminder of the Wordsworth of 1792, who returned to England to find himself like a "leaf cut off" and "whirled around in whirlwinds." The Soldier

> appeared
> Forlorn and desolate, a man cut off
> From all his kind, and more than half detached
> From his own nature.
>
> (ll. 57–60)

The Cumberland beggar is Wordsworth's anti-self, whose meaning is his assimilation to the environment; the discharged soldier is a version of an entirely deracinated self. The uncanniness of his presence is authenticated by the precise detail, "If but a glove had dangled in his hand / It would have made him more akin to Man" (ll. 66–7). Subduing his "specious cowardice," the narrator engages this walking ruin in conversation and finds that he has just returned from duty in the "tropic isles." In *The Prelude*, Wordsworth will suggest that the meeting had taken place in 1789, but in 1798, the time of the episode's composition, England was in the midst of its horrifying West Indian Campaign, in which thousands died in warfare and by disease. The soldier carries home with him the infection of colonialism, much like the Female Vagrant of "A Night on Salisbury Plain." But it is significant that in this case Wordsworth does not focus on the political provenance of the ruin. In the episode of 1798, the natural landscape is far less ravaged than it had been in 1793: it is the soldier who is at odds with the countryside and whose integration the narrator will assist. Even the soldier's alienation is attenuated by his placidity, finding himself in the woods, "much relieved" (l. 130). A "ghostly figure" (l. 125), he has not the unavoidable human facticity of the Cumberland beggar.

The soldier is reclaimed by the surroundings he moves through. Though Wordsworth does draw on a lexicon of waste and weariness, he uses it to describe the man, not the setting. The narrator's own rural ease offers a model of what the soldier might attain to, his own liberty and untrammeled subjectivity a vision of a freedom as yet unfelt by the returning trooper. But the agreeable "wise passiveness" recommended by the narrator of 'Expostulation and Reply," in the soldier takes the form of a

strange half-absence and a tone
Of weakness & indifference, as of one
Remembering the importance of his theme,
But feeling it no longer.

(ll. 143–6)

The utter absence of affect in the wraith prevents him from appearing "solemn & sublime" while he answers the narrator's questions of "what he had endured / from war & battle & the pestilence" (ll. 138–9). The sublime possibilities of such story-telling are annulled by the soldier's "ghastly mildness" (l. 163). We sense here the gap between the social reality which has led to the soldier's situation and the requirements of an aesthetic rendering of it. Yet the vigor of Wordsworth's criticism of the latent aesthetic material is not as harsh as it had been in "A Night on Salisbury Plain," and the episode concludes with the healing process that narrator, cottage, and nature begin to work on the returned soldier. Leaving the man in the care of a local cottager, the soldier thanks his benefactor "in a voice that seem'd / To speak with a reviving interest / Till then unfelt" (ll. 168–70). The soldier has metamorphosed from being a barely human "uncouth shape" into a "comrade." The process of the recovery of the human ruin by an alliance of poet and nature narrates both the narrator's mastery of the uncanniness of ruin and nature's palliative influence.

The 1797–8 human ruin poems modulate difficultly towards the ecological balance of a righted nature, which substitutes for the political imbalance of "A Night on Salisbury Plain," and offers the narrator a more solid ground. Yet each of these ruins continues to resist the tug of tranquillity that both nature and narrator appear to intend for each. The physical determination of the old man in the original fragment of "The Old Cumberland Beggar," the tenacity of the itinerant whose son lies in Falmouth, and the resistance offered by the soldier to the narrator's will ("I wished to see him move, but he remained / Fixed to his place," ll. 77–8) suggest that each of these men, like the woods at Condo Gorge, is "decaying, never to be decayed." Though Wordsworth decreases the recalcitrant autonomy of these men, in revision in the case of the first two poems and in the narrative itself in the Soldier sequence, all evince a human obstinacy exceeding ecological poise. They literally embody the ruins of

Wordsworth's earlier and powerful social criticism. Wordsworth's mastery of these ruins indexes his own political passage. The fulfillment of that mastery coincides with Wordsworth's own relinquishing of his antithetical political stance. In the opening month of 1798, the French invaded Switzerland, long the model for national autonomy and patriotism.[37] In a letter of December 1821 to his one-time political comrade James Losh, Wordsworth recalled that time: "after Buonaparte had violated the Independence of Switzerland, my heart turned against him, and against the Nation that could submit to be the instrument of such an outrage. Here it was that I parted, in feeling, from the Whigs . . ."[38] Having moved first from republican to Whig sympathy, in the poetry from this period and through the first decade of the nineteenth century Wordsworth will move even further away, going on to recover the ruins of nature and of nation, and in so doing, help construct a prospect of national identity and wholeness. Wordsworth's nationalism modulates from a kind of oppositional patriotism (his critique of poverty) to a nationalism whose function is to produce the homogeneity necessary for state cohesion: the production of a common language, the formulation of an abstract national rustic whose voice is the subjectivity of the *Lyrical Ballads*, and the creation of Wordsworth's own poetic persona as the representative man.

In "The Ruined Cottage," Wordsworth draws on the more traditional eighteenth-century topic of ruined structures, drafting an expressive interaction of decline between cottage and cottager. In "A Night on Salisbury Plain," the human ruin of the Female Vagrant had been set against the backdrop of the ruin and shrine of Stonehenge. "The Ruined Cottage" takes a more humble sort of building and raises its status to that of a monument, even as the actual fabric of the structure wears down.[39] In this sense, "The Ruined Cottage" can be classed, at least in its architectural reference, among "democratic" ruin poems.

As an example of a democratic ruin text, the poem belongs to the terrain inhabited also by Volney's *Ruins* (1791). One of the fairly consistent characteristics of eighteenth-century ruin sentiment had been the assumption that the viewer of the ruin might make sense of and easily read the mortal lessons suggested by structural decay. The ruin poem which celebrates national antiquity for the sake of ideological security, as in the example of ruined castle poems, shares the same epistemological stance as the speaker in Volney's more politically radical and aggressively democratic *Ruins*. Volney merely inverts political premises: in the invocation to the *Ruins*, he reverses the sense of desolation which the powerful feel at the sight of ruined imperial authority and instead exalts the voice of the historically disempowered. So he addresses the ruins: "you compensate the miseries of the poor by the anxieties of the rich; you console the wretched by opening to him a last asylum from distress."[40]

Wordsworth poetically redirects Volney's democratic theme – imaging the occupation of ruins by social marginals – in both a nostalgic and a nationalist direction. The two authors share the image of the ruin as the site of refuge for the destitute and homeless. But Volney does not conflate the refuge and the refugee, while Wordsworth constructs the physical structure as an objective correlative of domestic ruin. Volney's ruined palaces serve as a warning and the signal of the defeat of power, as well as the possibility of an international social transformation; Wordsworth's humble cottage lapses into a version of the domestic vernacular. Wordsworth's equation of liberty and Englishness points in a different direction from Volney's image of a "general assembly of nations," in which each originally isolated human type might become part of a global mutuality.[41]

In his excellent discussion of the intellectual climate of the English Romantics, Carl Woodring implies the naturalizing of politics when he writes: "English poetic nationalism is a political version of organic or divine union between people and land rather than an organic submission of land and people to an all-inclusive State."[42] This is clearly the atmosphere in "The Old Cumberland Beggar," but romantic poetic nationalism did eventually come to serve the needs of the state, as the state and the nation were blended into the mythology of British rurality. "The Ruined Cottage" – the longest and the most complex of Wordsworth's ruined nature poems – is particularly interesting because it was written just as the poet's politico-poetical development was in transition, and responsive to the internal pressures of national development. As Ernest Gellner argues, the internal conditions for nationalism are founded on a shift from agrarian to industrial culture, which requires an internal homogenization of peoples. The peculiarity of the birth of British nationalism, Tom Nairn argues, is that it not only derives from these conditions, but is able also to "pre-empt and politically arrest these conditions." The process of "concocting a viable popular patriotism" was one "from which the dangerous acids of populism and egalitarianism were bleached out."[43] Wordsworth's poetic gesture of returning social events to a soil of traditionalism participates in this British variation of nationalism and grounds his nostalgic view of the countryside. The persons who populate the *Lyrical Ballads* are exemplary of subjective states of mind. The long-standing debate over the originality of these poems and how they differ from a widespread antiquarian fascination with balladry, might be referred to the manner in which Wordsworth presents the subjectivity of representative individuals within an overarching national identity.

The subject matter of "The Ruined Cottage" – the decline of cottagers subjected to the purposes of a state in conflict with natural balance – makes a theme of the rift between nature and nation and then mends that rift through a poetic reparation.[44] The inhospitality of the environment in "The Ruined Cottage" is transformed by the pair of meditative minds of Armytage and the narrator. By the end of the poem the poet can find a "secret spirit of humanity" in the decay of the garden, which is retrospectively understood to be the engine of the entire experience. The reparation that the poem offers is a private and elegiac consolation, but the condition of its possibility is the restoration of the common field of nature. E. P. Thompson describes Wordsworth's psycho-political state when writing "The Ruined Cottage" as "Jacobinism-in-recoil" or a "Jacobinism-of-doubt."[45] It is certain, however, that this trade-off of political for personal comfort is poetically enabling, as if the fuel for a private poetic power must come directly out of a public political arena. Jonathan Wordsworth, who has written the most exhaustive study of "The Ruined Cottage," agrees with Thompson in viewing the poem as a poetic advance, a function of a poetic economy in which individuality is produced in the place of abstraction.[46] Wordsworth's political impulse, Thompson argues, "is transmuted in some way – from abstract political right to something more local, but also more humanely engaged."[47] The Wordsworthian humane is quite specifically a brand of nativism, offering the locality and its endowments as the ground of nationhood. It may be fair to say that for Wordsworth, the humane is local in origin, but representative in intention. The representative character of the local site is the synecdochic piece of the nation perceived as countryside. This is made explicit in *The Prelude*, but can be elicited contextually from the earlier "The Ruined Cottage." The human engagements Thompson and Jonathan Wordsworth observe in the poem, therefore, must be marked as counters in a natural dialectic Wordsworth builds, through which he finds the human in the natural by naturalizing the former in the presence of what he takes to be a natural pathology. Thus he moves closer to a version of restored nature: the kind glorified in "Tintern Abbey" and *The Prelude*.

In "The Ruined Cottage" Wordsworth takes the wasted, barren landscape of "A Night on Salisbury Plain" and turns it round, describing a mutant, burdensome, and equally inhospitable natural growth, as forbidding in its aspect of rank domesticity as it was in the shape of Sarum's monumental emptiness. In the revisions and additions of the spring of 1798, once Wordsworth was fully "parted in feeling from the Whigs," his evocation of nature's surfeit is bounded by an ordering poetic monumentality, born out of a humanized nature and recovering a version of the immortality-of-poetry *topos*, insofar as the narrator is able to poetically preserve Armytage's monument to Margaret.[48]

A way to take the measure of Wordsworth's poetic intention and outcome in "The Ruined Cottage" is to place it in the context of two other roughly contemporaneous ruin poems: Southey's "The Ruined Cottage," published as one of his *English Eclogues*, and John Clare's "The Ruins of Despair," written sometime around 1810.[49] The three poems varyingly reflect the distances between the picturesque and the experiential meanings of cottage life. Southey's version of the ruin approaches most closely to the picturesque norm instituted in the works of John Soane and others. James Malton writes in his *An Essay on British Cottage Architecture: Being an Attempt to perpetuate on Principle, that peculiar mode of Building, which was originally the effect of Chance*:

> When mention is made of the kind of dwelling called a Cottage, I figure in my imagination a small house in the country; of odd, irregular form, with various, harmonious coloring, the effect of weather, time, and accident; the whole environed with smiling verdure, having a contented, chearful inviting aspect, and door on the latch, ready to receive the gossip neighbor, or weary exhausted traveller.[50]

Armytage's narrative in Wordsworth's "The Ruined Cottage" appears at first to be something of a skeptical inquiry into this illustration of the aesthetic value of the cottage. The effects of war and government and a nature wrecked by those events plot a people's history of the realities of cottage life in the mid-1780s and the mid-1790s: bad harvests collude with warfare, impressment and unemployment. The problem of bad harvests was, of course, tied closely to the terrifically incapacitating Corn Laws, which passed off as nature's meanness the effects of agrarian protectionism.

Southey's "The Ruined Cottage" quite cheerfully endorses aestheticization. Though he asserts that "Nature steals on all the works of man / Sure conqueror she" (ll. 16–17), the overarching motif of the text is that of the decorative benignity of natural reclamation: the woodbine and hollyhock, "a stem / Bright with its roseate blossoms" (ll. 6–7). Southey tells a story of Joanna's sexual ruin, and what is presented as richness in nature is wantonness in the woman. The cottage is both the scene of Joanna's fall and the unviolated version of her personal ruin. Southey's nature offers humanity a moral, rather than a political reproach. Trading on a fairly obvious contrast between natural innocence and sexual knowledge, the poem transmits a sentimental moral message.

John Clare's "Ruins of Despair" is sharply anti-picturesque: "No whitewashed walls to pictured taste incline" (l. 25). The walls are made of mud, and the "dismal hearth is nothing but a hole" (l. 27). The ruin in this poem is the result of impoverished workmanship and materials, not the passage of time: "No shelves, no cupboards, no convenience there; / 'Twas planned in grief and finished in despair" (ll. 37–8). The utter degradation of the ruins does not invoke the ameliorative presence of natural renewal. The convention of counterpoising poem and ruin is subordinated to the reality principle; Clare begs his "Grief-searching Muse" to "stay thy too curious search, forbear!" (ll. 45, 47–8).

Clare, Southey, and Wordsworth all invoke the image of the shattered water-jar derived from *Ecclesiastes*. Clare's version of this emblem of mortality is altogether intractable. Symbolic nuances are shorn away:

> an old pitcher broke beyond excuse
> (For want concealed by them is little use)
> Stands with the filthy shadow of a pan
> Filthy and nauseous.
>
> (ll. 41–4)

For his part, Southey recalls the pitcher as it had been in a happier time, Joanna refreshing and trimming "the drooping plant" (l. 62) with her watering-pot, dispensing care to cultivated nature. Situated somewhere between the indomitable materiality of Clare's poem and the preciosity of Southey's, Wordsworth's poem is grounded in a social reality and yoked to the aesthetic of the picturesque. In Wordsworth's poem the "venerable Armytage" tells the narrator how, bending to drink at the well, he found "The useless fragment of a wooden bowl. / It moved my very heart" (ll. 91–2). Armytage, like a poet, uses the object to make a crucial symbolic and interpretive link between the woman who used the bowl and the object itself. Margaret imbues with her subjectivity the cottage and its effects, which are then transferred through the sympathetic powers of Armytage to his mental housing of them. This mental structure is then taken on by the narrator, himself transformed as he transmutes the ruin in nature into a poetic monument.

The monument-making is achieved in two stages. In Wordsworth's first addition to the poem, Armytage speaks with the voice of an eighteenth-century ruinist: "We have known that there is often found / In mournful thoughts, and always might be found / A power to virtue friendly" (ll. 227–9). The obvious insufficiency of this moralist reading – the distant narrator who abstracts a virtue from decay – is borne in upon us in the second half of the poem, in which we identify and suffer with Margaret as Armytage presents her to us. The deficit in the moralist's view is felt in the lesson which the narrator has learned by the time he leaves the scene, in Wordsworth's second addition to the poem. What the narrator learns is not an object-lesson, but a subject-lesson, in which sympathy takes the place of virtue: "I returned / Fondly and traced with milder interest / That secret spirit of humanity . . ." (ll. 501–3). In the very name of the speaker, "Armytage," we are alerted, however, to a complicated relationship between the natural world and the social one. As an archaic version of "hermitage," his name suggests that he will be Margaret's memorial until the collaboration of humanized nature and poet fully make her permanent through poetry. But within that hermitage, we hear the sound of the army, disruptively pulling local artisans into a national force.

Though the poem succeeds in giving access to poetic permanence, the excesses of an uncultivated nature distend across the poem's progress. The fulsome, almost frowzy cottage and its surroundings furnish a companion image to the malevolent intentions of a nature trying to prevent the narrator from crossing the "bare wide common" (l. 19), his "languid feet" (l. 20) "baffled still" (l. 21) by the "slippery ground" (l. 20). The resolved nature of "calm oblivious tendencies" (l. 504) which ends the poem is an early version of a "self" Wordsworth will later attribute to nature, which, "by human love / Assisted, through the weary labyrinth" (*The Prelude*, 1805, X, 922–3) will lead him to his place as poet and patriot and let him stand on the high moral ground of nationalism in the face of "this last opprobrium" (*The Prelude*, 1805, X, 934), Napoleon's coronation.

The human ruin poems place social detritus against a benign natural background. Wordsworth's "The Ruined Cottage" poetically integrates a sour nature and a human ruin, and in doing so, alters both. So the "rank speargrass" (l. 109) is transmuted into "high speargrass . . . / By mist and silent raindrops silver'd o'er" (ll. 574–5). But just as the discharged soldier's intransigence resists complete erasure, so the making of a restored nature through the sacrifice of Margaret not only undermines the "democratic" features of the poem, but also leaves us with a persistent uneasiness. The social troubles that face Margaret and her family share space in our affective response with our sense of her representative courage. In this sense, Wordsworth's intentions cannot quite overtake the relics of his social criticism.

The narrator opens the poem in a state of physical irritation: hot, tired, and bothered by flies. Consonant with this disagreeable climate, the ruin he comes upon is as graceless as the weather: "four naked walls / That stared upon each other" (ll. 31–2). There is a moment of poise as the Pedlar, linking human and natural worlds by means of his hat, "bedewed with water-drops" (l. 50) mediates the aridity of the common and the "wild" ground of the cottage garden. At this point in the poem, however, Armytage's enlarged vision of the place has not yet influenced the narrator's own perception and the first view of the garden is pervaded by the narrator's, by Wordsworth's, 1797 sensibility. As the poetic centerpiece of "The Ruined Cottage" the garden functions as an icon of the mutuality of human and natural intentions. The mutual imbalance, then, is not immanent to nature, but the result of some misalignment between humankind and nature.

The poetic vehicle by means of which Wordsworth accomplishes his naturally integrative intention is the picturesque. While "A Night on Salisbury Plain" points to the political underpinning of aesthetic categories, "The Ruined Cottage" first eschews the aesthetic rendering of the landscape, but then embraces the picturesque as a mode of transformation. In his impressive essay, "The Picturesque Moment," Martin Price remarks on two related elements of picturesque sensibility which have a particular bearing on "The Ruined Cottage." He notices the importance of "the dissociation of visual, pictorial, or generally aesthetic elements from other values in contemplating a scene."[51] When the local and social values are dissociated, the aesthetic remainder attains to a generalized form. And it is out of such generalized representations that local identities can become national ones. Within the fairly autonomous aesthetic realm of the picturesque, Price points also to the emphasis on arrangement as "interesting," producing a "complex or difficult harmony."[52] In "The Ruined Cottage," the narrator's first view of the garden is pre-picturesque. He sees the garden as wild, ripe with "matted weeds" (l. 55). The expected spots of curious harmonies appear unattractive. So, hedgerows grown together join in a "damp cold nook" (l. 62) in which the narrator comes across a well "half-covered up with willow-flower grass" (l. 63). The spot is "cheerless" (l. 60) and what fruit there is hangs from "leafless stems in scanty strings" (ll. 58–9). The peculiarity of this state is that it presents a kind of ruin whose force is not that of deprivation, but of an unorganized, uncultivated excess. Instead of producing a luxuriance, left unpruned the gooseberry trees grow haphazardly into "long lank slips" (l. 57).

A piece of nature set off from the countryside in general by its fence or wall, the garden provides an image of what culture, at any given time, imagines nature to be.[53] The cottage garden can be taken as the agricultural proletariat's counterpart to the enclosed landscape parks of the upper classes. The profitability of the massive park was more ideological than material: estate gardens "work" in the aesthetic sense, producing beauty as a kind of non-transitive commodity. In the rustic cottage garden, profit is marked as the outcome of productive work, particularly since this site of minor agriculture is the result of the expropriation of the workings of the common fields. For this reason, the problem of profit in the garden is centrally referred to by Armytage as an index of the cottager's decline. Untended, "the honeysuckle crowded round the door" (l. 308) and "worthless stonecrop ... grew like weeds" (ll. 310–11) against the window panes. Daisy, thrift, chamomile and thyme have taken over the pathways they were meant to border. The rose is bent down to the earth by the spreading foliage of "the unprofitable bindweed" (l. 314). "Waste," then, suggests not emptiness but unproductiveness. Armytage, as an active pedlar, provides a mediate persona between human ruin and poet. The conduit of natural sympathy, Armytage is the Wordsworthian rustic who can assert an economic and an aesthetic harmony with his surroundings. The narrator, who begins out-of-sorts with nature, exchanges his disorderly view of the environment for Armytage's harmonious one, and so undertakes his vocation as a poet in the presence of, and influenced by, the rustic.

It is Armytage, then, who prepares the ground for a picturesque reading of the garden. He delivers a hint of the picturesque "complex harmony" latent in the surroundings: "Often on this cottage do I muse / As on a picture ..." (ll. 117–18). Although he cannot actively identify himself as a poet, Armytage intuits the aesthetic response that liberates the poetic capacity for memorialization. As he invokes the poets' "elegies and songs" (l. 73), he makes it clear that poets must exist independently of nature: their separation from nature ensures the survival of the poetic memorial. Though not quite a poet himself, Armytage viscerally experiences the tranquil sympathy which forms the model for the poetic memorial as Wordsworth will come to consider it. Like Dorothy in "Tintern Abbey," Armytage bears on his person the memorializing function of the poet. This capacity is, however, finally antithetical to the poetic function, which is to make a monument separate from the self and thereby permanent.

As Wordsworth's vision shifts towards naturalizing cultural effects, he offers Armytage as the rustic mediator between political and natural actions. The result is the old man's language of natural disaster. Armytage's account of the 1780s blends together the 'blighting seasons" (l. 134) of bad harvests and war, in which war is metaphorized as a scourge from nature: "It pleased heaven to add / A worse affliction in the plague of war" (ll. 135–6). He describes Robert's degeneration as the mental decay that follows from idleness. Like the uncultivated garden running to an enervated excess, Robert turns from the structures of life: he whistles only snatches of tunes, and looks for something to do, not caring if his labor is for "use or ornament" (l. 168). Again in this instance, the political issue of unemployment is displaced through a metaphoric language in which nature predominates: "He blended where he might the various tasks / Of summer, autumn, winter, and of spring" (ll. 170–1). Though not absolving humans of their share in cruelty and economic distress ("Shoals of artisans / Were from their daily labour turned away / To hang for bread on parish charity," ll. 154–5), Armytage does not speak with the same indicting voice as the narrator of "A Night on Salisbury Plain." It is as a *local* disruption that the sense of dislocation is emphasized. "And of the poor did many cease to be / And their place knew them not" (ll. 143–4). Like Wordsworth's own experience on his return from France, and like the discharged soldier, the symptom of natural disunity is the unhomeliness of home. In "The Ruined Cottage," however, this condition is given as something which had been suffered in the past. The poem suggests that its monumentalizing repairs that suffering. Rather than presenting a nature responding to political turmoil, Wordsworth here replaces the very problematic of politics with a poetico-aesthetic solution.

In "Tintern Abbey," as noted in the previous chapter, we find the terminus of the picturesque ruin poem: the building entirely eradicated from the landscape, and the monument figured as the workings of a redemptive poetic memory. Wordsworth travelled the poetic passage from Salisbury Plain to the Wye Valley from 1793 to 1798, in the course of which he exchanged the contingencies of the political moment for the permanence of nature and of poetic monumentality. The ruins of nature are reclaimed through the poetic process of humanization, and the cultural ruins of cottage and abbey are settled into a benign soil. Still, we continue to read these early poems as "levelling" in the sense of party to a democratic ruin sentiment. Margaret and the other human ruins refuse to lie quiet.

III

In a "A Night on Salisbury Plain," Wordsworth presents the ruins of nature as an effect of political disequilibrium, and in "The Ruined Cottage," in keeping with the ideological-aesthetic preoccupations of his era, he engages, if fitfully, in the process of landscaping political and historical content out of the countryside, offering instead the consolations of poetic permanence. In *The Prelude*, Wordsworth reverses terms once again, and moves to fuse poetical and political matter within the context of a naturalized nation. Rather than using the language of natural occurrence to mask political content or to substitute for it, Wordsworth now asserts that the political coherence of the nation is entirely natural, and expressible in the language of the countryside. He thereby lays the foundation for his substantial body of nationalist poetry, from "Sonnets dedicated to Liberty" in his 1807 *Poems in Two Volumes*, through "Sonnets Dedicated to Liberty and Order," published in *Poems Chiefly of Early and Late Years* (1842). These latter poems xenophobically ward off "monstrous theories of alien growth, / Lest alien frenzy seize" the English people.[54] The preliminary narrative of *The Prelude* is the growth of the poet's mind as he encounters and triumphs over a personal crisis entailed by a political crisis. His emergence from that personal ruin into the poetic vocation is indissoluble from his reconciliation with his homeland. The epic poem of the growth of the poet is narrated congruently with the fulfillment of national identity.

Wordsworth conceived the 13-book *Prelude* in response to the final ruin of the Revolution, Napoleon's coronation, and as the retrospective narrative of his own recovery from personal wreckage, the "crisis of that strong disease" (1850, XI, 306). It is hardly surprising, then, that he would describe the poem in language close to the landscape ruin motif. In the architecture of *The Recluse*, *The Prelude* will occupy the place "the ante-chapel has to the body of a gothic church" (PW, V, 2). The structure of *The Prelude* is that of a self-contained fragment, fully shaped in itself, but leading on to a larger structure. Even without Wordsworth's own architectural metaphor to hand, reviewers discussed the poem when it was published in 1850 within the ruin/fragment ambiance. The critic in *The Eclectic Review* employed the fashionable lexicon of the new paleontological science to find an adequate descriptive language: "*[The Prelude]* seems a large fossil relic – imperfect and magnificent – newly dug up, and with the fresh earth and old dim subsoil meeting and mingling around it."[55] Ruin metaphors culled from eighteenth-century ruin sentiment had become, by 1850, only one source of imagery for describing the poem fragment. The vocabulary of the ruin was augmented by images and terms borrowed from Victorian evolutionary, geological, and archeological vocabularies. By the conclusion of the review, this scientific language has modulated from geology to Biblical archeology, predicting that Wordsworth's "fragments will be valued as if they were bits of the ark" (p. 554).

These are fragments as earthen ruins, pieces which yet survive some antique whole. To the Victorians such historicization of the earth – its shift from being the site of eternal and fixed objects to being a dense graveyard of obsolescent plants, animals and empires – created a terrific anxiety. Published in the same year as Tennyson's *In Memoriam*, *The Prelude* easily lent itself to being read as a remnant of an earlier and more innocent conception of the relations between humanity and nature. The *Eclectic* reviewer fosters a slightly patronizing attitude towards Wordsworth, finding the poet's attitude to nature naive, and imaging him as nature's ingenuous bridegroom who "loves her with the passion of a perpetual honeymoon" (p. 551). And certainly it is true that the "beauty and fear" through which nature teaches the child Wordsworth is perceptibly more benign than the ungentle nature who roars against humans and their world: "I care for nothing, all shall go."[56] We can discern here a split between a general transnational Nature of scientific inquiry and the mythic Nature of the national landscape.

The writer in *The Eclectic Review* commends *The Prelude* for portraying the triumph of personal survival; another contemporaneous critic more bleakly interprets *The Prelude* in the tones of the ruinist:

> *The Prelude*, therefore, complete as it is with regard to a brief period of the poet's life, is only a fragment, and one more example of the many which the last generation could produce of the uncertainty of human projects and of the contrast between the promise of youth and the accomplishment of manhood.[57]

Paradoxically, after reading the poem as a fragment whose shape mimes the condition it evokes, this same critic credits the poet with having accomplished the reassertion of national poetic power: in the atmosphere of political upheaval of the 1790s, "Childish things were put away, and poetry resumed the dignity and almost the stature, of its first manhood" (p. 468). The critic hails Wordsworth as "the great regenerator of English poetry" (p. 468), and suggests that *The Prelude*'s fragment form was the necessary price paid for Wordsworth's larger reparation of poetic ruin.

By 1850 the English fragment could claim its own kind of monumentality, having long been tacitly acknowledged generically through the public reception of such various fragment poems as "The Giaour," "Christabel," and "Hyperion. a Fragment." Yet however easily assimilated to the fragment genre in the minds of critics, *The Prelude* is undoubtedly whole and reparative in its theme of nature and self restored. The poem asserts the vitality of poetry's claim to immortality even as it refuses unequivocal poetic closure. Complete and incomplete, *The Prelude* both fixes poetry "in a visible home" (1805, I, 129) and acknowledges poetic insufficiency. We hear the inexpressibility *topos* as Wordsworth observes those country people whose tongue "is the language of the heavens," for whom "Words are but under-agents in their souls – / When they are grasping with their greatest strength / They do not breathe among them" (1805, XII, 270, 272–4). These people are Wordsworth's abstraction of the national rustic, and if *The Prelude* makes possible the regeneration of English poetry, it does so by celebrating and formulating a poetic expressed in the language of the English countryside. Poetry and nation are thus bound one to the other. In *Poetic Form and British Romanticism*, Stuart Curran describes important links between British insularity and revitalized poetic composition in the last decades of the eighteenth century. Social crisis, the result of colonial and European wars, prepared the way for an intellectual isolationism, resulting in what Curran calls a "renaissance of the Renaissance," a recovery of the English poetic past. This certainly formed a plank of the ideological strengthening required for the formation of the state of the late eighteenth and early nineteenth centuries.[58] Asa Briggs, in *The Age of Improvement*, cites a speech by Pitt (when Chancellor of the Exchequer) in which he "had painted in dismal colours the state of Britain and the Empire; the 'memorable era of England's glory' was in the past."[59] In that speech Pitt called the state of the nation a set of "scenes of ruin" and complained that "the visions of [England's] power and preeminence are passed away."[60] Briggs argues that it was Pitt's achievement by 1793 to have turned that sentiment and situation around and "rehabilitated" the place of Britain in Europe.[61] Thus Britain was prepared to take on the rival nationalist movement of France in the winter of 1793, and from that time to enlist whatever domestic forces became available in the making of national-imperialist ideology. Poetry was one such field of force, and as Curran points out, the age was "mad for poetry."[62]

The critic for the *British Quarterly Review* in 1850, calling attention to the bond between poetic achievement and native ground, points to the merits of Wordsworth's "intimate acquaintance with the joys and sorrows of rural English life; of his manly love for all that is noble and stirring in English history; and of his admirable and exquisite mastery over the resources of the English tongue."[63] Wordsworth provides access to the strength of the entire nation by his presentation of its *particular* rural "joys and sorrows," elevating at once locality and poetry into constitutive elements of the nation. What the reviewer in 1850 perceives about Wordsworth's national role, however, is never explicitly asserted in *The Prelude* itself. Rather, Wordsworth maintains that his interests are purely local and particular and that freedom can be found only in locality, in "nook[s] of English land" (1805, IX, 221). Nonetheless throughout the poem the presence of the political nation is implied in the recesses of nature. By presenting one local culture as the model for a common culture and a common language, *The Prelude* rhetorically enacts, by synecdoche, the homogenization of local cultures requisite to the coherent national identity of an industrial society and an imperialist state.

Whatever other claims the poem makes about the recovery of personal ruin and the growth of poetic identity, *The Prelude* is equally an epic of national identity, a triumphant response and correction to the defeatism of *Paradise Lost*, going a fair way toward repairing the historical manifestations of "the ruins of our first parents" in a phase of national development quite different from that to which Milton responded. *Paradise Lost* belongs to a period in which the oppositional patriotism of the English Revolution met in the Restoration its first major setback. This seventeenth-century impulse asserts the political autonomy of the nation against an aristocratic absolutism whose filiations are pan-European. *The Prelude* is both less oppositional in its purpose and more optimistic in its tone than was *Paradise Lost*. In producing an image of the nation which confirms the kind of homogeneity necessary to supply factories and the navy, Wordsworth makes the language of the country serve the needs of the Country. In his Preface to the *Lyrical Ballads*, Wordsworth theorizes the language of men speaking to men, substituting the unity of a generalized human voice for the heterogeneity of class and regional distinction.[64] That human voice is indubitably English. Paradoxically for its industrial usefulness, the image world Wordsworth calls on to enable this coherent nation derives from the pre-industrial countryside. Wordsworth thus lays foundations for the construction of "the myth of an England essentially rural and essentially unchanging" that Martin Wiener sees as central to late nineteenth- and twentieth-century British economic decline.[65] But before performing this atrophic service, Wordsworth's poem functionally, if not intentionally, participates in the more economically triumphant process which, along with the elimination of the peasantry and the integration of market economy into the countryside, resulted in there being "no longer a rural society distinctly different from the 'national' society based in the cities."[66] Yoking the regeneration of poetry and nation, *The Prelude* replies to Milton's epic of defeat by asserting national righteousness through the vehicle of the poet and the poetic imagination: Wordsworth becomes the representative man speaking to men. In a sense, then, Wordsworth accomplishes the recovery of the "lost bard," and by focusing in the second half of *The Prelude* on Britain in a martial, European context, situates Britain as the place where "Freedom now / Stands single in her only sanctuary" (1805, X, 981–2). While Milton presents his critique of and hopes for England as a political unit through a religious mythology, Wordsworth takes the secular language of personal identity and imagination and delivers a version of the nation through a self who is both individualized and representative.

By thinking about *The Prelude* in the frame of national epics, we can freshly resist a set of critical arguments about the fortunes of epic in English after *Paradise Lost*. The first is that the epic was "impossible" after Milton: in this view, the power of *Paradise Lost* was so immense as to pacify any attempts to match or outdo it, and as a poem significantly centered on subjectivity, *The Prelude* exemplifies the only possible reply to that overwhelming Miltonic power. Once we focus, however, on the centrality of the nationalist project to the epic poem in general, and observe the manner in which Wordsworth's local landscapes synecdochically operate both as particulars and as parts for the whole of the nation, *The Prelude* evinces its position as epically reparative, fulfilling its redemptive mission,

> Not in Utopia – subterraneous fields,
> Or some secreted island, heaven knows where –

> But in the very world which is the world
> Of all of us, the place in which, in the end,
> We find our happiness or not at all.
>   (1805, X, 723–7)

Though he criticizes Pitt and the policies of the English during the opening of the war, when he has sorted out British from French nationalism, Wordsworth poetically proffers his own version of England, and uses that local terrain as the basis for an alternative description of the whole of the nation.[67] In the course of the nineteenth century, when the nationalism that accompanies industrialization was corralled into the strength that accomplishes imperialism, Wordsworth's rural countryside was taken on and elaborated as an image of the homeland, and the solitary Romantic Poet embraced as a national psychological type.

At the center of the "end of the epic" theme in criticism (itself reflective of and born in the "end of ideology" period) is the contention that if *The Prelude* is epic at all, then it is so in such a fashion as to entirely reverse epic issues and to substitute psychological for national concerns. Harold Bloom and Thomas Vogler are the best exponents of this view, but it informs much subsequent discussion and pedagogy of the poem.[68] Bloom asserts that Wordsworth fundamentally altered the subject-matter of poetry by displacing all themes but that of the struggle between solipsism and imagination, which Bloom takes to be the superior contention to the Promethean struggle of a world-directed epicality. Vogler argues that in *The Prelude* the nation of the epic becomes the nation of Self. While many other and later poets have indeed read *The Prelude* as sanction for poetry of an idiosyncratic self, the epic intention and outcome of the poem is of a *representative* self shown in relation to and in the language of a natural economy within the nation, though the presentation is overtly subjective:

> Not of outward things
> Done visibly for other minds – words, signs,
> Symbols or actions – but of my own heart
> Have I been speaking, and my youthful mind.
>   (1805, III, 174–7)

Just as the poet in Wordsworth's conception is a man speaking to men, different not in kind but in degree, so the poet hero of *The Prelude* presents himself as both chosen and typical. His is the "poetic spirit" which is inborn in all people, though "By uniform controul of after years / In most abated and suppressed" (1805, II, 276–8). Wordsworth's epic hero is a subjective corollary to the Scot Wallace, whose deeds were left

> To people the steep rocks and river banks,
> Her natural sanctuaries, with a local soul
> Of independence and stern liberty.
> (1805, I, 218–20)

The naturalization of the nation helped by way of the picturesque aesthetic is the matrix within which the matter of Wordsworth's poem translates itself from subjectivity to nationalism. And the claim that Wordsworth's poem signals the end of external subject-matter is belied by the case of his own poetry, for much of Wordsworth's work following on the authorizing completion of *The Prelude* is poetry on the Matter of England. Shakespeare's Tudor nationalism, Milton's defeated nationalism, and Wordsworth's naturalized nationalism all play a part in the formulation of national consciousness through poetic production. What is surprising is our contemporary unwillingness to allow the poem to assume its function as national epic.

Earlier in this chapter we saw that in 1793–1794 Wordsworth had an uncertain sense of the relationship between British and French notions of liberty, a confusion giving rise to his poem of the political uncanny, "A Night on Salisbury Plain." *The Prelude* looks back to that period and revises it from Wordsworth's now more confident political position, offering an epic version of fall and recovery, carried through in the poet's own person, but defining and exemplifying that moment in the formulation of English national identity when the processes of internal homogenization and external rivalry only just began to generate the myths and metaphors of the chauvinistic imperialism of the later nineteenth century.[69]

In 1793 Wordsworth was not alone in identifying England as a model and ground for the French struggle. The very structure of the Corresponding Societies had been established through the centenary

celebrations of the Glorious Revolution.[70] Richard Price linked the
two events in his *Discourse on the Love of our Country*, finding in 1688
the start of "that aura of light and liberty by which we have been made
an example to other Kingdoms, and become the instructors of the
world." [71] The "forerunner [of the French Revolution] in a glorious
course," the native unity of natural grace and national liberty was an
assumption for many like the young Wordsworth of Book VI of *The
Prelude*.

From his position in 1805, Wordsworth begins his narrative by
measuring each episode of his French adventure against what he
takes to be English certainties. In Book VI, recalling his 1790 journey
with Jones, Wordsworth details how the French celebrate the two
young men precisely because they are representative of the English
nation. In Book IX, looking back to his relations with the Royalists
before his own conversion by Michel Beaupuy, Wordsworth interprets his intuitive aversion to the Royalist cause as a function of his
Englishness. Against the dazzle of "regal sceptre, and the pomp / Of
orders and degrees" (1805, IX, 213–14), Wordsworth sets a local
space, remarkably pre-Norman and non-aristocratic:

> For, born in a poor district, and which yet
> Retaineth more of ancient homeliness,
> Manners erect, and frank simplicity,
> Than any other nook of English land,
> It was my fortune scarcely to have seen
> Through the whole tenor of my schoolday time
> The face of one, who, whether boy or man,
> Was vested with attention or respect
> Through claims of wealth or blood.
>
> (1805, IX, 218–26)

Norman Yoke ideology, associated with the oppositional patriotism
and progressive nationalism of the Civil War period, here serves to
conjure a non-monarchical England against French claims and to set
the stage for Wordsworth's common cause with the revolutionaries,
insofar as he identifies their aims with English rights. There is, of
course, a palpable irony in taking on an anti-Norman tradition to
justify a link with the French, but the significance lies in the identification of a struggle against an *ancien régime*. The important aspect of
this passage is that Wordsworth selects a safe spot in England, free

from the pressures of social injustice and governmental repression, but also fantasized as free from the monarchical rule which structurally undermines the liberty of parliamentary sovereignty. Here Wordsworth takes a local situation to demonstrate his patriotism, yet specifies that patriotism as linked to a version of English liberty in which democracy is foundational to the nation. Wordsworth's early experience in the Lake District gives him the values which he will then mark in the French revolutionists. Having been brought up in "mountain liberty" (1805, IX, 242), it is not strange that he should "hail / As best the government of equal rights / And individual worth" (1805, IX, 247–9). By locating the general values of liberty in the specific place of his youth, Wordsworth both imbues the more general political position with the soil of his upbringing and takes those politics to be at source local and knowable. When he is converted by Beaupuy, it is through the apprehension of political meaning through local experience. The "hunger-bitten girl" (1805, IX, 512) who wanders with her heifer is the image which stirs Wordsworth into revolutionary vigor, its catalyst Beaupuy's words, " 'Tis against that / Which we are fighting" (1805, IX, 519–20).

The journeys recapitulated in Books VI and IX take Wordsworth into the center of France, where he discovers and deepens his sense of the affinities between his homeland and France, established most securely through his intuitive response to and spiritual kinship with Beaupuy. But in Book X Wordsworth reverses his physical and spiritual direction: he doubles back to England from the richness of the Loire Valley (associated for him with English traditions from his travels with Jones in 1790) and into the trial of Paris, the "fierce metropolis" (1805, X, 7). There Wordsworth lives like a man cut off from his own nature foreshadowing what will be his central experience back in England a few months later. In the city he is cut off from his intuitive judgments upon what he sees, watching the events around him like a man gazing

> Upon a volume whose contents he knows
> Are memorable but from him locked up,
> Being written in a tongue he cannot read.
> (1805, X, 50–3)

Only at this moment does language become a disabling barrier. We are suddenly reminded that the language of this city is French, not Wordsworth's native tongue. A gap has opened up within Wordsworth between his intuitions and his actions, signalling a more critical breach within his identification of English and French liberty. In Paris, language becomes a marker of political and national difference. Haunted by the September Massacres, Wordsworth prays for the deliverance of France from its own self-deceptions, a deliverance he imagines can be brought by men who have "the gift of tongues" (1805, X, 121). The poet fantasizes that he himself might be such a man, a political cosmopolitan hero, whose success will be to return France to traditional liberties: "Redeemed according to example given / By ancient lawgivers" (1805, X, 187–8). The implication is that this language will be the translation out of English into internationalism, "Transcendent to all local patrimony" (1805, IX, 139). In other words, just as French nationalism will describe itself as international in the Napoleonic period, so Wordsworth equates English liberty with universal liberty. It is only after returning to England and recovering his equanimity that Wordsworth can redraft his missed heroic vocation as being "to men / useless," resulting in the greater loss of being "a poet only to myself" (1805, X, 199–200). This direct exchange between the vocations of statesman and poet, savior of the revolution or national poet, invites us to consider the extent to which Wordsworth's life as poet *was* a version of statesmanship, his presentation of himself as representative man/poet enacting an identity between self and nation.

Wordsworth provides the link between his individuality and his typicality when he describes the reaction in England to the declaration of war, which produced a "revolution" (1805, X, 237): "Not in my single self alone I found, / But in the minds of all ingenuous youth, / Change and subversion from this hour" (1805, X, 231–3). The violence done by the Pitt administration was to tear "at one decisive rent / from the best youth in England their dear pride, / Their joy, in England" (1805, X, 276–8). This alienation is given a poignant expression in the image of the youth in church unable to feel part of the parish, the fundamental unit of English rural life: " 'mid the simple worshippers perchance / I only, like an uninvited guest / Whom no one owned, sate silent" (1805, X, 271–2). At once bound to the other youth of his time and cut off from the nation as a whole, Wordsworth typifies the unnaturalness of the moment.

We should note, however, that while Wordsworth was between worlds in the summer of 1793, finding no place homely and viewing the countryside itself as aberrant, he was physically far away from Britain's redemptive sites. Just as Wordsworth's epic blends Dorset, the Lake District, and Wales into representative British soil, so the pre-redemptive moment is presented as disparate and heterogeneous pieces of countryside. In this atmosphere, the "unnatural strife" (1805, X, 250) in the poet's heart mimics the external war and "patriotic love" (1805, X, 280) gives way; while on its side, France offers its own pathology: "The goaded land waxed mad; the crimes of few / Spread into madness of the many" (1805, X, 312–13).

At the end of "A Night on Salisbury Plain," Wordsworth had suggested that brief respites from the calamities and oppression of social injustice were all that might be expected from an nation as unnatural as England was in the deathly summer of 1793: "And think that life is like this desart broad, / Where all the happiest find is but a shed / And a green spot 'mid wastes interminably spread" ("A Night on Salisbury Plain," ll.421–3). In Book X of *The Prelude*, Wordsworth returns to this image and revises it, beginning his narration of the following summer of 1794 by once again calling on the figure of an oasis in the midst of waste:

> And as the desert hath green spots, the sea
> Small islands in the midst of stormy waves,
> So that disastrous period did not want
> Such sprinklings of all human excellence
> As were a joy to hear of.
> (1805, X, 440–444)

The green spot Wordsworth finds is an example of "human nature faithful to itself / Under worst trials" (1805, X, 447–8), a model for the repair of his own ruin. Thinking perhaps of the Female Vagrant's fealty to her memory of Keswick, Wordsworth finds in homely fortitude the possible counterpoint to social calamity: between the versions of 1794 and 1805 Wordsworth's emphasis has shifted from a critique of governmental injustice to a confidence in the strength of the rural memory.

Within this later retrospect of 1794, Wordsworth mentally retraces his 1790 walking tour with Jones. Grounded now in the "green spot" of England, Wordsworth discovers that his memory of that walking tour had been wrong or rather, that its meaning was very different from what he had earlier taken it to be. Arras, the town where he and Jones had found confirmation of the identity of the two nations at a festival which "Triumphal pomp for Liberty confirmed" (1805, X, 453), is now important chiefly as the birthplace of Robespierre, whom Wordsworth takes to be the suppressor of liberty. Wordsworth intimates that the festival had presaged this later betrayal, with its "rainbow made of garish ornaments" (1805, X, 452). The Enlightenment appears to have been an artificial light, the sun "that rose in splendour" and "moved / In exultation among the living clouds" had "put his function and his glory off, / And turned into a gewgaw, a machine" (1805, X, 936–40).

This retrospective reinterpretation allows the poet to reaffirm a nativist liberty and a native poetry. To make his point Wordsworth compares himself to Lear, the king who acted most unnaturally towards not only his daughters, but also his nation, dividing that which ought to have been kept whole. The double valence of Arras produces a kind of madness in the poet:

> As Lear reproached the winds, I could almost
> Have quarrelled with that blameless spectacle
> For being yet an image in my mind
> To mock me under such a strange reverse.
> (1805, X, 461–5)

Wordsworth learns of Robespierre's defeat on a glorious English day in the summer of 1794, riding under a "genial sun," with "distant prospect among gleams of sky / And clouds, and intermingled mountain-tops, / In one inseparable glory clad" (1805, X, 476–9). The sun shines alone on England and the poet recollects "few happier moments" than that in which he had learned of Robespierre's fall. But the illuminated happy moment is crossed by his memory of the equally happy moment when he had recognized the embodiment of liberty in the French Revolution. That the same place should be the site of two such exclusive yet connected joys is to Wordsworth not only extraordinary, but also maddening. This contradictory perception fuses the contradictory impulses of French and English nationalism. At the moment Wordsworth writes of, the nationalist enterprise of the French Revolution was reaching its overt mission, to be completed and fulfilled by Napoleon. That French expansionism and project of unification under a national banner – much like the process of homogenization going on in England to complete its transition from an agrarian to an industrial society – was clearly incompatible with English nationalist aspirations. Wordsworth conveys, though he cannot make explicable, the exclusivity of national "liberties."

This episode on Levern Sands admumbrates what will find full narrative form as Wordsworth's recovery from crisis on Mount Snowdon. The Levern Sands incident links him to his own past and to a greater English past, and the openness of the Plain provides a critical counter-place to the barrenness of Salisbury Plain where the poet had wandered the previous summer. The site is profound for the poet first of all because it is inhabited by the spirit of a man from one of the "nooks of English land" that so nurtured Wordsworth as a child, William Taylor, his school headmaster. Wordsworth is both physically and imaginatively grounded by Taylor's grave. He can more easily make sense to himself of this historical moment by interpreting Robespierre's fall by reference to a British context which predates the corruption of the Pitt government. The scene of revelation on Levern Sands is presented as an isolated, sheltered moment, but it suggests that sense of English freedom standing "single in her only sanctuary" that Wordsworth will announce in 1805. Unlike the empty eerie plain at Sarum, on Levern Sands "all the plain / Was spotted with a variegated crowd / Of coaches, wains, and travellers, horse and foot" (1805, X, 523–5). Wordsworth breaks spontaneously into a "hymn of triumph" (1805, X, 543), and his return along the shore, punctuated by "uneasy bursts / Of exultation" (1805, X, 557–8), recalls to him the childhood races from the ruin of St Mary's "mouldering fane" (1805, X, 561). This linking of past to present characterizes the manner in which Wordsworth will recover his identity and imagination through the offices of Dorothy and nature, and exemplifies, through the poet's persona and local habitation, the recovery and the instantiation of the recovered nation itself. It was, we are reminded by allusion, at that very spot that Wordsworth had been given a childhood signal of his calling, when he sat beneath the dripping ivy of the ruin and listened to the voice of an invisible bird which sang so beautifully "that there I could have made / My dwelling-place, and lived forever there / To hear such music" (1805, II, 132–4). In Wordsworth's recourse here to the familiar ruin motif, in which national history has been reduced to the scope of an individual's life, and the architectural artifact redeployed as an organic one, we sense the congeniality of *The Prelude* to the project already begun of presenting the nation as verdantly inevitable. And in his revisions of *The Prelude*, Wordsworth continued to add ruin motif touches. For example, in revising Book II, Wordsworth prepares for Furness Abbey by introducing elements that will then accrue around the race through the ruins. "A mouldered cave" (1805, II, 64) becomes "the ruins of a shrine" (1850, II, 63), and the addition of "some framed temple where of yore / The Druids worshipped" (1850, II, 101–2), helps to endow the atmosphere with a layer of mythic pastness.

But like the Ancient Mariner, having achieved a kind of relief from his unease on Levern Sands, the poet must do more penance. Wordsworth goes on to argue that the disease of mental abstraction was the price he had to pay for his involvement with the French Revolution and his disaffection from England. The second half of Book X traces the etiology and recovery from this illness, and we sense that this disease is the psychic counterpart to his political alienation from the English locale and the corollary unhomeliness of the countryside itself to his eye. In the economy of imagination and ratiocination, the growth of abstract thought entails a loss of the nativity of imaginative process. So, though Godwin may have been the domestic source for Wordsworth's rational ill, the association of imagination with nature, and nature with homeland, suggests that Wordsworth's strong disease is really a mental version of the "French disease." Conversely, the imagination is a native British trait. Wordsworth retrospectively comes to the conclusion that his desire to promulgate an abstract category of freedom was both unavoidable and misconceived, a project doomed because not grounded in the freedom of local English soil. He represents his deviation as an assertion of a deracinated self, who aims to

> with a resolute mastery shaking off
> The accidents of nature, time, and place,
> That make up the weak being of the past
> Build social freedom on its only basis,
> The freedom of the individual mind.
> (1805, X, 821–5)

This image of the self shaking off the constraining irritations of existence is meant to be an antithetical mirror to Wordsworth's experience on Mount Snowdon, in which "genuine liberty" (XIII, 122) is exalted in those who precisely *have* the ability to build up from, and take as foundational, the accidents of time, nature, and place: these "native selves"

> build up greatest things
> From least suggestions, ever on the watch,
> Willing to work and to be wrought upon.
> They need not extraordinary calls
> To rouze them – in a world of life they live,
> By sensible impressions not enthralled,
> But quickened, rouzed, and made thereby more fit
> To hold communion with the invisible world
> . . .
> Oh, who is he that hath his whole life long
> Preserved, enlarged, this freedom in himself? –
> For this alone is genuine liberty.
> (1805, XIII, 98–105, 120–3)

Wordsworth commends in others the synecdochic facility that he himself rhetorically employs. To build from "least suggestions," and to use the local detail to illuminate and produce the whole, is the method by which the individual preserves and enlarges genuine liberty within himself. It is this same method which enables Wordsworth, in his period of recovery in 1796, to enlarge the compass of his recovery from his person to the entire nation. Book XII traces this process, beginning with Wordsworth's interest in the minutiae of the vernacular world, his capacity

> To look with feelings of fraternal love
> Upon those unassuming things that hold
> A silent station in this beauteous world.
> (1805, XII, 50–3)

The poet both figures his mind as a landscape, "The horizon of my mind enlarged" (1805, XII, 57), and surveys the native world with its rustics to reinforce his situating of the recovery of self within a native and harmonious, homogeneous countryside.

In "A Night on Salisbury Plain," Wordsworth made class distinctions,

in which we understood that the vagrant and traveler were lucky to
have come upon a lowly cot since they might not have received such
good treatment at a richer family's house. By the time of his 1805
revisions, Wordsworth is more concerned with stressing the coherence of the populace, the "people" required for a sense of "nation,"
than with making domestic distinctions. He produces this harmonizing by stressing "the universal heart" (1805, XII, 219) above "The
differences, the outside marks by which / Society has parted man from
man" (1805, XII, 217–18). While the alienated analyst separates men
from men, the experience of walking amongst the rural world and
hearing "sounds in unison" (1805, XII, 183) convinces Wordsworth
of rural coherence.

Yet it is not entirely clear that Wordsworth's categories here are
any less abstract than those he rejects in rationalism. Certainly his
elaboration of the generalized "tale of honour" coming "From
mouths of lowly men," their voices a set of "sounds in unison" (1805,
XII, 182–4), condemns the poet to the irreducibility of abstraction. In
the process of homogenizing native peoples, Wordsworth cannot
emancipate himself from the tendencies he criticizes amongst the
theorists of the French Revolution. But Wordsworth does move
towards abstraction from intuition and not intellection. In his poem
"To William Wordsworth," Coleridge describes the poet's articula-
tion of "Truth" as "Not learnt, but native" (59–60):[72] Wordsworth's
poetic capacity proceeds from and is owed to nature. So Wordsworth
comes to find his own vocation amongst the people: he defines the
role of the poet as he who can elicit this homogeneity, "enabled to
perceive / Something unseen before" (1805, XII, 304–5) operating
amongst men and in the presence of nature, a nature which has by
now become entirely vernacular in its characteristics. The recovering
Wordsworth has the insight that

> the genius of the poet hence
> May boldly take his way among mankind
> Wherever Nature leads – that he hath stood
> By Nature's side among the men of old,
> And so shall stand forever.
>   (1805, XII, 293–8)

The central faculty of native intuition is the imagination, which is explicitly assimilated to the nation in Book XII, as Wordsworth brings the reader and the poet round again to Salisbury Plain, to the experience of 1793 recast in the light of very different poetical and political intentions. Once the site of personal and national ruin, Sarum is now the site of Wordsworth's poetic commission. Wordsworth explains that his intuition that he possessed a power "Enduring and creative," that "might become a power like Nature's", (1805, XII, 308, 310) produced in him an exultation:

> To such mood,
> Once above all – a traveller at that time
> Upon the plain of Sarum – was I raised.
> (1805, XII, 313–16)

Wordsworth locates his poetic calling in the geographical space of British antiquity: Stonehenge is now an emblem of not simply national coherence, but also of the inextricable links between poetic vocation and national destiny.

Immediately after the narration of his experience in Sarum, Wordsworth opens the final Book of the 1805 *Prelude* with his experience of Mount Snowdon. If Salisbury Plain sets out the possibility of the poetic vocation at the birth of the nation, Mount Snowdon embodies the fulfillment of that promise. While the Mount Snowdon episode is chronologically anterior to Salisbury Plain, it is episodically counterpoised to Wordsworth's trip to the Alps in Book VI. The external world is empty and stingy in Europe: the Alps do not give what they might, either refusing to match up to the imagination's possibilities or sending the imagination into a torrent of confusing and conflicting passions. The beauty of the Loire Valley turns out to be the displaced beauty of Wordsworth's native land. In Wales, on British Mount Snowdon, the self and the external world are balanced, and the reciprocity of imagination and nature is equally that between the representative self and the larger nation. On Mount Snowdon we are once again at the site of Gray's bardic curse, and the continuity of the bardic voice is established. Wordsworth as poet stands for himself and again for a large common group, while asserting that those who can embody such reciprocity are themselves locally grounded:

> They from their native selves can send abroad
> Like transformation, for themselves create

A like existence, and, when'er it is
Created for them, catch it by an instinct.
                        (1805, XIII, 93–6)

The mutual making of nation and self is the climax of the poem. The reparative action of the Imagination and of its nationalist function are inseparable: here in native geography, the country answers the poets, for here "had Nature lodged / The soul, the imagination of the whole" (1805, XIII, 64–5). To speak of nature is to speak of the nation: the fragments cohere into a whole, the ruin is repaired, and as the nation moves through each person, so each person moves through the nation.

5

The Sublime of Ruin: Blake's *Jerusalem*

I

Like *The Prelude*, Blake's *Jerusalem* can be considered both as a national epic and as a member of the family of ruin poems. We have seen that *The Prelude* was critically assimilated to the ruin/fragment kind, while thematizing the reparation of the ruins of the nation. *Jerusalem*, with its formal dislocations and narrative chaos, enacts a kind of poetic ruin in addition to presenting in its subject-matter the collapse and recovery of the Giant Man Albion, the visionary human form of the nation. Wordsworth's poem draws a nation anchored to the countryside and the picturesque aesthetic, yoking a particular rural locale to the larger terrain of the nation, while Blake's *Jerusalem* is a poem which images a nation born from and centered in the city, and aesthetically preoccupied with the sublime. Politically distinct in motive, Wordsworth's national epic functions as a nationalist epic, while Blake's national epic is overtly critical. Wordsworth's epic poem adumbrates the blossoming of official nationalism, which "stretch[es] the short, tight, skin of the nation over the gigantic body of the empire."[1] Blake's epic presents a version of oppositional nationalism.

While exploring the ground of the ruined castle poem, we caught the outline of an ideology of the picturesque which produced congenial images of a stable yet ancestral landscape. The word "immemorial" aptly describes this ruin-affect, the sensation that the origins of ruined buildings are comfortingly beyond the reach of historical record. Wordsworth's manipulation of the landscape theme in *The Prelude* alters the meaning of space as ruined castle poetry had altered that of time. The melancholic placidity inspired by the sight of ivy-covered ruined castles locates the viewer in an atemporal permanence unthreatened by linear change. For his part, Wordsworth evokes a landscape which is presented as representative of the larger nation, and whose representative character then substitutes for localism. This generalizable landscape is easily accommodated to the temporality of the myth of national origins and so points towards that homogenized population – the "people" – of industrial society. Ernest Gellner's argument that the shift into industrialization is accompanied by a change in social representations from heterogeneous layers to a homogeneous national representation is borne out by the examples of ruin poems and *The Prelude*.[2]

Wordsworth fell into step with his nation ideologically, and the public success of his poetry can hardly be overstated, while the public intellectual and economic failure of Blake's is a fact equally plain. It is also certain that Blake, for all the progressive utopianism of his communitarian vision, was in many ways facing the past. Guardian of an artisanal mode of book production in a world in which the massive distribution of verse was tied to an expanding publishing industry,[3] attached to the oppositional patriotism of the seventeenth century at a moment when the intellectual and military forces around him were marching towards the official national chauvinism of British imperial power, drawing his poetic lexicon out of the Antinomian rhetoric in which anti-monarchical nationalism had spoken during the period of the English Revolution, Blake clung to the ideal of a heterogeneous society whose community coherence would result from the willed labor of mutually dependent but distinct humans.

Within the milieu of picturesque ruin poetry, understood as collaborative with the production of a cohesive national identity, *Jerusalem* stands forward as a major challenge to what Blake might call the "Indefinites" (J 55: 58)[4] of the myth of the Country imaged as the countryside. *Jerusalem* raises the banner of sublimity against the picturesque, the activity of culture against the passivity of nature, the city against the country, and the history of British tyranny against the opacity of the self-constraining nation of "One King One God One Law" (*Urizen* 4: 40).

Jerusalem is a poem of the urban sublime, in which London is figured as a terrible place of conflicting and contradictory impulses that will not be mastered, and whose energy fuels the poet-prophet Los's furnaces of painful yet productive forging: "And Los's Furnaces how loud, living, self-moving, lamenting / With fury & despair" (J 73: 2–3). When these sites of labor are seen with multiple vision, they shine "Translucent," with forms made of "Beryl and Emerald immortal," but they remain "incomprehensible / To the Vegetated Mortal Eye's perverted and single vision" (J 53: 9–11). Wordsworth in London intuits but then flees from the terrors of urban sublimity, "all the ballast of familiar life . . . / Went from me, neither knowing me, nor known" (*The Prelude*, 1805, VII, 603, 608). Blake, on the other hand, locates in city terror a set of energies which test and expand poetic and political boundaries.

Strikingly different from the values of the rural picturesque ruin poem is Blake's emphasis on the centrality of human labor against ruin. The ruined castle gives itself up to nature; the builders of Golgonooza struggle against depredations. The attempt to formulate a poetic of ruin that will resist the drift towards figuring either poem or persona as terminally ruined is the laboring task of Blake and Los, the poet who continually builds and rebuilds the city of Golgonooza, "the spiritual fourfold London eternal, / In immense labours & sorrow, ever building, ever falling" (*Milton* 6: 1–2). The immortality-of-poetry *topos* presents the poetic monument as an achieved solution to the transience of built artifacts and so aids in the preservation of the image of the nation. The poet-speaker of a ruin text is often led to his pensive melancholy through a passive acceptance of natural ruin. Such passivity is anathematic to Blake. *Jerusalem* suggests that poetry can have no life apart from its function in world-building: the immortality of poetry is inextricable from the immortality of human labor. In stressing process over product, Blake's poetic suggests the importance of the temporal fragment as well as the ruin. The ruin faces the past, the fragment intimates the as yet immanent future. The cold state of Albion fallen can only be roused by Los's terrifying labors in the human locale – the city – and by the human undertaking. In *Jerusalem* Blake takes apart the image of the nation and uses his poetry to try to build a new kind of nation.

Making sense of *Jerusalem* in the family of ruin poems means not only changing physical venue from country to city and aesthetic orientation from the picturesque to the sublime, but also shifting political direction from the implicit nationalism of Wordsworth to a more didactic but avowedly oppositional version of the nation's history. Readers often experience Blake's didacticism as a strain on their aesthetic attention. It is therefore important to point out that the "preaching" is a sign of poetic labor. *The Prelude* presents itself as given, the untroublingly natural sound of a man speaking to men. *Jerusalem* is obviously worked on, and its mode of speaking calls attention to itself as a social practice. James Scully makes this point about "tendency" poetry in general in his excellent study of politics and poetry: "Preaching is discourse constituted as unembarrassed social practice. It *confronts*, troubling the hegemony of social silence."[5]

Blake's urban ruin poem calls on the terror of historicity while uncovering the layers of social silence which the picturesque language of ruin poetry naturalizes. Blake asserts that the foundations of British national identity were built on the tyranny and oppression of English government. Blake's alternate history to the state one begins with "Satan, Cain, Tubal" (J 73: 35) and moves right through the latest British monarchs:

> Arthur, Alfred, the Norman Conqueror, Richard, John,
> Edward, Henry, Elizabeth, James, Charles, William, George.
>
>   (J 73: 36–7)

But of course Blake's intention is not to make myth impossible, for he knows that myths are narratives to act by, and his *oeuvre* is famously mythological in intent and imagery. Rather, Blake reconceives the myth of nation as complex and differentiated, and seeks to take it out of the hands of "Priest and King" and give it over to human laboring agents. Blake takes on the burden of a mystified antiquarianism – which he figures in *Jerusalem* as the tradition of Druidical wisdom – and uses the counters of that tradition to criticize its oppressive intention and to forge a different myth to live by. Walter Benjamin identifies the necessity of this impulse: "In every era the attempt must be made to wrest tradition away from a conformism that is about to overpower it."[6] Blake inhabits and presses against the language of national myth.

The ambiguous outcome of that struggle must be acknowledged, however, and gauged by the way in which Blake's work itself has been mystified into the linear tradition of Britishness. For example, those stanzas from *Milton* which promise to build Jerusalem in "England's green and pleasant land" became part of the language of discipline through which the state tyrannized its Borstal boys even in the twentieth century. And critics of British nationalism, seeing the term "British" as a mask worn by the English ruling powers, argue that Blake is tied to the tradition he seeks to expose, and so contributes to the perpetuation of radical insularity. Neal Ascherson, an outspoken critic of official British nationalism, mistakenly sees Blake as his opponent rather than his comrade: "When Labour MPs dedicated to pulling Britain out of the Common Market sing 'Jerusalem,' they are actually singing about the Druidic origins of Christianity. Blake's mystical Anglo-centric nationalism suits them well"[7] Ascherson has either misread *Jerusalem*'s ridicule of such Christianity, or he has received a second-hand, official version of Blake. Another irritating misunderstanding of Blake's counterposition occurred in 1963, when the newly-formed British Circle of the Universal Bond of Druids, attempting to prove an ancestry for themselves, argued that an earlier head of their tribe had been Blake himself![8] While this outcome may be partially explained by the triumph of official nationalism in England, it must also be keyed to the tortured reversionary image world Blake constructed, whose most acute readers would have been the seventeenth-century English communists: those Muggletonians, Levellers, and Ranters raised to their radical historical importance by Christopher Hill in *The World Turned Upside Down*, but certainly not populous in the early nineteenth century.[9]

Yet what is crucial and distinctive about Blake's reparative intention in *Jerusalem*, and its legacy to later progressive poets, is the manner in which the poetic moves beyond being critical: rather than resting in a nostalgic meditation on and redescription of national origins, Blake insists upon the transformative outcome of criticism:

> Can you think at all & not pronounce heartily, That to Labour in Knowledge is to Build up Jerusalem: and to Despise Knowledge, is to Despise Jerusalem and her Builders.
>
> (J 77)

To insist upon the material, historical, and national meanings which make up significant thematic strands in *Jerusalem* is to reassess some of the received wisdom about Blake's political and poetic development. For critics who hold a transcendental conviction, *Jerusalem* is often credited as the finest of Blake's poems. Harold Bloom calls it "the only rival to Wordsworth's *The Prelude* as the supreme long poem in English since *Paradise Lost*."[10] In Bloom's reading, the center of the poem is the struggle of Los against his Spectre. Bloom interprets this combat as the creative impulse warring against a solipsistic Selfhood which threatens to overtake the Imagination and bind it to negativity. Victory by the Imagination is given shape in the regained unity of Albion.

M. H. Abrams also calls *Jerusalem* Blake's highest achievement:

Blake's "last and greatest epic," "the recovery by the mythical man of his fourfold unity is equated with every individual man's recovery of his flexible, imaginative and creative power of unifying vision."[11] These readings, while they resonate with interpretative truth, are allied to the judgment that poetry addressing the Imagination is better than that which addresses the social world.

Historical critics, on the other hand, have tended towards a nega-tive evaluation of *Jerusalem*. Marilyn Butler sees in the poem a falling off of Blake's poetic power in concert with "a turning away from the material world of political action, collective frustration, postponed hope."[12] Edward Larrissy, a Marxist reader of Blake's work, says of *Jerusalem* and *Milton* both: "The slow-moving tableaux of his later works are the index of a political despair which sees all history as telling one dire story, and the only way out as mental, rather than physical fight."[13] In his judgment the later poems are inferior be-cause, unlike the "Song of Liberty" which ends *The Marriage of Heaven & Hell* or the apocalyptic transformations of Night IX of *The Four Zoas*, *Jerusalem* is constructed neither as directly referable to a set of contemporary revolutionary events nor from a narrative struc-ture resolved by apocalypse. David Erdman sidesteps giving an overt assessment of *Jerusalem*, but he suggests his attitude when taking over without qualification Northrop Frye's description of the poem as "harsh," and gives disproportionately little space to an analysis of the work in *Blake: Prophet Against Empire*.[14]

Jerusalem appears to be a less revolutionary work within Blake's *oeuvre* because Albion's regeneration is not accompanied by the perfervid harvest of *The Four Zoas* but rather by the more romantic and Christian "Breath Divine" (J 94: 18). A. L. Morton's significant discussion of the content of Blake's Christian imagery as it carries into the nineteenth century the language of seventeenth-century radi-cal politics alerts us to the socially representational content of the Biblical rhetoric.[15] We should also remember that *Jerusalem*, unlike *The Four Zoas*, is a work that Blake chose to insert into a public world, even if the constraint of his artisanal commitment meant that he produced only six hand-printed copies. *The Four Zoas* is patently a poem of poetic crisis, a work finally left in an unpublished and almost unintelligible form. The completion and publication of *Jerusalem* suggests that the crisis has been resolved, and that resolution is closely tied to the kind of work – the kind of social practice – that the poem undertakes. For *Jerusalem* is an example of that kind of political poetry which does its work, not by commenting on, or reproducing, or even transforming political events into a poetic language, but instead, tackling that part of political life which takes place *in* language. Blake attacks that ideology of nationalism promulgated by men like Burke and sustained by the state in, for example, its domination of Ireland with its mystified presentation of Ireland as "united" with England when it was in fact, colonized and brutalized in the name of "Britain." That is, the focus of Blake's critical poetic in such work is the realm of national representations. In this sense the poem's primary intent is not to provide an imitation of or reflection upon a set of events taking place in the larger world, but to be itself a political intervention. In this way the intention of *Jerusalem* is fully poetico-political. In some of the earlier poems Blake violently represents redemption, and this work can be interpreted as figuratively correlative to the productive and energetic violences of revolutionary change. But a poetic strategy which produces, in a different register, support for or response to events in the political world, at the same time limits the poetic function itself to a mirroring of that world. In *Jerusalem*, however, what Blake does is to take on the transcendent homogeneous myth of Britain and critically differentiate it into an immanently utopian myth of liberation. The intention of *Jerusalem* is to fight repressive myth with liberating myth – exposing the former by parodying it in the image of the Druid past. Blake would produce an internationalism out of nationalism, communitarianism out of oppressive hierarchy. Though Blake may have indeed become disillusioned with the later stages of the French Revolution, a work like *Jerusalem* shows that he didn't abandon his political intentions. The poetry then may have no mimetic function, but a strikingly *interventionist* one. This is a politi-cally immanent poetic.

In *Jerusalem*, narrative transformation also is immanent, figured as the both necessary and unending building undertaken by Los. In *The Four Zoas*, apocalypse is not only violent, it is also precipitated externally to narrative events. Christ must descend in "Luvah's Robes" to begin the harvest. In *Jerusalem* Los's immanence operates as well in the thematic torsion of the poem, which first registers and then revolutionizes the antiquarian materials it works upon. In this sense the poem achieves (even if it is unable to make functional) a poetically political reparative wholeness.

II

To take the measure of Blake's urban sublime, we must draw out his antithetical version of Britain, at whose geographical center lies the material city of London, the spiritual city of Golgonooza, and the potential city of Jerusalem. The landscape of Britain in *Jerusalem* is marked by monuments of a revisionist myth of origin: Stonehenge, Tyburn, and London Stone. These sites reverse the meaning of the linear patriotic myth of Whig nationalism. The notion of the linear continuity of a British tradition is not the property only of Whigs, of course. It persists today in the fetish of "heritage," acutely observed and analyzed by social critics like Patrick Wright and Neal Ascherson.[16] Ascherson discusses the constraint of a past presented as a continuum when he articulates the late twentieth-century version of "tradition" as a condition in which "time is linear to a perfectly oppressive degree."[17] In his internally dislocative and anti-linear narrative Blake attacks the power of the "concept of the continuous nation" which "has been used to legitimize the *ancien régime* – the unreformed British State – and to discourage republican ideas."[18] Stonehenge, Tyburn, and London Stone appear and disappear in the course of the poem; their geographical and temporal meanings shift, combine, and loosen over the course of the four chapters of the text. What these monuments consistently mark in *Jerusalem* are the places of ancient druidical as well as contemporary juridical execution. So Blake memorializes the Britain which official nationalism would like to forget.

We will return to these three sites later in this discussion, after sketching the larger geography of Blake's visionary Britain. *Jerusalem* refuses to produce the imagery of the green land invoked in the prefatory lyric to *Milton*. The fecund countryside is eschewed for the imagery of metalworks and forging. The closest to a natural constant or reiterated image is that of stone: nature depleted of its vitality. Under Blake's critical gaze the earth which Britain encompasses is no "precious stone set in a silver sea" (*Richard II*, II, i, 7), but an "Ancient Druid Rocky Shore," the reciprocal outer boundary to the central Druid stone altar which is at the heart of a desolate wasted nation. Blake's version of nationalism, then, begins with the same insight that Wordsworth had in his republican experience on Salisbury Plain: the assessment that contemporary England is a place most unlike its possibility. When Blake writes of the "Briton, Saxon, Roman, Norman amalgamating / In Los's Furnaces into One Nation, the English; & taking refuge / In the Loins of Albion" (J 92: 1–3), his aim is not to mirror the available representation of the unified nation, but imagine a new one, in which every individual and every organ of every individual is given space and identity:

> & they walked
> To & fro in Eternity as One Man, reflecting each in each & clearly seen
> And seeing, according to fitness & order.
>
> (J 98: 39–41)

The difficulty of that imagining is evident in the state of ruin which is everywhere present in the poem. Jerusalem/Golgonooza are ruins of a particularly non-picturesque character. We can distinguish the sublime from the picturesque ruin by contrasting the activity of sublimity to the inertia of the landscape ruin. This runs parallel to the distinction between the apparent naturalness and therefore permanence of the picturesque ruin and the transience of Blake's urban ruins. The nation in *Jerusalem* is in a state of continual fallings-apart and recoveries. Demolishing and creating are the twin labors of Los:

> In fears
> He builded it, in rage & in fury. It is the Spiritual Fourfold
> London, continually building & continually decaying desolate.
> (J 53: 17–19)

Unlike the ruins at Netley Abbey, the ruins of Jerusalem are not covered with moss or lichen, evidence of the inertia of materials and of the triumph of nature over forms of culture. Blake's ruins will not submit to a victory by vegetative life: they remain stony and stark in their Urizenic state. Yet in their resistance, they function as well as the building blocks of the new world. Critics have most profoundly understood Blake's anti-naturalism as a reflex of his production and celebration of the Imagination unfettered to the "Vegetating Death" (J 69: 31).[19] Here we can augment this psycho-poetical analysis by referring Blake's claim that "Where man is not, nature is barren" (K 152) to his campaign against the oppressive myth of British homogeneity.

As Wordsworth had in "A Night on Salisbury Plain," Blake draws on the image of the Druid to focus his history of the nation. As noted earlier, in his work on the Druid image, A. L. Owen points out that there were two distinct lines of filiation in the representation of Druids in English literature.[20] Druids were variously interpreted as an elite class of thinkers and poets, and as a conspiratorial secret society, whose corrupt priests performed bloody sacrificial rites. Owen notices that in the eighteenth century, the bloodlust aspect of Druidism was considerably downplayed.[21] The assimilation of the Druid figure to incipient nationalism was aided by that strain of antiquarian research which argued that the Druids had been a help to the rise of English Christianity, rather than an oppositional force; and then went on to "prove" that the origins of Druidism were linked to the very origins of Judeo-Christian history.[22] Blake also adopts this conflation of Jerusalem and Albion, but in order to *criticize* the "Religion of Chastity & Uncircumsised Selfishness" (J 60: 48). A most telling reformulation of the image of the ancient British Druid was from conquered inhabitant to what Owen calls a "militant patriot," who was "regarded by poets, antiquaries, and historians as zealous defenders of the island's freedom."[23] A fined example of this representation is in Cowper's "Boadicea: An Ode," in which the national heroine turns to a Druid priest for martial advice, and the Druid replies with a prophecy foretelling the triumphs of British empire:

> Then the progeny that springs
> From the forests of our land
> Armed with thunder, clad with wings,
>   Shall a wider world command.

Boadicea drinks in the Druid's words, returns to battle and, like Gray's Bard dying at the end of a line, uses the patriotic language as her final weapon:

> She, with all a monarch's pride
> Felt [the words] in her bosom glow;
> Rushed to battle, fought, and died;
>   Dying, hurled them at her foe.[24]

In this military production of empire, Cowper includes a place for the permanence of poetic effort since, as in Gray's poem, the poetic curse takes effect after the speaker has collapsed. Imperial and poetic certitude are here closely interdependent.

We have seen how culture was refigured as nature in the landscaping of the ruined castle poem. In a similar manner, the figure of the Druid, interpreted in the seventeenth and early eighteenth century as a complex and sublime figure – poet and slaughterer, prophet and conspirer – was often desublimated and naturalized. The "fervent patriot" Druid passed out of fashion after Cowper and in its place moved a Druid pensive and sage. Owen cites poems by Mason and others from the 1760s through the 1780s, and comments that by the end of the century, "Trees were themselves openly speaking in dark prophetic numbers, while groves became 'pensive' and the mistletoe 'sage.' "[25] Owen implicitly attributes this naturalization to the formal metonymic pull of poetic association; but it appears also to be part of the evacuation of cultural labor from the naturalness of national identity. Once again, the sublimity of history – its terrors and the terror excited by the incongruity of poetry and blood cruelty – is translated into the stable benignity of the landscape.

Though we are used to thinking of Blake as eccentric, he was actually quite close to other mythologizers who drew on Druid imagery to describe the nation by way of mythic sources and analogues.[26] The genius of Blake's contestatory myth of origins does not derive from the identification of Jerusalem and Albion, for that assimilation had currency in one form or another from the seventeenth century.[27] Neither is the originality of the poem to be attributed to the reversal of historical and hence originary temporality, by which the origin of the Bible is made, startlingly, to depend upon the historical priority of England. This issue of priority was taken up, in fact, within the dominant myth of national identity, which Denis Saurat described in 1929 as a prevalent "strange, mystic imperialism," in which during the eighteenth century "respect for the Bible is giving way before erudition and national feeling."[28] Instead, the revisionist power of *Jerusalem* derives in part from Blake's adoption and modification of the communist voices of seventeenth-century radical oppositional nationalism, a popularly and biblically based set of ideas which had surged forwards making claims against property and towards internationalism but was recouped by the bourgeois forces of the Protectorate.[29] That orientation understood that the nation can be used to signify itself and also as a metaphor for an international community or brotherhood and rhetorically asks, "Are not Religion & Politics the Same Thing? Brotherhood is Religion" (J 57: 10). Blake takes on this set of images and makes his reference contemporary, writing what amounts to a parody of a national epic as he links the oppressions of early nineteenth-century Britain to those of a postulated druidical antiquity.

III

The shape of Britain in *Jerusalem* is drawn as rocky Druid territory: oppressive oaks and altars fill up the map, and this Druid strand within the narrative links the nineteenth-century world to the past. In making the poem contemporary in its reference Blake draws on his own city, London, as well as looking to the relations between England and Ireland. A subtle but tenacious theme in Blake's oppositional history of Britain is the way Ireland is linked to England in a manner manifestly subordinate but potentially the source of a reconception of the "One Nation." "Ireland, ancient nation" (*Milton* 39: 45) is as old as the Druid past of England, but is counterpoised to druidic cruelty. In a profound parody, the chaotic dispersion of the Ancient Man Albion, from whose "dreadful ruins / Let loose the enormous Spectre . . . fill'd with revenge and Law" (J 40 (36): 31–3), offers itself as a counter-image to the newly established Union of Great Britain with Ireland, which went into effect a few years before Blake began his epic. Blake exposes how the absorptive capacity of the British state limits the autonomous particularity of its members and produces instead the condition of stonification.[30]

Throughout *Jerusalem* we are reminded of the "Minute Particulars" (J 91: 21) that make up Britain: not only England, Wales, Scotland, and Ireland, but also the complex catalogue of internal differentiations whose separate names make up Plates 16, 71, and 72. Against this local multiplicity Blake sets the false unity of absorption, that "World of Opakeness" (J 73: 22) that becomes "a Limit, a Rocky hardness without form & void, / Accumulating without end" (J 73: 23–4). The contrast between constraining and liberating unity exemplifies the distinction Blake makes in the poem between a Negation and a Contrary: "Negations are not Contraries: Contraries mutually Exist; / But Negations Exist Not" (J 17: 33–4). The Kingdom of Great Britain and Ireland has achieved the negation of

"Brittannia" (J 96: 2), the name for heterogeneous proliferation in the risen Albion, whose interior space is kept vital by the interaction of contrarieties.

Blake begins with the fact of Ireland's absorption and takes this datum in two directions. He makes a contemporary political point about how Britain has achieved a formal unity at a cost observable both in Ireland and in England, and he generates out of this knowledge a vision of an alternate union situated in Ireland's visionary form as Erin.

The general expectation that unification with Ireland would lead to Catholic emancipation in England was not fulfilled, and was actually thwarted by the king, leaving emancipation until 1829, some years after Blake had completed *Jerusalem*. Between 1804 and 1820, three separate Relief Bills were defeated in Parliament, and in the year before Blake began work on *Jerusalem*, Emmet's rising had been defeated. The spiritual privations suffered by the Irish were inextricable from the material ones of poverty, compounded in Ireland itself in 1817 by the partial failure of the potato crop. (This point is not meant to suggest that Blake supported Catholicism: in fact, he shows us an Erin who has been drained by the Negation of religion: "By Laws of Chastity & Abhorrence I am wither'd up": J 49: 26.)

Blake shows the cost to the Irish people of absorption into Britain also as a reflex of the global trade empire Britain was building. Among the arguments which had convinced the Ascendancy parliamentarians to vote for unification was one which linked nation and commerce: "Under Union there would be free trade and the enterprising men of Ulster would be able to push their linen as a British product within every province of the British empire."[31] Unification with England, then, amounted to the strengthening of the British textile trade, one of the strongest arms of Britain's control over foreign peoples and markets. In *Jerusalem* Blake concretely images this trade as the veinous excrescences of the English Polypus:

> In Verulam the Polypus's Head, winding around his bulk
> Thro' Rochester and Chichester & Exeter & Salisbury
> To Bristol, & his Heart beat strong on Salisbury Plain
> Shooting out Fibres round the Earth thro' Gaul & Italy
> And Greece & along the Sea of Rephaim into Judea
> To Sodom & Gomorrha: thence to India, China & Japan.
> (J 67: 35–40)

Here Blake manages to wrap not only his contemporary world, but the history of that world, in the threads of British economic oppression. From Roman Britain to Biblical Palestine to the markets of the East, Blake images British absorption as a process which drains past into present as well as "there" into "here." Against the imbalance of British domination Blake poses Albion's memory of a mutually benefiting world of trade: "In the Exchanges of London every Nation walk'd, / And London walk'd in every Nation, mutual in love & harmony" (J 24: 42–3).

Closer to hand, Blake drew on the fact that the British move to unification with Ireland had been partially compelled by the desire for an official state unity in the place of the kind of diverse unity represented by the rebellion of the United Irishmen in 1798. The British state aggravated the differences between Catholic and Protestant to better undermine the solidarity of the non-sectarian revolutionary United Irishmen.[32]

When Blake introduces Ireland into the body of *Jerusalem*, he poetically materializes the cost to Ireland of subordination to England. That price can be measured by deformations within Ireland and also in London. At the center of the poem – Tyburn, the end point of the path towards death from Newgate Prison – Blake alludes to and poetically constructs the tenements of the Irish immigrants whose rotting houses lined the path and lay juxtaposed to the site of execution. M. Dorothy George describes the horrifying conditions of life in the Calmel Buildings, located just off Portman Square, near the temporary and badly built huts slightly to the north, at Lisson Grove, the junction of Marylebone and Paddington.[33] We cannot forget that it was among the ruinous dwellings of the Irish laboring and begging poor that Blake placed Los and the builders of Golgonooza on the road to Tyburn:

> What are those golden Builders doing
> Near mournful ever-weeping Paddington,
> Standing above that mighty Ruin
> Where Satan the first victory won?
>
> (J 27: 25–8)

But though contemporary Ireland and the immigrant Irish bear the marks of Albion's degeneration, in the form of Erin Blake recovers the utopian potentiality of Ireland. From early in Chapter 1 (Plate 9), we see Erin as a crucially reparative character. Erin is an alternate space, born out of the labors of Los and his Spectre. Los compels his Spectre to work the bellows, "Till the Spaces of Erin were perfected in the furnaces / Of affliction, and Los drew them forth" (J 9: 34–5). In these spaces Erin preserves and kindles the possibility of an alternate regime to that under which the Sons and Daughters of Albion are forced to live. This is a variegated unity, reflecting the diversity of humanness and its particulars, rather than the One Law of English sovereignty, "For every thing exists & not one sigh nor smile nor tear, / One hair nor particle of dust, not one can pass away" (J 13–14: 66–1). By recovering Erin as a site of refuge, Blake reimagines Ireland, for it is within the redemptive area of Erin's spaces that Los contacts the Sons, Daughters, and Emanations who pour out of his furnaces. Erin's spaces are sublime and Los is himself "Terrified at the Sublime Wonder" (J 12: 22) of these endless regions which are remarkable because they are able to coexist with, without blending into, the fiery works that Los and his Spectre drive and serve.

Erin functions as an agent as well as a space in the poem. Separated out as an Aged Pensive Woman (J 48: 28), Erin is "occupied in labours / Of sublime mercy" (J 48: 40–1) as she moves through Los's furnaces. Imaged as a set of embedded structures, Erin's restful spaces are refined out of the productive violence of the labor process, and will, in turn, allow the reconstruction of Jerusalem. As a formed distillate, Erin is able to counsel and address the Daughters of Albion, and her speech congeals into the form of a rainbow. Erin names the condition of the corrupted Albion, calling it "the Place / Of Murder & Unforgiving" (J 48: 57) In her extended speech (Plates 48, 49, 50), Erin urges the Daughters of Albion to distinguish carefully between humanness and those "States or Worlds in which the Spirit travels" (J 49: 74). She presents the fallen Albion as a transient condition and not as an essence, and hints in her pun on "state" that the cruelties of the condition are linked to an abstracted governmental structure. The ossifying of a state into *the* state is a horror to Erin and to Blake:

> A World where Man is by Nature the enemy of Man,
> Because the Evil is Created into a State, that Men
> May be deliver'd time after time, evermore.
>
> (J 49: 69–71)

Blake has understood a point that will be developed later by Marx: that the possibility of the revolutionary transformation of England turns on the Irish Question.[34] So it is that for the duration of Albion's helpless sleep on the cold rock beneath Los's furnaces Erin observes and guards the elements of the fallen condition, "sitting in the Tomb to Watch them unceasing night and day. / And the Body of Albion was closed apart from all Nations" (94: 13–14).

IV

Just as the poetry of picturesque ruin is intelligible in relation to the late eighteenth-century revaluing of the countryside, so Blake's ruin language can be illuminated by reference to his contemporary environment of urban ruin. The London in which Blake grew up and to which he returned after his "three years slumber" (J 3) in Felpham was a notoriously and anxiously ruinous city. Morton Paley has noted that the building of the beautiful Nash terraces near to Blake's house on South Molton Street may be heard amidst the clangor of Los's construction.[35] But Nash's buildings were raised on solid foundations, accommodations for the wealthier classes, and built to last. In the poorer sections of London, however, and in those places where Irish immigrants were housed, decaying tenements and shoddy, insubstantial new buildings were a constant of city life. To keep the population of the city down, laws prohibited building on many sites, and these regulations exacted large penalties if broken. But landlords were prepared to pay the fines in order to erect flimsy but lucrative buildings which could easily be demolished. It was in these tenements that the laboring and the unemployed poor were housed. M. Dorothy George describes the neighborhoods of collapsing "old ruinous houses" and the "collapse of new or half-built houses." And Blake echoes her in *Jerusalem* in his own voice, "I behold Babylon in the opening Streets of London. I behold / Jerusalem in ruins wandering about from house to house" (J 74: 16–17). Where laws forbade new building, the effect was to "set their owners upon patching up tumbledown buildings, adding to them and digging cellars under them."[36] The atmosphere of ruin in the East End, which Los tours in his entry into London, passing through Hackney and Stepney, was certainly not evidence of the fall of empire nor redolent of the slow moldering action of Time.[37] It was squalid. Blake harnesses the terror of poverty and ruin in the city to produce a parody of the ruin aesthetic – urban sublimity at the wrong end of the social scale. Blake's version of city ruin takes on the reality of decay and waste and provides a counter-image to the gentry calm of landscape ruin.

Blake's leveling of the ruin motif fixes his urban ruins somewhere between the grand Roman ruins which elicited some of the first poems of ruin sentiment, and the humble ruined cottages which occupy the rural landscapes of John Clare. In Diderot's *Encyclopédie*, an article on "Ruins" clearly catalogues the acceptable structures to promote ruin sentiment: "Ruine ne se dit que des palais, des tombeaux somptueux ou des monuments publics."[38] As noted in the discussion above of Wordsworth's "The Ruined Cottage," in 1791 in the *Ruins of Empire*, Volney appropriated the aristocratic ruin for the historically disempowered: "You compensate the miseries of the poor by the anxieties of the rich; you console the wretched by opening to him a last asylum from distress."[39] Blake further democratizes cultural debris by making urban ruin a new source of meaning for ruin poetry, finding in the stuff of decay raw materials to be transformed through labor. The landscape garden with its few and carefully chosen or built ruin pieces provided a barrier between the historicity of both agricultural world and country house prestige. Blake's ruined city, on the other hand, is manifestly the product of human labor over historical time. Los's work *makes* the city, and the sublimity of the city draws out the children of Albion:

> Yet ceas'd he not from labouring at the roarings of his Forge,
> With iron & brass Building Golgonooza in great contendings,
> Till his Sons & Daughters came forth from the Furnaces
> At the sublime Labours.
>
> (J 10: 62–5)

Building Golgonooza (i.e., the method for rebuilding Jerusalem) is also the method for building liberty, for "Jerusalem is called Liberty among the Children of Albion" (J 54: 5). Blake produces an anti-state language of ruins through the vehicle of the historical sublime figured as the sublime of squalor. Los is so striking a creator because he is moved not only by imagination, but also by terror. Los does not speak in the cool voice of the moralizing ruinist, nor in that anomically collapsed voice of the abjectly ruined poetic persona who compensates by elevating autonomous poetic expressivity. In Los, Blake refuses the sentiment which infuses John Martin's romantic portrait of the Bard's suicide, preferring instead to recover the politically oppositional element of Gray's triumphant curse against his oppressor. Los struggles to build and, when necessary, is not afraid to destroy, as when he smashes his deformed counter-persona, the Spectre:

> Los beheld undaunted, furious,
> His heav'd Hammer; he swung it round & at one blow
> In unpitying ruin driving down the pyramids of pride,
> Smiting the Spectre on his Anvil & the integuments of his Eye
> And Ear unbinding in dire pain, with many blows
> Of strict severity self-subduing, & with many tears labouring.
>
> (J 91: 42–7)

Los builds against ruin and destroys against ossification, that process by which the heterogeneity of experience is rendered undifferentiated, the manner in which Albion, and before him, Urizen, have been reduced to their comatose states: "Now fix'd into one stedfast bulk his features stonify" (*The Four Zoas* 5: 2).

The rigor mortis of the stony concretion of Albion is a unity which is a Negation. Blake's appeal to unity – the unity which accompanies liberty – is one which requires the mechanism of internal difference. Edward Larrissy has interestingly interpreted Blake by way of the linguistic principle of difference. While Larrissy is wrong that *Jerusalem* is best understood as an "index of a political despair," he makes a most elegant formulation of a significant contradiction in Blake's project: "Blake longs for a lost unity, but his creations belong to difference."[40]

Unity, however, is not an uncomplicated matter for Blake. In his remarks on Homer's poetry, Blake writes that "every Poem must necessarily be a perfect Unity," but he points out that attention to a superficial notion of unity shows that "Unity is the cloke of folly."

It is the same with the Moral of a whole Poem as with the Moral Goodness of its parts. Unity & Morality are secondary considerations, & belong to Philosophy & not to Poetry, to Exception & not to Rule, to Accident & not to Substance.[41]

In *Jerusalem*, Albion is now in ruins; that is, he is different to himself and disunified. Albion has been sundered and Jerusalem has been ruined into a set of fragments which Los must reunify, to produce Blake's version of "abundant recompense." But Blake's goal of unity itself *stresses* and does not reduce internal differences, which is where the meanings are: "he who wishes to see a Vision, a perfect Whole, / Must see it in its Minute Particulars" (J 91: 21–2). We can then counterpoise Albion's ruin, which Blake calls the Negation of unity, to its Contrary, the production of multiplicity. "The Negation must be destroy'd to redeem the Contraries" (*Milton* 40: 33). The complexity of Blake's category of unity is articulated in his vision of the One Man:

> Mutual in one another's love and wrath all renewing
> We live as One Man; for contracting our infinite senses
> We behold multitude, or expanding, we behold as one,
> As One Man all the Universal Family.
>
> (J 38 [34]: 16–19)

The principle of heterogeneity, which is the formal as well as the thematic mainspring of Blake's poetic and political resistance, results in a poem which presents both a challenging revised notion of unity as well as an untidy, and in places unwieldy, mythic heterodoxy.

The parody of the unity of "Great Britain" in the disunity of Albion stonified inhabits the same perspective as Blake's discrimination of unities in poetic orientation. Rather than taking on the inexpressibility *topos*, *Jerusalem* makes palpable that the immortality-of-poetry *topos* must be referred to a poetic labor. We witness the attempt to make an eternal poetic city, built up from "English, the rough basement" (J 40 [36]: 58). The necessity of poetic labor to the reparation of the nation gives new meaning to the *topos*: "Los built the stubborn structure of the Language, acting against / Albion's melancholy, who must clse have been a Dumb despair" (J 41 [36]: 59–60). Blake articulates here the close relationship between poetry and reparation. Building language is building against stonification, and language will be the agency of Albion's awakening. In his appeal to the labor of poetic permanence, Blake both acknowledges and toils against the claim and the isolation of poetic autonomy, the poetic crisis of his time. He refuses to give way to the *topos* of poetic inexpressibility, which gains ever greater currency as lyric privacy and the inadequacy of language appear as forms of romantic poetic ideology: thoughts that lie too deep for words. Yet, as we often take note, Blake's strategies of protection fold back against his works. The voices of seventeenth-century radicals hardly found ready listeners in the early nineteenth century, and the paucity of copies of *Jerusalem* amongst those hundreds of volumes that Stuart Curran has taxonomized[42] bears witness to the form of ruin which plagued Blake himself – *Jerusalem* collapses narratively just as surely as did the old ruined tenements of London.

V

Wordsworth's national epic radiates its meaning outwards and representatively from the regions of Wordsworth's own experiences. Blake's epic attack upon official nationalism begins with a version of the disunity which goes by the name of "Britain," and deepens the attack by destabilizing a set of monuments belonging to the myth of the nation. London Stone, a marker of the Roman antiquity of Britain, Stonehenge, the ancient temple believed to have belonged to the Druids, and Tyburn, the medieval outer boundary of London and the traditional site of execution, are all rhetorically and thematically linked in *Jerusalem*.

"Jerusalem is called Liberty" (J 54: 5), and therefore liberty lies in ruins. For Wordsworth, liberty and the state are yoked; for Blake, they are antithetical. In the city's form as the female emanation of Albion, her ruins chart and embody the nation's disunity. In the more local geography of London/Golgonooza, the limits of stony ruin are set by Tyburn and London Stone, which simultaneously bridge the temporal gap between ancient and contemporary oppression. Blake draws the two sites together within a larger portrayal of urban blight in the lyric which opens Chapter II, "The Fields from Islington to Marybone":

> What are those golden Builders doing
> Near mournful ever-weeping Paddington,
> Standing above that mighty Ruin
> Where Satan the first victory won,
>
> Where Albion slept beneath the Fatal Tree,

And the Druids' golden Knife
Rioted in human gore,
In Offerings of Human Life?

They groan'd aloud on London Stone,
They groan'd aloud on Tyburn's Brook,
Albion gave his deadly groan,
And all the Atlantic Mountains shook.

(J 27: 25–36)

In *Blake: Prophet Against Empire*, David Erdman suggests that Blake means Tyburn and London Stone to be interpreted as occupying exactly the same space, based on John Rogue's 1741 map of London, which indicates a "stone where soldiers are shot" in Hyde Park.[43] But it is more likely that the actual monument known as London Stone, a block of stone encased in a protective shell and built into the wall of St Swithin's Church on Cannon Street, not very far from Newgate Prison, is the monument Blake wants us to notice, as it served as the starting point in the deadly procession which took the condemned from Newgate prison to the scaffold at the end of Tyburn Road. Not surprisingly, such a procession takes place in Blake's vision along a temporal as well as a spatial route, driving people to their executions from the beginning of the nation until the present time as well as along the path across the city. So London Stone leads forward to the "Fatal Tree" at Tyburn and back in time to the bloody altar at Stonehenge. That Blake chose to represent a stone situated in a Christian church as a Druid remnant adds further ironic echoes to the meaning of London Stone, in tune with Blake's view of the corruptions of Natural Religion, whose origins both Blake and contemporary antiquarians linked to the Druids.[44] Not surprisingly, the value Blake accorded to that association was exactly the opposite from that endorsed by the enlightened deistical antiquarians.[45] To Blake's mind, it was the legacy of Druidical Natural Religion which accounted for warfare and tyranny: "Those who Martyr others or who cause War are Deists, but never can be Forgivers of Sin . . . All the Destruction, therefore, in Christian Europe has arisen from Deism, which is Natural Religion" (J 52).

The tradition associated with the actual London Stone came from Camden, who said that it originally was the center of the Roman

British network of roads. Christopher Wren agreed with this history, but argued also that London Stone was a ruin of a large Roman building. Since the prevailing view of the Druids by the mid-eighteenth century was that they had been "militant patriots," fighting for the national integrity of their homeland against the imperial incursions of the Romans, it is fitting that Blake's parodic appropriation of that tradition should identify Druids and Romans, suggesting the tyrannical similitude of the two. Situated so close to Newgate – itself the ruined remainder of the gatehouse of one of the city's original gates – London Stone thus draws into one image Druid, Roman, Christian, and governmental tyranny.

London Stone not only marks an eastern and ancient boundary of oppression, it also is the focus of a set of metonymic associations which thread through the whole of *Jerusalem*. Blake links it with both Tyburn and Stonehenge, thus making it the fulcrum of the relationship between the two sites of sacrifice, which also work together as an image cluster in the poem. The relationship between the tree of execution used in Blake's lifetime and the ancient Patriarchal rock of execution further yokes literal death at Tyburn with the deathly "Tree of Mystery" grown by the druidical priests of natural religion.

Blake's Druid image of the "Wicker Man" produces another antithetical icon of British tradition. In the *Commentaries*, Caesar describes a Druid sacrifice involving the use of "huge figures, whose wicker limbs they fill with living men and set on fire, and the men die, surrounded by flames."[46] In Chapter 2 of *Jerusalem*, Los implores the Sons of Albion to help him reverse Albion's perverse degeneration. Los catalogues the fallen nation's cruelties and wiles, including the discursive duplicity of ideology:

> A pretence of Art to destroy Art; a pretence of Liberty
> To destroy Liberty; a pretence of Religion to destroy Religion.
> (J 43 [38]: 35–6)

When Los looks around him, he sees a stony rather than a productive earth: "I see Worlds crusted with snows & ice. / I see a Wicker Idol woven round Jerusalem's children" (J 43 [38]: 64–5). This Druid idol takes the shape of a man filled with men, a mirror image of Albion as a nation filled with men. The Wicker Idol, the icon of cruel sacrificial destruction, parodies the potential redemption of Albion. The image of weaving links the Wicker Man with the British Empire, with the Fibres of the Polypus whose heart is at the central Druid monument, Stonehenge. Just as in the deformed form of Ireland strangling fibres cut off the vitality of the nation, these fibres and weavings are the disabled forms of the "Fibres of love from man to man" (J 4: 8) which will shape the fabric of Blake's alternate "One Nation."

Early in Chapter 2, the "Divine Vision" sets behind Tyburn, and its "Divine Voice" laments the ruins of Jerusalem, disclosing that "London is a stone of [Jerusalem's] ruins" (J 29 [43]: 19). London Stone is a synecdochic ruin of the larger ruin of London, itself a visible piece of the ruin of Jerusalem.[47] In these layerings of waste, the gap between Golgonooza and contemporary London grows ever wider. In Plate 6 of *Milton*, a plate which adumbrates the entire compass of *Jerusalem* by outlining Golgonooza and London, Albion and Jerusalem, as pairs of whole and ruined structures, London Stone lies at the center of a circular blanketing of England by the vegetating stuff of Mystery's growth:

> Albion's four Forests which overspread all the Earth
> From London Stone to Blackheath east: to Hounslow west:
> To Finchley north: to Norwood south.
>
> (*Milton* 6: 3–6)

The picturesque moss covering of ruins is here seen as the parasite strangling of humanity by vegetal life.

As a site of trial, London Stone asserts that the harshness of contemporary justice is born out of a tradition of juridical tyranny. When Los attempts to reanimate Albion by providing him with knowledge of his ignorance, the erring Albion sends out his emanative toadies, Hand & Hyle, to capture Los and "Bring him to justice before heaven here upon London stone" (J 42: 50). Fallen Albion holds fallen philosophical positions, once based on "demonstrative truth" (J 28: 11) and therefore trapped in the false logic of causal relations. He holds that "man lives by deaths of Men" (J 42: 49), an empirically verifiable "truth" in a world in which governmental patriotism forges homogeneous national identity for the sake of economic and martial imperialism, and in which the imaginative humanity of youth is bound

And all the Arts of Life they chang'd into the Arts of death in Albion.
The hour-glass contemn'd because its simple workmanship
Was like the workmanship of the plowman, & the water wheel
That raises water into cisterns, broken & burn'd with fire
Because its workmanship was like the workmanship of the shepherd;
And in their stead, intricate wheels invented, wheel without wheel,
To perplex youth in their outgoings & to bind to labours in Albion
Of day & night the myriads of eternity: that they may grind
And polish brass & iron hour after hour, laborious task,
Kept ignorant of its use: that they might spend the days of wisdom
In sorrowful drudgery to obtain a scanty pittance of bread,
In ignorance to view a small portion & think that All,
And call it Demonstration, blind to all the simple rules of life.

(J 65: 16–28)

Ernest Renan defined the essence of a nation as a group having many things in common and also having forgotten many things.[48] In Blake's antithetical version of the national myth, he remembers much of what has been forgotten, fragmenting the idea of the nation so as to reconstruct it at a more complex and anti-state level. When Blake recovers the terrifying sublimity of the Druid – the terror of the sacrificial past as well as the power of the prophetic voice – he takes the Druid of official patriotism and reveals it to be an image made by the reductionism of the state. Blake's Druid is not simply a benign lost minstrel or bard, but an active historical agent, whose actions lead to those of the Pittite state.

Ancient Druidism and contemporary oppression are often linked in *Jerusalem* by way of the image of London Stone in conjunction with Stonehenge. One of the more interesting narrative moments occurs when Albion's children, having made a blood sacrifice of Luvah, are compelled by Vala to build Stonehenge, the monument whose arches are "Natural Religion and its Altars Natural Morality" (J 66: 8). This building is "A building of eternal death, whose proportions are eternal despair" (J 66: 9). Blake binds Stonehenge up

with chains
Of rocks round London Stone, of Reasonings, of unhewn Demonstrations
In labyrinthine arches (Mighty Urizen the Architect) thro' which
The Heavens might revolve & Eternity be bound in their chain.

(J 66: 2–5)

Here at Stonehenge the Daughters of Albion perform their blood rite, a sacrifice which stains them with the very blood they exact from their victim, much like the blood which stains the palace walls in "London," or the images of "human gore" and the Rhine "red with human blood" in the lyric "The Fields from Islington to Marybone." It is here, at Stonehenge, that Blake's latest version of the Tree of Mystery is planted. This is now "Albion's Tree," and will also be associated, in contemporary time, with Tyburn. This tree is figured in a Druid simile, made even more critical as it suggests that parasitism of nature on humanity: "As the Mistletoe grows on the Oak, so Albion's Tree on Eternity. Lo!" (J 66: 55).[49]

When Albion awakens and England rises from her tormented dreams, recognizing that she has murdered Albion in "Dreams of Chastity and Moral Law" (J 94: 23), she blames her delusive dreams on the Druids. They are the source of those laws, and she recognizes London Stone as a Druid site: "In Stone-henge & on London Stone & in the Oak Groves of Malden / I have Slain him in my Sleep with the Knife of the Druid. O England!" (J 94: 24–5).

As he uses Stonehenge and London Stone as poetic icons, and links them to "Natural Religion," Blake follows contemporary antiquarian taste. In the rush to provide historical background for Britain as a nation, the antiquarians coined a language of ancestry which made the present and past coincide. Antiquarianism, that is, was the voice which articulated the tradition. Blake occupies that language, but presses against it until it releases a counter-tradition of tyranny and subjection. The myth of Druid benevolence, then, is complicated by Blake and show to contain within itself an explosive terror. The sublime shatters the amnesiac benignity of Natural Religion.

The poet travels across time from Stonehenge to London Stone: from London Stone to Tyburn Tree the prisoner travels to death. Tyburn marks the western boundary of Blake's urban geography. While in the reparative vertical movement of the poem, Los and his builders labor to rebuild Jerusalem, the horizontal movement passes from Newgate to Tyburn, tracking the extent of the nation's ruined shape and witnessing the slums of contemporary London. In the medieval period, the site was the western limit of Westminster, marked by the River Tyburn, hence Blake's persistent epithet,

"Tyburn's Brook." [50] Tyburn was the city limit, but also, according to Blake, the place where Beulah is linked to the stony wastes of the fallen nation: "Where Beulah lovely terminates in rocky Albion, / Terminating in Hyde Park on Tyburn's awful brook" (*Milton* 11: 4–5). Most recently, for Blake, Tyburn has been the site of the limit of governmental law, where the right to take life was exercised by the conspiracy of Priest & King. By the time Blake composed *Jerusalem*, the scaffold at Tyburn had been leveled, and so could be construed as another ruin monument of governmental oppression. Blake voices the interrelationship of this site of public execution with the morality which made that execution possible when Albion, behaving very Urizenically, sits down by "Tyburn's brook,"

> and underneath his heel shot up
> A deadly Tree: he nam'd it Moral Virtue and the Law
> Of God who dwells in Chaos hidden from the human sight.
> (J 28: 14–16)

In choosing Tyburn as a central location in *Jerusalem*, Blake was referring to a popular tradition of Tyburn lore. The executions there had not only a long history, dating from the fifteenth century, but were also considered a holiday attraction in the eighteenth century.[51] Usually held eight times a year, they were taken as days off work by journeymen and apprentices.[52] Bernard Mandeville recorded that "All the way from Newgate to Tyburn is one continued Fair for whores and rogues of the meaner sort."[53] Ironically, the spectacle of public execution produced a suspension of everyday morality, as though the condemned prisoner was a scapegoat whose taking on of punishment relieved others of their quotidian obligations. The greater irony to Blake was, of course, that the parade and execution were conducted in public for the sake of the King & Priest's morality. The prevalence of popular, folk practices among state ones at Tyburn executions contributed also to the sense of festivity which jostled with the injunction to penance. Children were hauled up onto the gallows to be given the touch of the hanged person's corpse since, Edward Cadogan tells us, "the 'death sweat' of a man who had been hanged [was] held to be a cure for scrofulous diseases."[54] Peter Linebaugh, in a recent work of social history, writes: "The possibilities of resuscitation after hanging, the widespread belief in the therapeutic powers of the malefactor's corpse, the view that the spirit of the dead could return to the living, and the treatment of a hanging as a wedding were some of the attitudes to death present among the condemned and the Tyburn crowd."[55] It is hardly surprising that the government began to think that this public display was being diverted from its exemplary intentions. Henry Angelo recalled:

> The malefactors being exposed thus publicaly through the main street for three miles, it was supposed, would tend to morality, by deterring many who were witnesses of the agony of the miserable culprits from the perpetration of those vices which had brought them to their pitiable fate. This, however, was at length discovered to be a mistaken policy, for these cruel spectacles drew thousands from their lawful occupations, emptied the manufactories and workshops and filled the public houses with drunkenness and riot."[56]

As a result, after 1783 "Tyburn Fair" was no longer held, and executions took place right outside the Newgate prison. In the age of Victorian secrecy, public executions were abolished altogether, though capital punishment was still enforced. In Angelo's account, it is the mob which is pictured as the criminal. Blake turns the meaning of the Tyburn Tree around, and indicts the judicial system as the culprit. Moreover, by associating Tyburn with Stonehenge and Natural Religion, Blake names Tyburn as a source, and not simply the symptom, of his society's corruptions – the monument "on Tyburn's Brook among the howling Victims in loveliness" (J 90: 48) that connects past to present.

In the image of Tyburn, Blake gives a poetic form to governmental oppression; he produces the agony of fallen Albion's victims and labors in order to construct the continuity of governmental violence from the past into the present:

> & the Wheels of Albion's Sons turn'd hoarse
> Over the mountains, & the fires blaz'd on Druid Altars,
> And the Sun set in Tyburn's Brook where Victims howl & cry.
> (J 62: 32–4)

Gazing at the ruins of Jerusalem, Los mourns, "Instead of Albion's lovely mountains & the curtains of Jerusalem, / I see a Cave, a Rock, a Tree deadly and poisonous, unimaginative" (J 43 [38]: 59–60). The

Druid Rock and the fatal tree are alike deadly because they inhibit vision, imagination. The Tree of Mystery, subjecting particularity to homogeneity, is the deadly counterforce to "benevolence / Who protects minute particulars every one in their own identity" (J 43 [38]: 22–3). The dialectic of Blake's encounter with the traditions he calls upon produces Tyburn first as the site of death, but then, as the site of a truly new gate, whose stones are "precious" and which "To Tyburn's deathful shades admits the wandering souls / Of multitudes who die from Earth . . . It is the Gate of Los" (J 38 [34]: 58–9; 39 [35]: 3). Los builds Golgonooza to remember Albion, Blake remembers Tyburn to heterogenize the myth of national linear history. In excavating Tyburn and its terrors, Blake recalls that which the nation tries to forget when it produces itself coherently and homogeneously.

At the Tyburn hanging spectacle, often the crowd and the condemned together sang Psalm 51, known as the "hanging song."[57] In that psalm, the speaker is presented as a solitary "I" who has transgressed and now petitions for a purgation: "Purge me with hyssop, and I shall be clean; / Wash me, and I shall be whiter than snow." As actually sung by a large crowd, however, the psalm ironically indicts the nation which has produced the petitioner's song, suggesting that the execution itself will be unacceptable to God because it derives from a transgressive nation: "For thou hast no delight in sacrifice; / Were I to give a burnt offering, thou would'st not be pleased." The speaker of the psalm asks to be delivered from "bloodguiltiness," but such guilt belongs to the larger nation which is offering the condemned as an unacceptable sacrifice. The psalm ends with a plea to "rebuild the walls of Jerusalem," for only then "wilt thou delight in new sacrifices." In popular expression, then, Tyburn and Jerusalem were already yoked, but Blake rivets the allegorical possibilities of the psalm to political interpretation. What appears in the psalm to be a transgression against the nation is rather to be understood as the transgression of the nation, which keeps its city, the walls of Jerusalem, in deliberate ruin.

VI

The energy that the government had unwittingly summoned up in the public execution – popular, unconstrained, anti-state – is the same energy that Blake wants to recover. It derives from the nation as the reservoir of variousness, "all / Human Forms identified, living, going forth & returning wearied / Into the Planetary lives of Years, Months, Days & Hours" (J 99: 1–3). Blake figures London as a place of terror and waste, but also as a place of enormous activity and potential, for Cities / Are Men, fathers of multitudes" (J 38 [34]: 46–7). It is through such activity that Los experiences the magnificent visions of Jerusalem while at his labors:

> I see the New Jerusalem descending out of Heaven,
> Between thy Wings of gold & silver, feather'd, immortal,
> Clear as the rainbow, as the cloud of the Sun's tabernacle.
>   . . .
> Thus Los sings upon his Watch, walking from Furnace to Furnace.
> He siezes his Hammer every hour; flames surround him as
> He beats, seas roll beneath his feet, tempests muster
> Around his head, the thick hail stones stand ready to obey
> His voice in the black cloud, his Sons labour in thunders
> At his Furnaces, his Daughters at their Looms sing woes,
> His Emanation separates in milky fibres agonizing
> Among the golden Looms of Cathedron, sending fibres of love
> From Golgonooza with sweet visions for Jerusalem, wanderer.
>   (J 86: 19–21; 33–41)

Those "milky fibres" are the counterstrands to those woven by "The Shuttles of death" that work "black melancholy as a net" (J 41 [37]: 7–8) over London. Terror and beauty, the components of the sublime experience, enable the poet, speaking in his own voice, to produce his vision of reparation:

> I behold London, a Human awful wonder of God!
>   . . .
> I write in South Molton Street what I both see and hear
> In regions of Humanity, in London's opening streets.
>   (J 38 [34]: 29; 42–3)

London is at once the fallen Golgonooza and an "immortal Guardian" (J 38 [34]: 40) who calls out to rouse Albion:

> [London] says: "Return, Albion, return! I give myself for thee.

"My Streets are my Ideas of Imagination.
"Awake Albion, awake! and let us wake up together.
"My Houses are Thoughts: my Inhabitants, Affections,
. . .
"For Albion's sake and for Jerusalem thy Emanation
"I give myself, and these my brethren give themselves for Albion."
(J 38 [34]: 30–3; 38–9)

In Chapter 1, Los enlists his workers to build Golgonooza, and the work is both "terrible" and necessary: "Terrified at the sublime Wonder, Los stood before his Furnaces. . . . And they builded Golgonooza: terrible eternal labour!" (J 12: 21, 24). Terror and beauty unite in the urban sublime, "perfect in its building, ornaments & perfection" (J 12: 53). Of greatest importance in the making of the poem is the value assigned to this urban labor, its reparative as well as its interventionist and adumbrative meanings: "Go on, builders in hope, tho' Jerusalem wanders far away / Without the gate of Los, among the dark Satanic wheels" (J 12: 43–4). Labor is intervention: "The blow of his Hammer is Justice, the swing of his Hammer Mercy, / The force of Los's Hammer is eternal Forgiveness" (J 88: 49–50).

In Chapter 3, a retrospective history remembers the fall of the Eternals into the Four Zoas, and the dialectic of ruin and reparation is succinctly imaged:

All fell towards the Center, sinking downwards in dire ruin.
In the South remains a burning Fire: in the East, a Void:
In the West, a World of raging Waters: in the North, solid Darkness
Unfathomable without end; but in the midst of these
Is Built eternally the sublime Universe of Los & Enitharmon.
(J 59: 17–21).

Golgonooza, the eternal form of London, is built up out of the ruin to prevail over ruin. Sublimity, then, emerges out of the confrontation of the poet figure with an oppressive national history. His task is to dismantle the oppression of that history and make something new out of it. Los is characteristically imaged as being in terror, the essential sublime response. Always, however, Blake insists that the confrontation must take place amongst particularities, not generalities, and it is the particular that must be released from bondage: "Minute Particulars in slavery I behold among the brick-kilns / Disorganiz'd" (J 89: 17–18).

In a letter to George Cumberland, Blake complained, "since the French Revolution Englishmen are all Intermeasurable One by Another, Certainly a happy state of Agreement to which I for One do not Agree."[58] Blake and his surrogate, Los, both struggle against that "happy state" of historical amnesia. The myth which they produce is not historically verifiable, but it includes the possibility of national complexity, which official nationalism seeks to exclude.

Blake's project of countering "intermeasurability" by an interventionist poetics of heterogeneity is clearly stated in the preface to Chapter 1 of *Jerusalem*, in which the poet articulates the political relationship between poetry and national identity. The "Monotonous Cadence" is to be challenged by the metrical variety of *Jerusalem*: "Poetry Fetter'd Fetters the Human Race" (J 3: 46–47). The various disposition of "terrific numbers" and "gentle ones" will not only relieve monotony, but will poetically embody the principle of Minute Particulars. Such a program, however, has built-in drawbacks. The variety of numbers demands a reader as willing to work as hard as Los and the poetic lexicon demands a reader knowledgeable in the politico-religious rhetoric of the seventeenth century.

Through the poetic constructions of Blake and the workings at Los's furnaces, Albion lies cold and stony on his rocks. The end of the poem is the waking of Albion to his best self, a transpersonal self and nation. The awakening of Albion is the summoning together of the various names of Albion, also: "As the Sun & Moon lead forward the Visions of Heaven & Earth, / England, who is Brittannia, entered Albion's bosom rejoicing" (J 96: 1–2). Here Blake acknowledges the customary conflation of England with Britain, since the British state principally serves the needs and desire of England, and turns that priority around, as England enters Albion as one agent amongst the many.

Los's triumph is to have overcome "Albion's Spectre, the Patriarch Druid," and overcome as well the imperialism of the fallen Albion, whose "Oak Groves . . . cover'd the whole Earth beneath his Spectre," and "the Fruit of Albion's Poverty Tree" that is "the Kingdoms of the World & all their glory that grew on Desolation" (J 98: 50–3). Blake's triumph is to have made the tokens of official nationalism – Druid wisdom, the aged British oak, the tentacular spread of textile markets – bear contradictory and oppositional meanings. Blake de-natures the nation.

The poem ends by asserting that Jerusalem, that is Liberty, will prevail, an assertion that the variousness which is Liberty/Jerusalem/Brittannia is neither the negation of sameness nor the multiplicity of fragmentation, but the overturning of One Law for Lion and Ox.

In the poetry of picturesque ruin, the building quietly subsides into the landscape, and the poetic voice recovers an elegiac pleasure in contemplating the return of humanly made structures to their natural origins – the pleasure of entropy. Blake's project in *Jerusalem* is anti-natural in the sense that it is committed to recovering historicity as sublimity in a narrative of human labor in a humanly built world: Los builds amidst ruin and amidst oppressive regimes. Walter Benjamin suggests that "to articulate the past . . . means to seize hold of a memory at a moment of danger."[59] Blake seizes the constructedness of the world at a moment when it is being threatened by the encroachment of national naturalness, by a veil of forgetfulness hung by the state over the landscape.

Ineluctable, however, are the facts of *Jerusalem*'s social history. Progressive in content but anachronistic in rhetoric, anti-imperialist in the main age of the British empire, claiming heterogeneity as a good in a world increasingly homogeneous, *Jerusalem* remembers and speaks a great deal of what the nation has forgotten, but hardly anyone can hear.

6

Conclusion

We leave the ruin theme after *Jerusalem* in its own temporary state of decay: Blake's communitarian language imagines a community but cannot bring it into being, while the authority of hegemonic nationalism moves ever more securely into place. The affective power of Wordsworth's epic in inculcating values of nationalism had succeeded in part because its complex psychological field braids together private and public interests: the explicit themes of personal exploration in *The Prelude* transmit the deeper purpose of national monumentalization. Once the "common man" has become a recognizable identity, the rhetoric of the imperial nation is free to become more mythic and more explicit, calling on each Briton to recognize both heritage and duty. The triumphant age of imperialism hooks the myth of the past to a global mission: the Victorian fashion for things medieval helps to cast a benign romance halo around the values of expansion. At the same time, as Martin Wiener points out, "One promise held out by Imperial expansion was that of escape from the pressure of unwelcome change at home,"[1] the natural nation retaining its rural stability. The frictionless later nineteenth-century national epic reflects and produces this absolute separation of past from present: the transformation of antiquarianism into a codified mythology for the state. Tennyson's *Idylls of the King*, completed in 1872, is a chief example of epic medievalism and we might recall that the poem begins with a prefatory ode to Victoria on the benefits of maintaining the strength of the Empire.[2]

The ruin motif is keyed to larger national and poetic crises, and the security of mythic presentations prevents the abysses of ruin-thought. Accordingly, the next period of ruin sentiment takes shape during the imperialist crisis of World War I: hence the resonance of *The Waste Land*. But *sentiment* had by this time ceased to be the right term, for Eliot's ruin mode in the postwar period is *ironic*. Eliot as ironist creates a simulacrum of a world in his assemblage of cultural materials, yet he cannot make that world temporal. His modernist ruin differs, also, from an earlier age's figure of time's wasting action, for Eliot's ruin poem describes a tremendous explosion. Nothing has worn down over time: time has itself blown up. Furthermore, Eliot the ruinist cannot be sure whether or not his collated fragments will be taken simply as junk. *The Waste Land*'s irony is, however, built on Eliot's deeply held belief in what he takes to be the British cultural mandate. Rather like the aristocratic ruinists of the renaissance, Eliot conceives the reparation of imperial ruin as a genealogical rather than a geographical task and so as he transcends European ruin with the Sanskrit "Shanti"; assimilating it to the Christian West through his gloss as "The peace that passeth understanding," he occludes the complex relations between the origins in European imperialism of his reparative project and his appeal to Indic knowledge.

A profound probing of the claims of nation and ruin in the imperialist war can be found in the work of Blake's modernist heir, Isaac Rosenberg, whose trench poems use ruin language to criticize and to expose British social and poetic complacency. As a working-class first-generation Jewish private in the British army, Rosenberg experienced British racism as well as the oppression exerted on the working-class soldiery.[3] An artisan engraver with strong poetic ties to the tradition of Biblical prophecy, Rosenberg makes critical sense of the Great War, and presents an internationalist rather than an imperialist poetic. Rupert Brooke's patriotic poems naively promise the kind of transcendence and monumentality associated with the immortality-of-poetry *topos*: "We have built a house that is not for Time's throwing," he writes in his war sonnet sequence, *1914* ("Safety"). In the claim that " there's some corner of a foreign field / That is forever England," he extends the identification of individual psychology and national interest which Wordsworth figured as his experience on Mount Snowdon.[4] Rosenberg, on the other hand, writes war poems which present the conflict in a critical unmasking and judgment against formulating poetic tradition in collusion with martial nationalism. Rather, he tries to disentangle the motives of poetic and national intention. In a letter from the field, he writes of Shakespeare, "that old hawker of immortality, how glad one feels, he is not a witness of these terrible times – he would only have been flung into this terrible destruction, like the rest of us."[5] Brooke's poem "Safety" proffers an obsolete rhetoric of the poem as preservative of the nation. In "Returning, We Hear the Larks," Rosenberg juxtaposes the lark's song to the sound of death by gunfire and knows that transcendence cannot be willed. The bird's song exposes the betraying dream of lyric reparation, "Like a girl's dark hair for she dreams no ruin lies there, / Or her kisses where a serpent lies."[6]

Rosenberg's strength as ruinist derives from his Blakean refusal to mistake war for martyrdom or to conceive of poetry as indifferent to social experience. In a letter to Rosenberg's ambivalent patron, Edward Marsh, in the summer of 1917, Harold Munro wrote that the task of poetry editors in wartime was to "show as clearly as possible that English poetry does not allow itself to be distracted by such a passing event as war."[7] Rosenberg persistently yokes the ruinations of war and poetry and the national past: "The darkness crumbles away – / it is the same old druid Time as ever," he literalizes in "Break of Day in the Trenches" (ll. 1–2). He views a world in which "The roots of a torn universe are wrenched" (*The Unicorn*, l. 134), and he antithetically tropes Shakespeare's bare ruined choirs by presenting "a tower of skulls / Where birds make nests" (*The Unicorn*, ll. 210–11). In "A Worm Fed on the Heart of Corinth," Rosenberg turns a ruinist's glance to the Blakean worm eating through the *translatio imperii*:

> England! famous as Helen
> Is thy betrothal sung
> To him the shadowless
> More amorous than Solomon.
> (ll. 7–10)

The war was only one brutal instance of the inter-European competition involving violence against distant lands and unseen and unheard people. From this site of ruin we move, in the second half of the twentieth century, to the domestic experience of the breakup of the British Empire in a homeland ruining its social democratic institutions. In our contemporary ruin sentiment, and it has become something of a sentiment again, the ironist does not make judgments because irony itself has been displaced. The high moral ground of the ironist is eroded by the coming to pass of that "unwelcome change at home" feared in the nineteenth century – the ineluctable results of empire's origins and ends. In the place of irony we find, on the one hand, the truly sentimental and dangerous call to return to "Victorian values" which presents "British heritage" as a contemporary equivalent to eighteenth-century myth-making; and on the other, a kind of aesthetic celebration of urban ruin coupled with savage indignation and apocalyptic pessimism. The two attitudes, though different in political intention, are functionally linked: both serve to displace the possibility of present agency into either the nostalgic re-presentation of earlier models now disconnected from their material foundation or the immobility and cultural "flat affect" which symptomatizes the condition of disaster.

Notes

Chapter 1 Introduction: The Ruin Poem in English

1 Rose Macauley, *Pleasure of Ruins* (London: Thames and Hudson, 1953), p. 454.
2 See Martin J. Wiener, *English Culture and the Decline of the Industrial Spirit 1850–1980* (Harmondsworth: Penguin, 1985), and Alan Sked, *Britain's Decline: Problems and Perspectives* (Oxford: Basil Blackwell, 1987).
3 See Patrick Wright, *On Living in an Old Country: The National Past in Contemporary Britain* (London: Verso, 1985); Michael Bommes and Patrick Wright, "'Charms of Residence': The Public and the Past," in *Making Histories: Studies in History-writing and Politics*, ed. Richard Johnson, Gregor McLennan, Bill Schwarz and David Sutton (London: Hutchinson, 1982); David Lowenthal, *The Past is a Foreign Country* (Cambridge: Cambridge University Press, 1985).
4 Cited in Greil Marcus, *Lipstick Traces: A Secret History of the Twentieth Century* (Cambridge: Harvard University Press, 1989), p. 8.
5 For discussions of the ruin sentiment in eighteenth-century art see Macauley, *Pleasure of Ruins*; Paul Zucker, *Fascination of Decay: Ruins: Relic – Symbol – Ornament* (Ridgewood, New Jersey: The Gregg Press, 1968); Stuart Piggott, *Ruins in a Landscape: Essays in Antiquarianism* (Edinburgh: Edinburgh University Press, 1976); Jean Clay, *Le Romantisme* (Paris: Hachette, 1980); Sir Kenneth Clark, *The Gothic Revival: An Essay in the History of Taste* (London: John Murray, 3rd edn, 1962); David Watkin, *The English Vision: The Picturesque in Architecture, Landscape and Garden Design* (London: John Murray, 1982).
6 Benedict Anderson, *Imagined Communities: Reflections on the Origin and Spread of Nationalism* (London: Verso, 1983), p. 15.
7 ibid., p. 16.
8 M. W. Thompson, *Ruins: Their Preservation and Display* (London: British Museum Publications, 1981), p. 14.
9 "The *world which arises* arises on the ruins of prior states of affairs." See Allen Grossman, "Why is Death in Arcadia? Poetic process, literary humanism, and the example of pastoral," *Western Humanities Review*, 41 (1987), 160.
10 William Shakespeare, *The Sonnets*, ed. C. Knox Pooler (London: Methuen, 1931), Sonnets LV and LXXIII, pp. 57, 74.
11 William Gilpin, *Observations relative chiefly to Picturesque Beauty, Made in the Year 1772, on . . . the Mountains, and Lakes of Cumberland, and Westmorland* (London, 1796, 2 vols), I, 188. Cited in Lowenthal, *The Past is a Foreign Country*, p. 157.
12 Anderson, *Imagined Communities*, p. 49.
13 Matthew Arnold, *English Writers and Irish Politics*, ed. R. H. Super (Ann Arbor: University of Michigan Press, 1973), p. 55.

14 *The Exeter Book*, ed. George Philip Krapp and Elliott Van Kirk Dobbie (New York: Columbia University Press, 1961), pp. xv, xiv. Text on pp. 227–9.

15 The translation of the poem is by Cecilia A Hotcher, *Wessex and Old English Poetry, with Special Consideration of "The Ruin"* (New York: 1939).

16 See, for example, Michael McKeon, "Politics, Literature, and the Division of Knowledge," presented at the English Institute, Harvard University, 1988.

17 John Dyer, *Grongar Hill*, ed. Richard C. Boys (Baltimore: Johns Hopkins University Press, 1941), pp. 90–1.

18 Arnold, *English Writers*, p. 53.

19 Francis Jeffrey, rev. of "The Giaour," *Edinburgh Review*, 21 (1813), 299.

20 D. F. Rauber, "The fragment as romantic form," *Modern Language Quarterly*, 30 (1969), 213. In his beautiful *The Form of the Unfinished: English Poetics from Spenser to Pound* (Princeton: Princeton University Press, 1985), Balachandra Rajan offers readings of unfinished poems from *The Faerie Queene* through *The Cantos*. See my review of his book in *The Wordsworth Circle*, 17 (1986), 326–8.

21 Thomas McFarland, *Romanticism and the Forms of Ruin: Wordsworth, Coleridge, and the Modalities of Fragmentation* (Princeton: Princeton University Press, 1981).

22 Marjorie Levinson, *The Romantic Fragment Poem: A Critique of a Form* (Chapel Hill: University of North Carolina Press, 1987).

23 ibid., p. 48.

24 M. H. Abrams, "Structure and Style in the Greater Romantic Lyric," in *From Sensibility to Romanticism: Essays Presented to Frederick A. Pottle*, ed. Frederick W. Hilles and Harold Bloom (Oxford: Oxford University Press, 1965), pp. 527–57.

25 Laurence Goldstein, *Ruins and Empire: The Evolution of a Theme in Augustan and Romantic Literature* (Pittsburgh: University of Pittsburgh Press, 1972), p. 5.

26 John Hughes, "Ode to the Creator of the World," in *The Works of the English Poets*, ed. Alexander Chalmers (21 vols, London: 1810), X, 45; John Dyer, "The Ruins of Rome," in Chalmers, XIII, 228.

27 Goldstein, *Ruins and Empire*, p. 236.

28 See Anne Mellor, *English Romantic Irony* (Cambridge: Harvard University Press, 1980).

29 Friedrich Schlegel, *Lucinde and the Fragments*, trans. Peter Firchow (Minneapolis: University of Minnesota Press, 1971), p. 175; *Literary Notebooks*, ed. Hans Eichner (London: Athlone, 1957), p. 116.

30 Philippe Lacoue-Labarthe and Jean-Luc Nancy, "Genre," *Glyph*, 7 (1981), 2.

31 Thomas McFarland, *Romanticism and the Forms of Ruin: Wordsworth, Coleridge, and the Modalities of Fragmentation* (Princeton, New Jersey: Princeton University Press, 1981), p. 8.

32 See Jerome McGann, *The Romantic Ideology: A Critical Investigation* (Chicago: University of Chicago Press, 1983).

33 Thomas Percy, *Reliques of Ancient English Poetry . . .* (London: J. Dodsley, 1763); Edward Said's discussion of the chrestomathy as the Orientalist's model of knowledge can be found in his *Orientalism* (New York: Pantheon, 1978), pp. 127–9.

34 See the illuminating discussions of this problem by Paul de Man, "Intentional Structure of the Romantic Image," in *Romanticism and Consciousness: Essays in*

Criticism, ed. Harold Bloom (New York: Norton, 1970), pp. 65–77, and by Robert F. Gleckner, "Romanticism and the self-annihilation of language," *Criticism*, 18 (1976), 173–89, in which he describes the romantic problem of an alternating overconfidence in, and despair about, the efficacy of poetic language in general.

35 Stuart Curran, *Poetic Form and British Romanticism* (Oxford: Oxford University Press, 1987), p. 15.

36 ibid., p. 18.

37 Graham Pechy, "1789 and After: Mutations of 'Romantic' Discourse," in *1789: Reading Writing Revolution*, ed. Francis Barker (Colchester: University of Essex, 1982), p. 62.

38 Jeffrey, review of "The Giaour," p. 299. See also E. A. Poe, "The Poetic Principle" (1850), *Complete Works of Edgar Allan Poe*, ed. James A. Harrison (1902; rpt New York: AMS Press, 1965), p. 267.

39 Francis Turner Palgrave, *The Golden Treasury of the Best Songs and Lyrical Poems in the English Language* (Cambridge: Sever and Francis, 1863), pp. vii, xii, xiii.

40 Mary Shelley, "Preface of 1824," in Shelley, *Complete Works*, ed. Roger Ingpen and Walter E. Peck (New York: Gordian Press, 1965), I, lviii.

41 *The Poems of Percy Bysshe Shelley*, ed. C. D. Locock (London: Methuen, 1911), II, 140.

42 See Caroline Robbins, *The Eighteenth-century Commonwealthman* (Cambridge, MA: Harvard University Press, 1959).

43 See Mark Girouard, *The Return to Camelot: Chivalry and the English Gentleman* (New Haven: Yale University Press, 1981).

Chapter 2   Ruinists in Rome

1 *The Works of Edmund Spenser: A Variorum Edition*, ed. Edwin Greenlaw, Charles Grosvenor Osgood, Frederick Morgan Padelford, and Ray Heffner (Baltimore: The Johns Hopkins Press, 1947), *The Minor Poems*, II, 27–189. All references to the *Complaints* will be from this edition and will be cited in the text by sonnet number, and in the case of *The Ruins of Time* (RT), by line number.

2 The classical sources of the immortality-of-poetry *topos* display a literary confidence that is quite exhilarating to listen to in our own diminished culture of poetry. In some version of the *topos*, it is the individual poetic agent who is immortalized by Fame:

> parte tamen meliore mei super alta perennis
> astra ferar, nomenque erit indelebile nostrum,
> quaque patet domitis Romana potentia terris,
> ore logar populi, perque omnia saecula fama,
> siquid habent veri vatum praesagia, vivam.
>
> Ovid, *Metamorphoses*, XV, 875–9

[Still in my better part I shall be borne immortal far beyond the lofty stars and I shall have an undying name. Wherever Rome's power extends over the conquered world, I shall have mention on men's lips and, if the prophecies of the bards have any truth, through all the ages shall I live in fame.]

In others, as in this example from Horace, the poet gives fame to the object of praise:

> vixere fortes ante Agamemnona
> multi; sed omnes inlacrimabiles
> urgentur ignotique longa
> nocte, carent quia vate sacro.
>
> *Odes*, IV. 9

[Many heroes lived before Agamemnon; but all are overwhelmed in unending night, unwept, unknown, because they lacked a sacred bard.]

But more important than either agent or object is the permanence of the poetic structure itself: "'Tis the Muse forbids the hero worthy of renown to perish."

> non incisa notis marmora publicis,
> per quae spiritus et vita rodit bonis
> post mortem ducibus, non celeres fugae
> reiectaeque retrosum Hannibalis minae,
> non incendia Carthaginis impiae
> eius, qui domita nomen ab Africa
> lucratus rediit, clarius indicant
> laudes quam Calabrae Pierides neque,
> si chartae sileant quod bene feceris,
> mercedem tuleris.
>
> *Odes*, IV.8

[Not marble graven with public records, whereby breath and life return to goodly heroes after death, nor the swift retreat of Hannibal and his threats recoiling on himself, nor the burning of wicked Carthage, declare more gloriously the fame of him who came back home, having won his name from Africa's subjection, than do the Muses of Calabria; nor wouldst thou reap thy due reward, should the parchment leave thy worldly deeds unheralded].

Ovid, *Metamorphoses*, trans. Frank Justus Miller (New York: Putnam's Sons, 1916), II, 426–7; Horace, *The Odes and Epodes*, trans. C. E. Bennett (Cambridge: Harvard University Press, 1914), pp. 320–1, 314–15.

3 "'The Afflatus of Ruin': Meditations on Rome by Du Bellay, Spenser, and Stevens", in *Roman Images: Selected Papers from the English Institute, 1982*, New series, No. 8, ed. with an Introduction by Annabel Patterson (Baltimore: Johns Hopkins University Press, 1982, p. 24.

4 Benedict Anderson, *Imagined Communities: Reflections on the Origin and Spread of Nationalism* (London: Verso, 1983), p. 45.

5 Thomas Greene, *The Light in Troy* (New Haven: Yale University Press, 1982), p. 241.

6 Anderson makes the argument that the rise of the vernacular and hence, nationalism, rides on the coat-tails of the spread of Protestantism: "Protestantism

was always fundamentally on the offensive, preciesly because it knew how to make use of the expanding vernacular print-market being created by capitalism, while the Counter-Reformation defended the citadel of Latin." (*Imagined Communities*, p. 43).

7 Laurence Goldstein, *Ruins and Empire: The Evolution of a Theme in Augustan and Romantic Literature* (Pittsburgh: University of Pittsburgh Press, 1972), p. 35. Goldstein gives a very judicious reading of the poem, one of the very few interpretations in print of this work.

8 See the discussion of Gibbon's attitude to Augustus in Howard D. Weinbrot, *Augustus Caesar in "Augustan" England* (Princeton: Princeton University Press, 1978), pp. 101–8.

9 John Dyer, *The Ruins of Rome* (London: 1740). All further references to this work will be made by line number in the text.

10 Jean Clay, *Le Romantisme* (Paris: Hachette, 1980), p. 264.

11 ibid., p. 266.

12 Michel Foucault, *The Order of Things*, trans. Alan Sheridan (New York: Pantheon Books, 1971), p. 130.

13 Thomas Spratt, "History of the Royal Society," in *Critical Essays of the Seventeenth Century*, ed. J. E. Spingarn (Oxford: Clarendon Press, 1908), p. 118.

14 Cited in Ralph M. Williams, "The publication of Dyer's *Ruins of Rome*," *Modern Philology*, 44 (1946–7), 99.

15 See Michael McKeon, "Literature and Politics in Eighteenth-Century England," unpublished manuscript, in which he develops this point of the relation between aesthetic and historical distance.

16 "The Ruin," in *Georg Simmel: 1858–1918: A Collection of Essays with Translations and a Bibliography*, ed. Kurt H. Wolff (Columbus: Ohio University Press, 1959), p. 261.

17 Foucault, *The Order of Things*, p. 104.

18 John Keats, *The Complete Poems*, ed. Miriam Allott (London: Longman, 1977), p. 426.

19 Neil Hertz, "Medusa's Head: Male Hysteria Under Political Pressure," in Hertz, *The End of the Line: Essays on Psychoanalysis and the Sublime* (New York: Columbia University Press, 1985), pp. 161–93.

20 *The Complete Poetical Works*, ed. Neville Rogers (Oxford: Oxford University Press, 1975), II, 48.

21 *The New Century Classical Handbook*, ed. Catherine B. Avery (New York: Appleton-Century-Crofts, 1962), s.v. "Lake Avernus."

22 Neil Hertz argues that a conflation of Medusa's head and the Phrygian Cap of the French Revolution reveals to the analyst an instance of male castration anxiety: "The representation of what would seem to be a political threat was as if it were a sexual threat" ("Medusa's Head," p. 161).

23 Horace, *Odes and Epodes*, V, Book I, Ode V, p. 19.

24 All further references to Canto IV in the text are by stanza number. They are taken from Lord Byron, *The Complete Poetical Works*, ed. Jerome J. McGann, II, *Childe Harold's Pilgrimage* (Oxford: Clarendon Press, 1980).

25 Ernst Robert Curtius, *European Literature and the Latin Middle Ages*, trans. Willard

R. Trask (Princeton: Princeton University Press, 1973), p. 159.

26 Bernard Blackstone, *Byron: A Survey* (London: Longman, 1975), p. 219.

27 John Hobhouse, *Historical Illustrations of the Fourth Canto of "Childe Harold"* (London: John Murray, 1816), p. 196.

28 ibid.

29 Rev. Joseph Jefferson, *The Ruins of a Temple: a Poem, etc.* (London: 1793), l. 13.

30 Henri Lefebvre, *Production de l'espace* (Paris: Editions Anthropos, 1974) p. 253.

31 ibid., pp. 258–9.

32 Carolyn Springer, *The Marble Wilderness: Ruins and Representation in Italian Romanticism, 1775–1850* (Cambridge: Cambridge University Press, 1987), p. 84.

33 Byron, *Letters and Journals*, ed. Leslie A. Marchand (London: John Murray, 1978), VIII, 53.

34 Springer, *Marble Wilderness*, p. 86.

35 Cited in Lorenz Eitner, *Neoclassicism and Romanticism: 1750–1850, Sources and Documents* (New Jersey: Prentice-Hall, 1970), I, 18.

36 Sigmund Freud, *Civilization and its Discontents* (New York: Norton, 1961), p. 16. All further references to this work will be cited by page number in the text.

37 On the following page, Freud reiterates this problem, when considering using an embryological analogy: "The fact remains that only in the mind is such a preservation of all the earlier stages alongside of the final form possible, and that we are not in a position to represent this phenomenon in pictorial terms" (p. 20).

38 This idea, echoed as the "rabbit/duck" illusion in Wittgenstein's *Philosophical Investigations* and cited by E. H. Gombrich in *Art and Illusion: A Study in the Psychology of Pictorial Representation* (Princeton: Princeton University Press, 1960), p. 5, as an irreducible fact of visual psychology, has been significantly challenged in the course of the twentieth century: Pound's superimpositional method of poetic composition, Michel Foucault's theory of the "statement" in *The Archaeology of Knowledge* (London: Tavistock, 1974), pp. 79–88, and current theories of the "palimpsestic" qualities of literary texts all suggest that perhaps we may now, in fact, be able to see both rabbit and duck without overloading our cognitive faculties.

39 For a psychoanalytic reading of this passage, see Susan Cassirer Bernfeld, "Freud and archaeology," *The American Imago*, 8 (1951), 118–20. "Freud's great interest in the layer structure of ancient cities, as well as that of the mental apparatus, probably goes back to early childhood efforts to comprehend his family structure and master its emotional demands. Dating each person and assigning each to his proper place was a significant achievement, the pleasure of which recurred in the intellectual satisfaction of dating layers, and of recognizing in the tiniest pottery fragment the time and place to which it belongs" (p. 120). For a thorough political and psychoanalytic discussion of Freud's use of Rome in the *The Interpretation of Dreams*, see Carl E. Schorske, *Fin-de-Siècle Vienna: Politics and Culture* (New York: Knopf, 1980), pp. 181–207.

Chapter 3   History into Landscape: Vernacular Ruin Poetry

1 Published also as *Antiquities or Venerable Remains of above 400 Castles . . .* (London, 1711–1753), 4 vols.

2 See, for example, Henry V. S. Ogden and Margaret S. Ogden, *English Taste in Landscape in the Seventeenth Century* (Ann Arbor: University of Michigan Press, 1955); Eino Railo, *The Haunted Castle* (New York: 1927; rpt New York: Gordon Press, 1974); Montague Summers, "Architecture and the Gothic Novel," *Architectural Design and Construction*, 2 (1931), 78–81; Warren Hunting Smith, *Architecture in English Fiction* (New Haven: Yale University Press; rpt Hamden, CT: Archon, 1970); Rose Macauley, *Pleasure of Ruins* (London: Thames and Hudson, 1953); Paul Zucker, *Fascination of Decay: Ruins: Relic – Symbol – Ornament* (Ridgewood, New Jersey: The Gregg Press, 1968).

3 A comprehensive set of bibliographies of topographical poems was compiled by R. A. Aubin and published in his *Topographical Poetry in Eighteenth Century England* (New York: Modern Language Association, 1936). Among the periodicals in which ruined castle poems appear are: *The Gentleman's Magazine*; *London Magazine*; *Scots Magazine*; *European Magazine*, etc.

4 John Barrell, *The Idea of Landscape and the Sense of Place: 1730–1840* (Cambridge: Cambridge University Press, 1972), pp. 1–64, *passim*.

5 George Lyttleton, *The Progress of Love* (London: 1732), II, 21–2, cited in Barrell, *The Idea of Landscape*, p. 38.

6 George Harding, "Kenelworth Castle" (1790), *Miscellaneous Works in Prose and Verse* (London: 1818), II, 48–50.

7 Aubin defines and characterizes the building-poem in *Topographical Poetry*, pp. 148–93.

8 Historical Pontefract, from *The Sieges of Pontefract Castle*, edited by Richard Holmes (Pontefract, 1887); Picturesque Pontefract, from J. S. Fletcher, *Pontefract* (London, 1920); both reproduced at the front of this volume.

9 The best and most thoroughgoing critique of the myth of the permanence of the landscape is Raymond Williams, *The Country and the City* (Oxford: Oxford University Press, 1973).

10 Francis Drake, "On the Ruins of Pomfret Castle," written 1750, *The London Chronicle*, 8 (1760), 588. All further references to this poem will be made by line number in the text.

11 "Lines written among the Ruins of Crookstoun Castle," *Scots Magazine*, 95 (1825), 467, ll. 60–4.

12 John Langhorne, "Written amongst the Ruins of Pontefract Castle, 1756," *Poetical Works* (London: 1766), I, 17–20 and 155–9. All further references to this poem will be made by line number in the text.

13 "G. J.," "Spontaneous Thoughts, written in the Ruins of Winchelsea Castle, near Rye, in Sussex," *Universal Magazine*, 59 (1776), 147–8.

14 "C. H.," "Lines, Written at Kenilworth Castle, Warwickshire," *Monthly Magazine; or, British Register*, 26 (1808), 456.

15 In his *Nations and Nationalism* (Oxford: Basil Blackwell, 1983), Ernest Gellner elaborates a theory of the movement from agricultural to industrial society as

linked to the shift from heterogeneous to homogeneous social relations.

16 As Habbakuk put it: "From some eighteenth-century memoirs, one might suppose that England was a federation of country-houses." H. J. Habbakuk, "England," in *The European Nobility in the Eighteenth-Century*, ed. Albert Goodwin (London: Black, 1953), p. 4. Cited in Harold Perkin, *Origins of Modern English Society* (London: Routledge and Kegan Paul, 1985), p. 125.

17 Lawrence Stone and Jeanne C. Fawtier Stone, *An Open Elite? England 1540–1880* (Oxford: Oxford University Press, 1986), abridged edn, p. 202.

18 Stone and Stone, *An Open Elite?*, p. 199.

19 David Watkin, *The English Vision: The Picturesque in Architecture, Landscape and Garden Design* (London: John Murray, 1982), p. 48.

20 Stone, *An Open Elite?*, p. 308.

21 See Gellner, *Nations and Nationalism*, pp. 39–52.

22 A good discussion of the range of enclosure acts in the period can be found in Michael Turner, *Enclosures in Britain: 1750–1830* (London: Macmillan, 1984).

23 Walter Benjamin, *The Origins of German Lyric Tragedy*, trans. John Osborne (London: New Left Books, 1977), p. 139.

24 "B.," "Clackmannan Tower" (1804), *Scots Magazine*, 67 (1805), 296. All further references to this poem will be made by line number in the text.

25 "Delta," "Lines Written at Kelburne Castle, Ayrshire," *Blackwood's Magazine*, 31 (1832), 953–5, ll. 111–21.

26 Kenneth Clark, *The Gothic Revival: An Essay in the History of Taste*, 3rd edn (London: John Murray, 1962), p. 48.

27 Margaret Anne Doody, *The Daring Muse: Augustan Poetry Reconsidered* (New York: Cambridge University Press, 1985).

28 See Roy Porter, *English Society in the Eighteenth Century* (London: Allen Lane, 1982); John Brewer, *Party Ideology and Popular Politics at the Accession of George III* (Cambridge: Cambridge University Press, 1976); H. T. Dickinson, *Liberty and Property: Political Ideology in Eighteenth Century Britain* (New York: Holmes and Meier, 1977); E. P. Thompson, *Whigs and Hunters: the Origin of the Black Act* (Harmondsworth: Penguin, 1977).

29 Thomas Gray, "The Bard," *The Poems of Thomas Gray, William Collins, Oliver Goldsmith*, ed. Roger Lonsdale (London: Longman, 1969), pp. 177–200; Walter Scott, *The Lay of the Last Minstrel* (New York: 1854). All further references to these poems will be made by line or stanza number in the text.

30 John Brown, *A Dissertation on the Rise, Union, and Power, the Progressions, Separations, and Corruptions of Poetry and Music* (London: 1763), p. 157.

31 Thomas Percy, *Reliques of Ancient English Poetry . . .* (London: 1839) I, xxvi.

32 ibid., p. xxix.

33 Brown, *Dissertation*, p. 158.

34 ibid., p. 222.

35 The dialectic of that division is explored in Michael McKeon's "Politics, Literature, and the Division of Knowledge," presented at the English Institute, Harvard University, 1988: His thesis is that "the close association of politics and literature in eighteenth-century England is most instructively seen as part of a larger historical process – the modern division of knowledge – that consists in their discrimination."

36 Brown, *Dissertation*, p. 159.

37 ibid., p. 222.

38 Christopher Hill, "The Norman Yoke," in *Puritanism and Revolution: Studies in the Interpretation of the English Revolution of the Seventeenth Century* (London: Secker and Warburg, 1965), p. 91.

39 J. G. A. Pocock, *The Ancient Constitution and the Feudal Law: A Study of English Historical Thought in the Seventeenth Century*. 2nd edn (Cambridge: Cambridge University Press, 1987).

40 Brown, *Dissertation*, p. 77.

41 ibid., p. 222.

42 Edward Snyder, *The Celtic Revival in English Literature: 1760–1800* (Cambridge, MA: Harvard University Press, 1926), p. 91.

43 John Sitter, *Literary Loneliness in Mid-Eighteenth-Century England* (Ithaca: Cornell University Press, 1982), p. 83.

44 Thomas Gray, *Cambri*, cited in R. W. Ketton-Cremer, *Thomas Gray: A Biography* (Cambridge: Cambridge University Press, 1955), p. 133.

45 See Arthur Johnston, "Gray's use of the Gorchest y Beirdd in *The Bard*," *Modern Language Review*, 59 (1964), 335–8.

46 J. B. Leishman, *Themes and Variation in Shakespeare's Sonnets* (London: 1961), p. 27.

47 *The Works of Thomas Gray . . . To Which are added Memoirs of His Life and Writings by W. Mason, M. A.* (London: 1807), I, 73.

48 ibid.

49 Walter Jackson Bate, *The Burden of the Past and the English Poet* (Cambridge, MA: Harvard University Press, 1970).

50 Mason, I, 73.

51 Cited in Ketton-Cremer, p. 135.

52 Pocock, *Ancient Constitution*, p. 245.

53 "Conway Castle," *Poetical Magazine*, 1 (1809), 315–16. Further references to this poem will be by line number in the text.

54 Paul Henderson Scott, *Walter Scott and Scotland* (Edinburgh: William Blackwood, 1981), p. 73.

55 Cited in ibid., p. 69.

56 *Poems of Samuel Taylor Coleridge*, ed. Ernest Hartley Coleridge (Oxford: Oxford University Press, 1912), pp. 264–7.

57 Marjorie Levinson, "Insight and Oversight: Reading 'Tintern Abbey,'" in *Wordsworth's Great Period Poems* (Cambridge: Cambridge University Press, 1987), pp. 14–57.

58 Sneyd Davies, from "A Voyage to Tintern Abbey," in *The New Oxford Book of Eighteenth Century Verse*, ed. Roger Lonsdale (Oxford: Oxford University Press, 1984), pp. 398–9.

59 Christopher Smyth, "On the Ruins of Kenilworth Castle," *Literary Magazine and British Review*, 4 (1790), 467–8.

60 William Wordsworth, *The Prelude: 1799, 1805, 1850*, ed. Jonathan Wordsworth, M. H. Abrams, and Stephen Gill (New York: Norton, 1979), II, 128–35.

61 Jerome McGann, *The Romantic Ideology: A Critical Investigation* (Chicago: University of Chicago Press, 1983).

62 Benjamin Boothroyd, *The History of the Ancient Borough of Pontefract...* (Pontefract: 1807), pp. 311–12.

63 For an interesting discussion on how objects move from the category of "rubbish" into "value," see Jonathan Culler's review of Michael Thompson, *Rubbish Theory: The Creation and Destruction of Value* (Oxford: Oxford University Press, 1979), in *Diacritics*, 15, No. 3 (1985), 2–12.

64 Christopher Mulvey, *Anglo-American Landscapes: A Study of Nineteenth Century Anglo-American Travel Literature* (New York: Cambridge University Press, 1983), p. 18.

65 "M.," "Lines written on visiting the celebrated Castle of Dornadilla in Strathnaver," *Scots Magazine*, 66 (1804), 456–9.

66 Percy, *Reliques*, I, 46.

67 *Oxford Dictionary of English Place-Names* (Oxford: Clarendon Press, 1960), p. 370, s.v. "Pontefract."

68 "T. H.," "Donnington Castle, near Newbury," *Gentleman's Magazine*, 78 (1808), 146–7.

69 Chalmers, Alexander, ed., *The Works of the English Poets* (London: 1810), 21 vols, XIV, 443–5.

70 Georg Simmel, "The Ruin," *in Georg Simmel: 1858–1918; A Collection of Essays with Translations and a Bibliography*, ed. Kurt H. Wolff (Columbus: Ohio University Press, 1959), p. 259.

71 "Lines written among the Ruins of Crookstoun Castle," *Scots Magazine*, 95 (1825), 467. All further references to this poem will be made by line number in the text.

72 For a survey of this "myth of greenness," see Martin J. Wiener, *English Culture and the Decline of the Industrial Spirit, 1850–1980* (Harmondsworth: Penguin, 1985).

Chapter 4 Out of the Wasteland: Wordsworth's Repair of Ruins

1 *The Prelude: 1799, 1805, 1850*, ed. Jonathan Wordsworth, M. H. Abrams, and Stephen Gill (New York: Norton, 1979), p. 372. All further references will be made in the text by year, book, and line number.

2 *The Salisbury Plain Poems*, ed. Stephen Gill (Ithaca: Cornell University Press, 1975), pp. 31–8. All further references will be made in the text by line number.

3 F. W. Bateson, *Wordsworth: A Re-Interpretation* (New York: Longman's, 1956), p. 110. Bateson goes on: "Between this pastoral realism [of the Female Vagrant's description of Keswick] and the eerie picture of Salisbury Plain at night that precedes it no connection whatever is established. Like oil and water, the two elements do not mix" (p. 111). Stephen Gill, editor of the poem, also finds "A Night on Salisbury Plain" to be an inferior poem to "Adventures on Salisbury Plain." See his "Wordsworth's breeches pocket: attitudes to the didactic poet," *Essays in Criticism*, 19 (1969), 385–401.

4 "The Uncanny," in *The Pelican Freud Library: Art and Literature*, General Editor, James Strachey, this volume ed. Albert Dickson (Harmondsworth: Penguin, 1985), XIV, 340.

5 *The Poetical Works of William Wordsworth* (hereafter PW in citations in text), ed. Ernest de Selincourt and Helen Darbishire (Oxford: Clarendon Press, 1949), V, 79.

6 William Gilpin, *Observations of the Western Parts of England . . .* (London: 1798; 2nd edn, 1808), pp. 84–5.

7 The most significant discussion of Wordsworth's debt to Burke is James Chandler, *Wordsworth's Second Nature: A Study of the Poetry and of the Politics* (Chicago: University of Chicago Press, 1984).

8 Z. S. Fink, "Wordsworth's interest in seventeenth century English republican thought," *Journal of English and Germanic Philology*, 47 (1948), 110.

9 David Erdman, "Treason trials in the early romantic period," *The Wordsworth Circle*, 19 (1988), p. 76.

10 Clive Emsley, *British Society and the French Wars, 1793–1815* (Totowa: Rowan and Littlefield, 1979), pp. 27–8.

11 E. J. Hobsbawm, *The Age of Revolution: 1789–1848* (London: Sphere, 1977), p. 80.

12 C. B. Macpherson, *Burke* (Oxford: Oxford University Press, 1980), pp. 61, 63.

13 A. L. Owen, *The Famous Druids: A Survey of Three Centuries of English Literature on the Druids* (Oxford: Oxford University Press, 1962), p. 154.

14 J. H. Grainger. *Patriotisms: Britain 1900–1939* (London: Routledge and Kegan Paul, 1986), p. 14.

15 ibid., p. 17.

16 Fink, "Wordsworth's interest," pp. 116–17.

17 "The burial of popular sovereignty," *New Statesman*, 11 March 1988, pp. 16–21. See also Perry Anderson, "Origins of the present crisis," *New Left Review*, 23, and Tom Nairn, *The Enchanted Glass: Britain and its Monarchy* (London: Radius, 1988).

18 "Two Addresses to the Freeholders of Westmorland," in *The Prose Works of William Wordsworth*, ed. W. J. B. Owen and Jane Worthington Smyser (Oxford: Clarendon Press, 1974), III, 175.

19 Harold Bloom, "Enlightenment and Romanticism," Charles Eliot Norton Lecture, Harvard University, 20 April 1988. Published as *Ruin the Sacred Truths: Poetry and Belief from the Bible to the Present* (Cambridge, MA: Harvard University Press, 1989), p. 119.

20 Gilpin, *Observations*, pp. 80–1.

21 Bloom, *Ruin the Sacred Truths*, p. 131.

22 Gilpin, *Observations*, p. 83.

23 See, for example, Cleanth Brooks, "Wordsworth and Human Suffering: Notes on Two Early Poems," in *From Sensibility to Romanticism: Essays Presented to Frederick A. Pottle*, ed. Frederick W. Hilles and Harold Bloom (New York: Oxford University Press, 1965), pp. 373–87; James A. Averill, *Wordsworth and the Poetry of Human Suffering* (Ithaca: Cornell University Press, 1980).

24 Geoffrey Hartman goes on, writing of "Tintern Abbey," "There is nothing patently archaic or poetically archaizing in Wordsworth's use of a belief which he grounds so deeply in the human passion for continuity, for binding together the wisdom of the dead and the energy of the living." "Wordsworth, Inscriptions, and

Romantic Nature Poetry," in Hilles and Bloom, *From Sensibility to Romanticism*, p. 403.

25 Kenneth R. Johnston, *Wordsworth and The Recluse* (New Haven: Yale University Press, 1984), pp. 36–52.

26 Freud, "The Uncanny," pp. 347–8.

27 *Lyrical Ballads*, edited by R. L. Brett and A. R. Jones (London: Methuen, 1963), p. 200.

28 "A Night Piece," ed. Beth Darlington, "Two Early Texts," in *Bicentenary Studies in Wordsworth in Memory of John Alban* (Ithaca: Cornell University Press, 1970), p. 431.

29 *The Letters of William and Dorothy Wordsworth: The Early Years 1787–1805*, ed. Ernest de Selincourt; 2nd edn revised by Chester L. Shaver (Oxford: Clarendon Press, 1967), p. 162 and note. We can sense the ambivalence of Wordsworth's consciousness of the nation in Dorothy's letter describing Wordsworth's witness of the "glory" of the fleet before the shoreline was littered with corpses.

30 "Lyrical Ballads," *Monthly Review*, 29 (1799), p. 209.

31 In his interesting essay of 1974, "Home at Grasmere: ecological holiness," *Publications of the Modern Language Association*, 89 (1974), 132–41, Karl Kroeber argues for Wordsworth's positive ecological feeling in the *Recluse* poem: "He speaks for the profound, biologically-rooted need for territorial security common to all men" (p. 132). I read that ecological orientation specifically in "The Old Cumberland Beggar" to be regressive. That is not to say, however, that I find contemporary conservationism always to be so.

32 As James Chandler has ably pointed out, when "habit does the work of reason," we are in that region occupied also by Burke, and so "feeling [does] the work of willing, divine law the work of human law, providence the work of political science." Chandler, *Wordsworth's Second Nature*, p. 89. Harold Bloom's reading of "The Old Cumberland Beggar" as a portrait of a man who exemplifies "a mode of consciousness which both intends nature for its object and at length blends into that object," conforms most exactly to the intenton Wordsworth settles on in the poem. The narrator quiets that poverty of the beggar by embedding it in the necessity of benevolent connectedness. Harold Bloom, *The Visionary Company: A Reading of English Romantic Poetry* (London: Faber and Faber, 1962), p. 178.

33 Johnston, *Wordsworth and The Recluse*, p. 52.

34 But see Brooks, "Wordsworth and Human Suffering," p. 376, calling the beggar "a kind of inverse scapegoat: instead of bearing away the sins of the community into the wilderness, he bears back and forth *through* the community a memory of its good offices and charities."

35 Geoffrey Hartman, *Wordsworth's Poetry: 1787–1814* (New Haven: Yale University Press, 1964), pp. 19–22.

36 Theodor Adorno, *Minima Moralia* (London: New Left Review, 1974), p. 87.

37 See Alan D. McKillop, "Local Attachment and Cosmopolitanism – the Eighteenth Century Pattern," in Hilles and Bloom, *From Sensibility to Romanticism*, 205–8. But also see Benedict Anderson, *Imagined Communities: Reflections on the Origin and Spread of Nationalism* (London: Verso, 1983), p. 124: ". . . the first real Swiss citizenship, the introduction of direct (male) suffrage, and the ending of

'internal' tolls and customs were achievements of the Helvetic Republic forcibly brought into being by the French occupation of 1798."

38 *The Letters of William and Dorothy Wordsworth: The Later Years. Volume I: 1821–30*, ed. Ernest de Selincourt (Oxford: Clarendon Press, 1939), p. 57.

39 All references to "The Ruined Cottage" will be by line number and will refer to the following edition: William Wordsworth, *Poems: The Ruined Cottage, The Brothers, Michael*, ed. Jonathan Wordsworth (Cambridge: Cambridge University Press, 1985), pp. 27–47.

40 Constantin François Chasseboeuf, Comte de Volney, *A New Translation of Volney's Ruins*. Reprint of the 1802 edn printed for Levrault, Paris. (London: Garland Publishing, 1979), pp. xi, 16.

41 "The Laplander with his pointed bonnet and his snow-shoes; the Samoyede with his feverish body and his strong odour; the Tongouse with his horned cap, and carrying his idols pendant from his neck; the Yakoute with his freckled face . . . the Chinese, attired in silk, with their hair hanging in tresses," *Ruins*, p. 170.

42 Carl Woodring, *Politics in English Romantic Poetry* (Cambridge, MA: Harvard University Press, 1970), p. 45.

43 Nairn, *The Enchanted Glass*, p. 136. See Ernest Gellner, *Nations and Nationalism* (Oxford: Basil Blackwell, 1983).

44 See Jerome McGann's interesting discussion of the poem in his *The Romantic Ideology: A Critical Investigation* (Chicago: University of Chicago Press, 1983), pp. 82–6.

45 E. P. Thompson, "Disenchantment or Default? A Lay Sermon," in *Power and Consciousness*, ed. Conor Cruise O'Brien and William Dean Vanech (New York: New York University Press, 1969), p. 152.

46 Jonathan Wordsworth, *The Music of Humanity: A Critical Study of Wordsworth's Ruined Cottage* (London: Nelson, 1969).

47 Thompson, "Disenchantment or Default?," p. 152.

48 But see Marjorie Levinson's discussion in *The Romantic Fragment Poem: A Critique of a Form* (Chapel Hill: University of North Carolina Press, 1987), p. 224.

49 Southey, *Poetical Works*, ed. Maurice H. Fitzgerald (Oxford: Oxford University Press, 1909), p. 415–17; John Clare, *Poetical Works*, edited by J. W. Tibble (London: Dent, 1956), pp. 19–21.

50 James Malton, *An Essay on British Cottage Architecture: being an Attempt to perpetuate on Principle, that peculiar mode of Building, which was originally the effect of Chance* (London: 1795), p. 5.

51 Martin Price, "The Picturesque Moment," in Hilles and Bloom, *From Sensibility to Romanticism*, p. 260.

52 ibid., p. 277.

53 "'the natural' is the meaning extracted from nature, and there is an invisible but impenetrable barrier between the two. 'The Natural' is the meaning given by culture to nature; that it is socially determined and not a fixed quality is shown by the change in what constitutes 'the natural' from age to age. It becomes the justification for whatever society approves and desires. But precisely because of this reference to Nature as the determinant of what is good, as though it were an independent arbiter, 'the natural' becomes the meaning given to culture by nature

– although it is culture that determines 'the natural' anyway." Judith Williamson, *Decoding Advertising. Ideology and Meaning in Advertising* (London: Marion Boyars, 1978). Quoted in Simon Pugh, *Garden-Nature-Language* (Manchester: Manchester University Press, 1988), p. 136.

54 "In Allusion to Various Recent Histories and Notices of the French Revolution," "Concluded," *Poetical Works*, ed. de Selincourt and Darbishire, IV, 131.

55 "The Prelude," *Eclectic Review*, 28 (1850), 551.

56 Alfred, Lord Tennyson, *The Poems*, ed. Christopher Ricks, (London: Longman's, 1969), p. 911. "In Memoriam A. H. H.," LVI, 3–4.

57 "Wordsworth's Autobiographical Poem," *Gentleman's Magazine*, 34 (1850), 468.

58 Stuart Curran, *British Romanticism and Poetic Form*, p. 14.

59 Asa Briggs, *The Age of Improvement* (London: Longman's, 1979), p. 124.

60 Quoted in Charles Whibley, *William Pitt* (Edinburgh and London: William Blackwood and Sons, 1906), pp. 50–1.

61 Briggs, *Age of Improvement*, p. 118.

62 Curran, *Poetic Form and British Romanticism*, p. 15.

63 "The Prelude," *British Quarterly Review*, 12 (1850), 579.

64 Jon Klancher, in *The Making of English Reading Audiences: 1790–1832* (Madison: University of Wisconsin Press, 1987), writes that "Wordsworth's writing aims at last to make an audience somewhere beyond the determination of class and the material habitus it effects" (p. 147). While Klancher sees in this the burden of a liberal humanist discourse, it is as well a nationalist language.

65 Martin J. Wiener, *English Culture and the Decline of the Industrial Spirit 1850–1980* (Harmondsworth: Penguin, 1985), p. 55.

66 ibid., p. 48.

67 Asa Briggs points out that the taste for the Lakes was not confined to the Wordsworth circle: "The discovery of the mountains of the Lake District was an important event in English social history, part of the turn towards the picturesque, and by 1788, according to Wilberforce, 'the banks of the Thames are scarcely more public than those of Windermere." (*Age of Improvement*, pp. 47–8.)

68 See Harold Bloom, "The Internalization of Quest Romance," in *Romanticism and Consciousness*, ed. Harold Bloom (New York: Norton, 1970), pp. 3–24; Thomas A. Vogler, *Preludes to Vision: The Epic Venture in Blake, Wordsworth, Keats, and Hart Crane* (Berkeley: University of California, 1971), pp. 60–117.

69 E.J. Hobsbawm, *The Age of Revolution: 1789–1848* (London: Weidenfeld and Nicolson, 1977), p. 80. "No doubt the French nation, and its subsequent imitators, did not initially conceive of its interests clashing with those of other peoples, but on the contrary saw itself as inaugurating, or taking part in, a movement of the general liberation of peoples from tyranny. But in fact national rivalry (for instance that of French businessmen with British businessmen) and national subordination (for instance that of conquered or liberated nations to the interests of *la grande nation*) were implicit in the nationalism to which the bourgeois of 1789 gave its first official expression. 'The people' identified with 'the nation' was a revolutionary concept; more revolutionary than the bourgeois-liberal programme which purported to express it."

70 Albert Goodwin, *The Friends of Liberty: The English Democratic Movement in the Age*

of the French Revolution (Cambridge, MA: Harvard University Press, 1979), pp. 85–7; 106–9.

71 Quoted in ibid., p. 108.
72 Samuel Taylor Coleridge, *Poetical Works*, ed. E. Hartley Coleridge (Oxford: Clarendon Press, 1912).

Chapter 5   The Sublime of Ruin: Blake's Jerusalem

1 Benedict Anderson, *Imagined Communities: Reflections on the Origins and Spread of Nationalism* (London: Verso, 1983), p. 82.
2 Ernest Gellner, *Nations and Nationalism* (Oxford: Basil Blackwell, 1983), pp. 19–24.
3 Stuart Curran, *Poetic Form and British Romanticism* (Oxford: Oxford University Press, 1987), pp. 14–18.
4 All references to Blake's work are from *Complete Writings of William Blake* (Oxford: Oxford University Press, 1972), ed. Geoffrey Keynes, and will be indicated in the text by poem title, plate and line numbers, except in the case of *Jerusalem*, which will be indicated by the abbreviation J, plate and line numbers.
5 James Scully, *Line Break: Poetry as Social Practice* (Seattle: Bay Press, 1988), p. 60.
6 Walter Benjamin, "Theses on the Philosophy of History," in *Illuminations*, ed. Hannah Arendt, trans. Harry Zohn (New York: Schocken Books, 1969), p. 257.
7 Neal Ascherson, "Druids," in Ascherson, *Games with Shadows* (London: Radius, 1988) p. 91.
8 Stuart Piggott, *The Druids* (London: Thames and Hudson, 1968), p. 181.
9 Christopher Hill, *The World Turned Upside Down: Radical Ideas During the English Revolution* (Harmondsworth: Penguin, 1975).
10 Harold Bloom, *Blake's Apocalypse* (New York: Doubleday, 1963), p. 365.
11 M. H. Abrams, *Natural Supernaturalism: Tradition and Revolution in Romantic Literature* (New York: Norton, 1971), pp. 262, 342.
12 Marilyn Butler, *Romantics, Rebels and Reactionaries: English Literature and its Background 1760–1830* (Oxford: Oxford University Press, 1982), p. 51.
13 Edward Larrissy, *William Blake* (Oxford: Basil Blackwell, 1985), p. 154.
14 David Erdman, *Blake: Prophet Against Empire* (Princeton: Princeton University Press. 1954); for a politically astute critique of the kind of premises upon which my argument is based, see Jerome McGann's as yet unpublished "Blake and the Peace of Amiens."
15 A. L. Morton, *The Everlasting Gospel* (London: Lawrence and Wishart, 1958). "Blake's tragedy was that he was speaking a language which was already becoming obsolete. He was the greatest English Antinomian, but also the last" (p. 36).
16 Patrick Wright, *On Living in an Old Country: The National Past in Contemporary Britain* (London: Verso, 1985).
17 Ascherson, "Ancient Britons and the Republican Dream," in *Games with Shadows*, p. 153.
18 ibid., p. 154.
19 See Harold Bloom, "The Internalization of Quest Romance," in *Romanticism and*

Consciousness: Essays in Criticism, edited by Harold Bloom (New York: Norton, 1970).

20 A. L. Owen, *The Famous Druids: A Survey of Three Centuries of English Literature on the Druids* (Oxford: Oxford University Press, 1962), pp. 138–68.

21 ibid., p. 158.

22 ibid., pp. 59–82.

23 ibid., p. 138.

24 William Cowper, *The Poetical Works*, ed. H. S. Milford (London: Oxford University Press, 1950), pp. 310–11; see also Owen, *The Famous Druids*, pp. 152–153.

25 Owen, *The Famous Druids*, pp. 170–71.

26 See Ruthven Todd, "William Blake and the Eighteenth-Century Mythologists," in *Tracks in the Snow: Studies in English Science and Art* (London: Grey Walls Press, 1946), pp. 29–60.

27 See Harold Fisch, *Jerusalem and Albion: The Hebraic Factor in Seventeenth Century Literature* (London: Routledge Kegan Paul, 1964).

28 Denis Saurat, *Blake and Modern Thought* (London: Constable, 1929), pp. 82, 53.

29 Hill, *World Turned Upside Down*, pp. 14–15.

30 See Tom Nairn, *The Break-Up of Britain: Crisis and Neo-Nationalism*, 2nd edn (London: New Left Books, 1977): "Absorption, not federation [has] always been the principle of British development" (p. 12).

31 J. Steven Watson, *The Reign of George III: 1760–1815* (Oxford: Clarendon Press, 1960), p. 400.

32 I want to thank Andrew Murphy, graduate student at Brandeis University, for pointing this out to me. It appears in his unpublished term paper on Blake and Ireland.

33 M. Dorothy George, *London Life in the Eighteenth Century* (Harmondsworth: Penguin, 1965), p. 121.

34 See, for example, letter to Ludwig Kugelman, November 29, 1869, Karl Marx and Frederick Engels, *Selected Correspondence: 1846–1895*, trans. Dona Torr (Westport, CT: Greenwood Press), pp. 278–9.

35 Morton Paley, *The Continuing City: William Blake's Jerusalem* (Oxford: Clarendon Press, 1983), p. 75.

36 George, *London Life*, p. 79.

37 See John Adlard, "Los enters London," *English Studies*, 54 (1973), 227–30, for a detailed mapping of Los's entry into London.

38 Cited in Roland Mortier, *La Poétique des ruines en France: ses origines, ses variations de la renaissance à Victor Hugo* (Geneva: Droz, 1974), p. vii.

39 Volney, *Ruins*, p. xi.

40 Larissy, *William Blake*, p. 154.

41 *Complete Writings of William Blake*, ed. Keynes, p. 778.

42 Curran, *Poetic form*.

43 Erdman, *Blake*, p. 429. The map appears affixed to the endpapers of Walter Besant's *London in the Eighteenth Century* (London: Adam and Charles Black, 1902).

44 Piggott, *The Druids*, pp. 154–7.

45 ibid., p. 156.

46 S. Foster Damon, *A Blake Dictionary: The Ideas and Symbols of William Blake* (London: Thames and Hudson, 1973), s.v. "Wicker Man."

47 Erdman makes the same point, *Blake*, pp. 428–9.

48 "Or l'essence d'une nation est que tous les individus aient beaucoup de choses en commun, et aussi que tous aient oublié bien des choses." Cited in Anderson, *Imagined Communities*, p. 15.

49 Owen, *The Famous Druids*, pp. 169–78, for a discussion of the Druid symbolism of Oak and Mistletoe.

50 George Bebbington, *London Street Names* (London: Batsford, 1972), s.v. "Tyburn Way."

51 George, *London Life*, p. 207.

52 ibid.

53 Quoted in Edward Cadogan, *The Roots of Evil* (London: John Murray, 1937), p. 133.

54 ibid., p. 140.

55 Peter Linebaugh, "The Tyburn Riot Against the Surgeons," in Douglas Hay, Peter Linebaugh, John G. Rule, E. P. Thompson and Cal Winslow, *Albion's Fatal Tree: Crime and Society in Eighteenth Century England* (London: Allen Lane, 1975), p. 115.

56 Henry Angelo, *Reminiscences* (London: Henry Colburn, 1828), I, 465.

57 Linebaugh, "The Tyburn Riot", p. 116.

58 *Complete Writings of William Blake*, ed. Keynes, p. 878.

59 Benjamin, "Theses on the Philosophy of History," p. 257.

Chapter 6   Conclusion

1 Martin J. Wiener, *English Culture and the Decline of the Industrial Spirit 1850–1980* (Harmondsworth: Penguin, 1985), p. 56.

2 Mark Girouard, *The Return to Camelot: Chivalry and the English Gentleman* (New Haven: Yale University Press, 1981), p. 227.

3 Jon Silkin, *Out of Battle: The Poetry of the Great War* (London: Routledge and Kegan Paul 1972; rpt 1987), p. 271.

4 "Safety" and "The Soldier" reprinted in Robert Giddings, *The War Poets* (London: Bloomsbury Press, 1988), pp. 24–5.

5 Isaac Rosenberg to R. C. Trevelyan, late 1917, *The Collected Works of Isaac Rosenberg*, ed. Ian Parsons (New York: Oxford University Press, 1979), p. 265.

6 *Collected Works of Isaac Rosenberg*, p. 109.

7 Cited in Jean Liddiard, *Isaac Rosenberg: The Half-Used Life* (London: Victor Gollancz, 1975), p. 224.

Selected Bibliography

Abrams, M. H. *Natural Supernaturalism: Tradition and Revolution in Romantic Literature*. New York: Norton, 1971.

Adlard, John. "Los enters London." *English Studies*, 54 (1973), 227–30.

Anderson, Benedict. *Imagined Communities: Reflections on the Origin and Spread of Nationalism*. London: Verso, 1983.

Arnold, Matthew. *English Writers and Irish Politics*. Ed. R. H. Super. Ann Arbor: University of Michigan Press, 1973.

Ascherson, Neal. *Games with Shadows*. London: Radius, 1988.

Aubin, R. A. *Topographical Poetry in Eighteenth Century England*. New York: Modern Language Association, 1936.

Averill, James A. *Wordsworth and the Poetry of Human Suffering*. Ithaca: Cornell University Press, 1980.

"B." "Clackmannan Tower." *Scots Magazine*, 67 (1805), 296.

Barrell, John. *The Idea of Landscape and the Sense of Place: 1730–1840*. Cambridge: Cambridge University Press, 1972.

Bate, Walter Jackson. *The Burden of the Past and the English Poet*. Cambridge: Harvard University Press, 1970.

Bateson, F. W. *Wordsworth: A Re-Interpretation*. New York: Longman's, 1956.

Benjamin, Walter. *The Origins of German Lyric Tragedy*. Trans. John Osborne. London: New Left Books, 1977.

Bernfeld, Susan Cassirer. "Freud and archaeology." *The American Imago*, 8, No. 1 (1951), 107–28.

Blackstone, Bernard. *Byron: A Survey*. London: Longman's, 1975.

Blake, William. *Complete Writings of William Blake*. Ed. Geoffrey Keynes. Oxford: Oxford University Press, 1972.

Bloom, Harold. *Blake's Apocalypse*. New York: Doubleday, 1963.

—— *Ruin the Sacred Truths: Poetry and Belief from the Bible to the Present*. Cambridge: Harvard University Press, 1989.

Bommes, Michael, and Patrick Wright. "'Charms of Residence': The Public and the Past." In *Making Histories: Studies in History-writing and Politics*. Ed. Richard Johnson, Gregor McLennan, Bill Schwarz and David Sutton. London: Hutchinson, 1982, pp. 253–302.

Boothroyd, Benjamin. *The History of the Ancient Borough of Pontefract . . .* Pontefract: 1807.

Brewer, John. *Party Ideology and Popular Politics at the Accession of George III*. Cambridge: Cambridge University Press, 1976.

Briggs, Asa. *The Age of Improvement*. London: Longman's, 1979.

Brown, John. *A Dissertation on the Rise, Union, and Power, the Progressions, Separations, and Corruptions of Poetry and Music*. London: 1763.

Buck, Samuel and Nathaniel. *Antiquities or Venerable Remains of above 400 Castles . . .* 4 vols. London: 1711–53.

Butler, Marilyn. *Romantics, Rebels and Reactionaries: English Literature and its Background 1760–1830*. Oxford: Oxford University Press, 1982.

"C. H." "Lines, Written at Kenilworth Castle, Warwickshire." *Monthly Magazine; or, British Register*, 26 (1808), 456.

Chalmers, Alexander, ed. *The Works of the English Poets*. 21 vols. London: 1810.

Chandler, James. *Wordsworth's Second Nature: A Study of the Poetry and of the Politics*. Chicago: University of Chicago Press, 1984.

Clark, Kenneth. *The Gothic Revival: An Essay in the History of Taste*. 3rd edn. London: John Murray, 1962.

Clay, Jean. *Le Romantisme*. Paris: Hachette, 1980.

Coleridge, Samuel Taylor. *Poems*. Ed. Ernest Hartley Coleridge. 2 vols. Oxford: Clarendon Press, 1912.

"Conway Castle." *Poetical Magazine*, 1 (1809), 315–16.

Culler, Jonathan. Review of *Rubbish Theory: The Creation and Destruction of Value*, by Michael Thompson. *Diacritics*, 15, No. 3 (1985), 2–12.

Curran, Stuart. *Poetic Form and British Romanticism*. Oxford: Oxford University Press, 1987.

Curtius, Ernst Robert. *European Literature and the Latin Middle Ages*. Trans. Willard R. Trask. Princeton: Princeton University Press, 1973.

"Delta," "Lines Written at Kelburne Castle, Ayrshire." *Blackwood's Magazine*, 31 (1832), 953–5.

de Man, Paul. "Intentional Structure of the Romantic Image." In *Romanticism and Consciousness: Essays in Criticism*. Ed. Harold Bloom. New York: Norton, 1970, pp. 65–77.

Dickinson, H. T. *Liberty and Property: Political Ideology in Eighteenth Century Britain*. New York: Holmes and Meier, 1977.

Doody, Margaret Anne. *The Daring Muse: Augustan Poetry Reconsidered*. New York: Cambridge University Press, 1985.

Drake, Francis. "On the Ruins of Pomfret Castle." *The London Chronicle*, 8 (1760), 588.

Dyer, John. *Grongar Hill*. Ed. Richard C. Boys. Baltimore: Johns Hopkins University Press, 1941.

—— *The Ruins of Rome*. London: 1740.

Eitner, Lorenz. *Neoclassicism and Romanticism: 1750–1850, Sources and Documents*, vol. I. Englewood Cliffs, New Jersey: Prentice-Hall, 1970.

Emsley, Clive, *British Society and the French Wars, 1793–1815*. Totowa: Rowan and Littlefield, 1979.

Erdman, David. *Blake: Prophet Against Empire*. Princeton: Princeton University Press, 1954.

—— "Treason trials in the early romantic period." *The Wordsworth Circle*, 19 (1988).

The Exeter Book. Ed. George Philip Krapp and Elliott Van Kirk Dobbie. New York: Columbia University Press, 1961.

Ferguson, Margaret. "'The Afflatus of Ruin': Meditations on Rome by Du Bellay, Spenser, and Stevens." In *Roman Images: Selected Papers from the English Institute, 1982*. Ed. with an Introduction by Annabel Patterson. New Series, No. 8. Baltimore: Johns Hopkins University Press, 1982, pp. 23–50.

Fink, Z. S. "Wordsworth's interest in seventeenth century English republican thought." *Journal of English and Germanic Philology*, 47 (1948).

Fletcher, J. S. *Pontefract*. London: 1920.

Foucault, Michel. *The Order of Things*. Trans. Alan Sheridan. New York: Pantheon Books, 1971.

Freud, Sigmund. *Civilization and its Discontents*. New York: Norton, 1961.

"G. J." "Spontaneous Thoughts, written in the Ruins of Winchelsea Castle, near Rye, in Sussex." *Universal Magazine*, 59 (1776), 147–8.

Gellner, Ernest. *Nations and Nationalism*. Oxford: Basil Blackwell, 1983.

George, M. Dorothy. *London Life in the Eighteenth Century*. Harmondsworth: Penguin, 1965.

Gill, Stephen. "Wordsworth's breeches' pocket: attitudes to the didactic poet." *Essays in Criticism*, 19 (1969), 385–401.

Gilpin, William. *Observations of the Western Parts of England* . . . London: 1798; 2nd edn 1808.

—— *Observations relative chiefly to Picturesque Beauty, Made in the Year 1772, on* . . . *the Mountains, and Lakes of Cumberland, and Westmorland*, vol. I. London, 1796.

Girouard, Mark. *The Return to Camelot: Chivalry and the English Gentleman*. New Haven: Yale University Press, 1981.

Gleckner, Robert F. "Romanticism and the self-annihilation of language." *Criticism*, 18 (1976), 173–89.

Goldstein, Laurence. *Ruins and Empire: The Evolution of a Theme in Augustan and Romantic Literature*. Pittsburgh: University of Pittsburgh Press, 1972.

Gombrich, E. H. *Art and Illusion: A Study in the Psychology of Pictorial Representation*. Princeton: Princeton University Press, 1960.

Goodwin, Albert. *The Friends of Liberty: The English Democratic Movement in the Age of the French Revolution*. Cambridge: Harvard University Press, 1979.

Grainger, J. H. *Patriotisms: Britain 1900–1939*. London: Routledge and Kegan Paul, 1986.

Gray, Thomas. *The Poems of Thomas Gray, William Collins, Oliver Goldsmith*. Ed. Roger Lonsdale. London: Longman's 1969.

Greene, Thomas. *The Light in Troy*. New Haven: Yale University Press, 1982.

Grossman, Allen. "Why is Death in Arcadia? Poetic process, literary humanism, and the example of pastoral." *Western Humanities Review*, 41 (1987), 152–88.

Harding, George. *Miscellaneous Works in Prose and Verse*. London: 1818.

Hartman, Geoffrey. *Wordsworth's Poetry: 1787–1814*. New Haven: Yale University Press, 1964.

Hertz, Neil. *The End of the Line: Essays on Psychoanalysis and the Sublime*. New York: Columbia University Press, 1985.

Hill, Christopher. *Puritanism and Revolution: Studies in the Interpretation of the English Revolution of the Seventeenth Century*. London: Secker and Warburg, 1965.

Hilles, Frederick W. and Harold Bloom, eds. *From Sensibility to Romanticism: Essays*

Presented to Frederick A. Pottle. Oxford: Oxford University Press, 1965.

Hobhouse, John. *Historical Illustrations of the Fourth Canto of "Childe Harold."* London: John Murray, 1816.

Hobsbawm, E. J. *The Age of Revolution: 1789–1848.* London: Weidenfeld and Nicolson, 1977.

Holmes, Richard, ed. *The Sieges of Pontefract Castle.* Pontefract: 1887.

Jefferson, Rev. Joseph. *The Ruins of a Temple: a Poem, etc.* London: 1793.

Jeffrey, Francis. Review of "The Giaour" by Lord Byron. *Edinburgh Review,* 21 (1813), 299–309.

Johnston, Arthur. "Gray's use of the Gorchest y Beirdd in *The Bard.*" *Modern Language Review,* 59 (1964), 335–8.

Johnston, Kenneth R. *Wordsworth and The Recluse.* New Haven: Yale University Press, 1984.

Ketton-Kremer, R. W. *Thomas Gray: A Biography.* Cambridge: Cambridge University Press, 1955.

Klancher, Jon. *The Making of English Reading Audiences: 1790–1832.* Madison: University of Wisconsin Press, 1987.

Kroeber, Karl. "Home at Grasmere: ecological holiness." *Publications of the Modern Language Association,* 89 (1974), 132–41.

Langhorne, John. *Poetical Works.* London: 1766.

Larrissy, Edward. *William Blake.* Oxford: Basil Blackwell, 1985.

Lefebvre, Henri. *Production de l'espace.* Paris: Editions Anthropos, 1974.

Levinson, Marjorie. *The Romantic Fragment Poem: A Critique of a Form.* Chapel Hill: University of North Carolina Press, 1987.

—— *Wordsworth's Great Period Poems.* Cambridge: Cambridge University Press, 1987.

Liddiard, Jean. *Isaac Rosenberg: The Half-Used Life.* London: Victor Gollancz, 1975.

Linebaugh, Peter. "The Tyburn Riot Against the Surgeons." In Douglas Hay, Peter Linebaugh, John G. Rule, E. P. Thompson and Cal Winslow, *Albion's Fatal Tree: Crime and Society in Eighteenth Century England.* London: Allen Lane, 1975.

"Lines written among the Ruins of Crookstoun Castle." *Scots Magazine,* 95 (1825), 467.

Lonsdale, Roger, ed. *The New Oxford Book of Eighteenth Century Verse.* Oxford: Oxford University Press, 1984.

Lowenthal, David. *The Past is a Foreign Country.* Cambridge: Cambridge University Press, 1985.

"M," "Lines written on visiting the celebrated Castle of Dornadilla in Strathnever." *Scots Magazine,* 66 (1804), 456–9.

Macauley, Rose. *Pleasure of Ruins.* London: Thames and Hudson, 1953.

McFarland, Thomas. *Romanticism and the Forms of Ruin: Wordsworth, Coleridge, and the Modalities of Fragmentation.* Princeton: Princeton University Press, 1981.

McGann, Jerome. *The Romantic Ideology: A Critical Investigation.* Chicago: University of Chicago Press, 1983.

McKeon, Michael. "Politics, Literature, and the Division of Knowledge," presented at the English Institute, Harvard University, 1988.

Macpherson, C. B. *Burke.* Oxford: Oxford University Press, 1980.

Marcus, Greil. *Lipstick Traces: A Secret History of the Twentieth Century*. Cambridge: Harvard University Press, 1989.

Mason, M. A. *The Works of Thomas Gray . . . To Which are added Memoirs of His Life and Writings . . .*, vol. I. London: 1807.

Mellor, Anne. *English Romantic Irony*. Cambridge: Harvard University Press, 1980.

Morton, A. L. *The Everlasting Gospel*. London: Lawrence and Wishart, 1958.

Mulvey, Christopher. *Anglo-American Landscapes: A Study of Nineteenth Century Anglo-American Travel Literature*. New York: Cambridge University Press, 1983.

Nairn, Tom. *The Enchanted Glass: Britain and its Monarchy*. London: Radius, 1988.

O'Brien, Conor Cruise and William Dean Vanech. *Power and Consciousness*. New York: New York University Press, 1969.

Ogden, Henry V. S. and Margaret S. Ogden. *English Taste in Landscape in the Seventeenth Century*. Ann Arbor: University of Michigan Press, 1955.

Owen, A. L. *The Famous Druids: A Survey of Three Centuries of English Literature on the Druids*. Oxford: Oxford University Press, 1962.

Paley, Morton. *The Continuing City: William Blake's Jerusalem*. Oxford: Clarendon Press, 1983.

Palgrave, Francis Turner. *The Golden Treasury of the Best Songs and Lyrical Poems in the English Language*. Cambridge: Sever and Francis, 1863.

Pechy, Graham. "1789 and After: Mutations of 'Romantic' Discourse." In *1789: Reading Writing Revolution*. Ed. Francis Barker. Colchester: University of Essex, 1982, pp. 52–66.

Percy, Thomas. *Reliques of Ancient English Poetry . . .* London: J. Dodsley, 1763.

Perkin, Harold. *Origins of Modern English Society*. London: Routledge and Kegan Paul, 1985.

Piggott, Stuart. *The Druids*. London: Thames and Hudson, 1968.

—— *Ruins in a Landscape: Essays in Antiquarianism*. Edinburgh: Edinburgh University Press, 1976.

Pocock, J. G. A. *The Ancient Constitution and the Feudal Law: A Study of English Historical Thought in the Seventeenth Century*. 2nd edn. Cambridge: Cambridge University Press, 1987.

Porter, Roy. *English Society in the Eighteenth Century*. London: Allen Lane, 1982.

Railo, Eino. *The Haunted Castle*. New York, 1927; rpt New York: Gordon Press, 1974.

Rajan, Balachandra. *The Form of the Unfinished: English Poetics from Spenser to Pound*. Princeton: Princeton University Press, 1985.

Rauber, D. F. "The fragment as romantic form." *Modern Language Quarterly*, 30 (1969), 212–21.

Review of *The Prelude*. *Eclectic Review*, 28 (1850), 550–62.

Review of *The Prelude*. *British Quarterly Review*, 12 (1850), 549–79.

Robbins, Caroline. *The Eighteenth-century Commonwealthman*. Cambridge, MA: Harvard University Press, 1959.

Rosenberg, Isaac. *Collected Works*. Ed. Ian Parsons. New York: Oxford University Press, 1979.

Said, Edward. *Orientalism*. New York: Pantheon, 1978.

Saurat, Denis. *Blake and Modern Thought*. London: Constable, 1929.

Schlegel, Friedrich. *Lucinde and the Fragments*. Trans. Peter Firchow. Minneapolis: University of Minnesota Press, 1971.

—— *Literary Notebooks*. Ed. Hans Eichner. London: Athlone, 1957.

Schorske, Carl E. *Fin-de-Siècle Vienna: Politics and Culture*. New York: Knopf, 1980.

Scott, Paul Henderson. *Walter Scott and Scotland*. Edinburgh: William Blackwood, 1981.

Scott, Sir Walter. *The Lay of the Last Minstrel*. New York: 1854.

Scully, James. *Line Break: Poetry as Social Practice*. Seattle: Bay Press, 1988.

Silkin, Jon. *Out of Battle: The Poetry of the Great War*. London: Routledge and Kegan Paul. 1972; rpt 1987.

Simmel, Georg. *Georg Simmel: 1858–1918: A Collection of Essays with Translations and a Bibliography*. Ed. Kurt H. Wolff. Columbus: Ohio University Press, 1959.

Sitter, John. *Literary Loneliness in Mid-Eighteenth-Century England*. Ithaca: Cornell University Press, 1982.

Smyth, Christopher. "On the Ruins of Kenilworth Castle." *Literary Magazine and British Review*, 4 (1790), 467–8.

Snyder, Edward. *The Celtic Revival in English Literature: 1760–1800*. Cambridge, MA: Harvard University Press, 1926.

Spenser, Edmund. *The Minor Poems*. Vol. II, pp. 27–189. In *The Works of Edmund Spenser: A Variorum Edition*, ed. Edwin Greenlaw, Charles Grosvenor Osgood, Frederick Morgan Padelford, and Ray Heffner (Baltimore: The Johns Hopkins Press, 1947).

J. E. Spingarn, ed. *Critical Essays of the Seventeenth Century*. Oxford: Clarendon Press, 1908.

Springer, Carolyn. *The Marble Wilderness: Ruins and Representation in Italian Romanticism, 1775–1850*. Cambridge: Cambridge University Press, 1987.

Stone, Lawrence, and Jeanne C. Fawtier Stone. *An Open Elite? England 1540–1880*. Abridged edition. Oxford: Oxford University Press, 1986.

Summers, Montague. "Architecture and the Gothic Novel." *Architectural Design and Construction*, 2 (1931), 78–81.

"T. H." "Donnington Castle, near Newbury." *Gentleman's Magazine*, 78 (1808), 146–7.

Thompson, E. P. *Whigs and Hunters: the Origin of the Black Act*. Harmondsworth: Penguin, 1977.

Thompson, M. W. *Ruins: Their Preservation and Display*. London: British Museum Publications, 1981.

Todd, Ruthven. *Tracks in the Snow: Studies in English Science and Art*. London: Grey Walls Press, 1946.

Turner, Michael. *Enclosures in Britain: 1750–1830*. London: Macmillan, 1984.

Vogler, Thomas A. *Preludes to Vision: The Epic Adventure in Blake, Wordsworth, Keats, and Hart Crane*. Berkeley: University of California Press, 1971.

Watkin, David. *The English Vision: The Picturesque in Architecture, Landscape and Garden Design*. London: John Murray, 1982.

Weinbrot, Howard D. *Augustus Caesar in "Augustan" England*. Princeton: Princeton University Press, 1978.

Wiener, Martin J. *English Culture and the Decline of the Industrial Spirit 1850–1980*.

Harmondsworth: Penguin, 1985.

Williams, Ralph M. "The publication of Dyer's *Ruins of Rome.*" *Modern Philology*, 44 (1946–7), 97–101.

Williams, Raymond. *The Country and the City*. Oxford: Oxford University Press, 1973.

Woodring, Carl. *Politics in English Romantic Poetry*. Cambridge: Harvard University Press, 1970.

Wordsworth, Jonathan. *The Music of Humanity: A Critical Study of Wordsworth's Ruined Cottage*. London: Nelson, 1969.

Wordsworth, William. *The Prelude: 1799, 1805, 1850*. Ed. Jonathan Wordsworth, M. H. Abrams, and Stephen Gill New York: Norton, 1979.

—— *The Salisbury Plain Poems*. Ed. Stephen Gill. Ithaca: Cornell University Press, 1975.

—— *The Poetical Works of William Wordsworth*. Ed. Ernest de Selincourt and Helen Darbishire. 2nd edn. 5 vols. Oxford: Clarendon Press, 1952.

—— *Poems: The Ruined Cottage, The Brothers, Michael*. Ed. Jonathan Wordsworth. Cambridge: Cambridge University Press, 1985.

—— *The Prose Works of William Wordsworth*, vol. III Ed. W. J. B. Owen and Jane Worthington Smyser. Oxford: Clarendon Press, 1974.

"Wordsworth's Autobiographical Poem." Review of *The Prelude. Gentleman's Magazine*, 34 (1850), 459–468.

Wright, Patrick. *On Living in an Old Country: The National Past in Contemporary Britain*. London: Verso, 1985.

Zucker, Paul. *Fascination of Decay: Ruins: Relic – Symbol – Ornament*. Ridgewood, New Jersey: The Gregg Press, 1968.

Index

Index by Ken Hirschkop